78 Tax Tips For Canadians
FOR
DUMMIES®

by Christie Henderson, CA, CFP, TEP
Brian Quinlan, CA, CFP, TEP
Suzanne Schultz, CA, CFP

WILEY

John Wiley & Sons Canada, Ltd.

78 Tax Tips For Canadians For Dummies®

Published by
John Wiley & Sons Canada, Ltd
6045 Freemont Boulevard
Mississauga, Ontario, L5R 4J3

www.wiley.com

Copyright © 2010 by John Wiley & Sons Canada, Ltd.

Published by John Wiley & Sons Canada. Ltd.

Trademarks: Wiley, the Wiley Publishing logo, For Dummies, the Dummies Man logo, A Reference for the Rest of Us!, The Dummies Way, Dummies Daily, The Fun and Easy Way, Dummies.com, Making Everything Easier, and related trade dress are trademarks or registered trademarks of John Wiley & Sons, Inc. and/or its affiliates in the United States and other countries, and may not be used without written permission. All other trademarks are the property of their respective owners. Wiley Publishing, Inc., is not associated with any product or vendor mentioned in this book.

For general information on John Wiley & Sons Canada, Ltd., including all books published by Wiley Publishing, Inc., please call our distribution centre at 1-800-567-4797. For reseller information, including discounts and premium sales, please call our sales department at 416-646-7992. For press review copies, author interviews, or other publicity information, please contact our publicity department, Tel. 416-646-4582, Fax 416-236-4448.

For technical support, please visit www.wiley.com/techsupport.

Wiley also publishes its books in a variety of electronic formats. Some content that appears in print may not be available in electronic books.

Henderson, Christie

78 tax tips for Canadians for dummies / Christie Henderson, Brian Quinlan, Suzanne Schultz.

Includes index.

ISBN 978-0-470-67658-5

1. Income tax—Law and legislation—Canada—Popular works. 2. Tax returns—Canada—Popular works. 3. Tax planning—Canada—Popular works. I. Quinlan, Brian, 1960- II. Schultz, Suzanne, 1971– III. Title. IV. Title: Seventy-eight tax tips for Canadians for dummies.

KE5682.H45 2010   343.7105'2   C2009-906378-6

KE5682   KF6290.ZA2H45 2010

Printed in the United States

1 2 3 4 5 RRD 14 13 12 11 10

WILEY

About the Author

Christie Henderson, CA, CFP, TEP, is managing partner of Henderson Partners, LLP, a mid-sized firm in Oakville, Ontario. She obtained her Chartered Accountant designation with Ernst & Young serving high net worth clients in the Tax and Wealth Management Practice. She is a Certified Financial Planner and a Trust and Estate Practitioner. In addition, she has completed the CICA's In-Depth Tax Course, the Canadian Securities Course, the Canadian Investment Funds Course and is a member of the Canadian Tax Foundation.

Christie's clientele consists largely of entrepreneurial owner managers and their businesses, professionals, executives and their families. Her expertise is in providing comprehensive tax and financial planning. She also specializes in retirement, investment, estate and business succession planning.

Christie is a respected media expert on tax and personal finance to CBC, *The Globe and Mail*, Global/CH TV and others.

Christie was the recipient of the 2009 Institute of Chartered Accountants of Ontario's Award of Distinction and has been nominated one of Canada's "Top 40 under 40" and for the RBC Canadian Women Entrepreneur Awards. Christie enjoys a busy life at home with her husband, Kirk, and their three boys. She spends her spare time running marathons, hiking and skiing.

Brian Quinlan, CA, CFP, TEP, is a partner with Campbell Lawless Professional Corporation in Toronto. He works with individuals and owner-managed businesses to maximize cash by minimizing tax. Brian serves as a contributing editor at *Canadian MoneySaver Magazine*; he has been a guest on a number of TV and radio call-in shows and is a frequent speaker at tax and financial planning seminars. He has instructed tax courses for Ryerson University and the Institute of Chartered Accountants of Ontario.

Brian has two income-splitting vehicles: Andrew, 19, and Tara, 16.

Suzanne Schultz, CA, CFP, is a financial planner with RBC Dominion Securities in Hamilton, Ontario. She is the host of the HGTV series *House Poor* and is regularly featured in the media providing practical financial advice to Canadians on matters ranging from tax to investing to renovating on a budget.

Suzanne graduated from Dalhousie University, then went on to obtain her chartered accountant designation while working for KPMG. She completed the CICA's in-depth tax course, the certified financial planner designation, and is securities and insurance licensed. Suzanne has spent many years working in the investment industry providing tax and estate planning advice to clients across the country. She has helped a wide range of clients with their concerns, including high-net-worth individuals, owner-managers, and those with cross-border issues. She also enjoys teaching and has been a featured speaker at many Canadian financial services events.

Aside from her career, Suzanne enjoys a busy family life with her husband, Kevin, sons Carter and Ben and daughter Claire, and can usually be found at the arena during the hockey and lacrosse seasons.

Acknowledgments

With three authors contributing to this book, we'd like to recognize the following people for their assistance: First, a special thank you to our families for their patience and support while we wrote. It's no small feat keeping up with family and work obligations while writing a book on the side, and the encouragement of our families was essential to getting this project done. Another thanks to our co-workers, too numerous to mention, for being there to throw tax ideas around with, making us all better tax professionals.

A sincere thanks to our editor, Robert Hickey, copy editor, Kelli Howey, Project Coordinator, Pauline Ricablanca, and the staff at John Wiley & Sons Canada for helping to transform what is normally a very dry subject into one that is fun to read and easy to understand.

Publisher's Acknowledgements

We're proud of this book; please send us your comments at http://dummies.custhelp.com. For other comments, please contact our Customer Care Department within the U.S. at 877-762-2974, outside the U.S. at 317-572-3993, or fax 317-572-4002.

Some of the people who helped bring this book to market include the following:

Acquisitions and Editorial

Editor: Robert Hickey

Copy Editor: Kelli Howey

Project Editor: Pauline Ricablanca

Cartoons: Rich Tennant
(www.the5thwave.com)

Composition

Project Coordinator: Lynsey Stanford

Layout and Graphics: Samantha Cherolis, Timothy Detrick, Melissa K. Jester, Christine Williams

Proofreader: Leeann Harney

Indexer: Claudia Bourbeau

John Wiley & Sons Canada, Ltd

Bill Zerter, Chief Operating Officer

Karen Bryan, Vice-President, Publishing Services

Jennifer Smith, Publisher, Professional & Trade Division

Publishing and Editorial for Consumer Dummies

Diane Graves Steele, Vice President and Publisher, Consumer Dummies

Kristin Ferguson-Wagstaffe, Product Development Director, Consumer Dummies

Ensley Eikenburg, Associate Publisher, Travel

Kelly Regan, Editorial Director, Travel

Composition Services

Debbie Stailey, Director of Composition Services

Table of Contents

Introduction

. . . .

*O*kay, we know what you're thinking. This is a tax book. How fun a read can it be? How can it possibly keep my attention? How will I ever get through enough of this tome to learn how to do my own tax planning, plus what I need to prepare my tax return accurately and on time? We're pretty good mind readers, aren't we? But you're right on only one account: This is a tax book. You'll be pleasantly surprised, though (amazed and astounded, really), to find that this book does hold your attention, and you don't have to pore over it from start to finish to get out of it what you need to pay less tax. As for the fun part, well . . . we promise this will be more fun than a root canal!

About This Book

Excuse us while we give ourselves a collective pat on the back, but we really couldn't have assembled a better team of authors to put this book together. Each author is a chartered accountant and certified financial planner with considerable expertise in tax matters. Our combined years of experience span more decades than even an accountant can count. Trust us, at the hourly rates we charge, this book is a deal — just a few cents per tip! (To be honest, we've slipped in even more than 78 tips, but we figured you wouldn't mind getting a few extra.) The bottom line? You can't beat the advice you get in this book, and the value is outstanding.

We've been writing For Dummies tax books since 2000. But you'll find this version quite different. This book is really a set of tips, with each part geared toward different kinds of taxpayers. You'll find these tips come in handy throughout the year, not just come tax-filing time. For example, maybe you just had a new baby and are wondering what types of tax relief you might have, or how to save tax-effectively for your child's education. Well, you can jump right to Part IV, Tips for Families, to get lots of great tips. Or maybe you want to get a head start on estate planning. Part V, Tips for Special Tax Planning Circumstances, is for you. But you'll also find the book comes in extra handy during tax-filing time, when you can be sure you're aware of all the deductions and credits you're eligible for. Talk about useful!

How This Book Is Organized

78 Tax Tips For Canadians For Dummies is organized into six distinct parts, each covering a different set of tax concerns.

Part 1: Tips for Everyone

This part offers tax advice that applies to just about everyone. We help you understand Canada's tax system, including our tax rates and our provincial/territorial tax systems, too. We also talk about how to organize your receipts and other tax information, and the various ways to file your return (no, it's not good enough to simply stuff your receipts in an envelope and mail them to the tax collector!). Additionally, we look at one tax-reducing strategy that everyone can do: donating to charity. Finally, we cover what happens after you file your return, and offer some hints on how to deal with disagreements with the Canada Revenue Agency (CRA).

Part 11: Tips for Employees and Business Owners

If you're part of the working world, you definitely want to read this part. Whether you work for yourself or someone else, you need to know what income and benefits are taxable and what types of deductions and credits you can claim. This can make a huge difference in how much tax you pay each year. For those of you who are out of work or looking for a new job, we have tips for you too, including what to do with severance pay, negotiating non-taxable benefits from your employer, and deducting moving costs if you have to move to find work. No matter what your situation, a thorough read of Part II is a must for anyone working for a living!

Part 111: Tips for Investors

Investors come in many shapes and sizes. Some are working away, and saving for the day they can retire. Some are already retired, and living off their savings. For some work is a hobby, for others it's a chore. Some investors are conservative, others aggressive. Some like stocks, some like property.

Wherever you fit in, one thing's for sure. Taxes make a difference. If you're an investor of any kind, be sure to read this part, chock full of tips for your situation. We explore how to use RRSPs and TFSAs to your best advantage, how to invest tax-efficiently, how to minimize the tax on capital gains or make the most of capital losses, and more!

Part IV: Tips for Families

A whole part just for families? Yes! Here you find which deductions and credits you can claim for you and your family, along with tax tips for everything from buying or renovating a house, to divorce (remember, we're sticking to tax tips here; your lawyer and your friends will likely have some tips of their own). We also offer a tonne of income splitting tips to help your family tax plan to pay less tax — together! Finally, we offer tips for families that include students, whether they're kids heading off to school for the first time, or adults hitting the books once more to freshen up their skills.

Part V: Tips for Special Tax-Planning Circumstances

We admit that this part's name is a bit mysterious. But what else could we call a part that covers tips for donating to charity, medical expenses, pension income, estate planning, and more! (Really, what else? We're open to suggestions.) Get out the sticky notes; this part is sure to be well used throughout the year.

Part VI: The Part of Tens

Every book should have a place for a top-ten list. Enter the Part of Tens — Part VI. We pack invaluable tidbits of useful information into this perennial For Dummies favourite.

Icons Used in This Book

Running down the left margin of these pages are cute little drawings. Here's a guide to what they mean.

This nerdy guy appears beside discussions that aren't critical when you just want to know the basic concepts and get answers to your tax questions — that is, when you're using the book as a quick reference days before your return is due (you wouldn't do that, now, would you?). However, actually reading these little information gems can deepen and enhance your tax knowledge. You'll be the tax-savviest person around the office water cooler.

The bull's-eye marks the spot for smart tax tips and timesavers to help you get your tax return done quickly and with a minimum amount of pain. This is definitely the icon to look for if you're pulling an all-nighter on April 29.

When you see this icon, you'll find a friendly reminder of stuff we discuss elsewhere in the book or of points we really, really want you to remember.

Don't make these common but costly mistakes with your taxes! Aren't we nice folks to point them out?

Where to Go from Here

We organized this book so you can flip to any part or tip based on your needs. Locked in a struggle with the CRA? Check out Part I. Trying to figure out the most tax-savvy way to handle your small business? Part II is for you. Have some investment money you want to shelter from tax, but you've maxed out your RRSPs? Tip #41 has your name on it.

We hope you find this book useful year-round, a helpful one-stop shop for all your tax questions. So dive in, and start saving money!

Part I
Tips for Everyone

In this part . . .

Tips for Everyone; the title says it all! Take some time to read through this part, no matter what stage of life you are in. Don't worry, there are very few numbers and complicated calculations lurking among these tips. Instead, we ease you in gently: Have you ever wanted to understand what sorts of taxes you have to worry about? Or if you qualify for "free money" from the taxman? If so, you've come to the right place. We also give you some handy pointers on how to stay organized, or — for all you procrastinators out there — how to get organized in the first place. We also have some helpful advice on how to make your charitable donations give you the best tax breaks. And for those who are about to get audited, don't stress, we've got tips for you, too!

Understand the Essentials

●●

*W*e get it. Most Canadians aren't tax geeks like us. We understand that tax is not known to be the most exciting of subjects. But if you don't care about your money, who will? Having a basic understanding of the Canadian tax system is an imperative first step to ensure you don't pay more tax than you should. So, that being said, congratulations on taking this step to know more about taxes! We promise it won't be too painful.

Though it can be confusing at times, Canada's income tax system has two very straightforward purposes. The first is to finance government expenditures. The second is to encourage Canadians to make certain expenditures. That's right — our government cuts you a tax break when you spend money in ways it approves of. For example, the government wants to encourage you to:

- **Pursue post-secondary education.** Tuition fees, textbooks, and interest incurred on student loans are eligible for a tax credit. Even better, scholarships, fellowships, and bursaries are completely tax free!

- **Work.** If you hire someone to look after your kids so you can work, you can deduct childcare expenses. And all employees are eligible for a Canada employment credit — the government's way of recognizing that we all incur some out-of-pocket expenses in order to work.

- **Save for retirement.** Tax rules are favourable for registered retirement savings plans (RRSPs).

- **Invest.** Dividends from Canadian corporations are taxed at a favourable rate, and only one-half of the capital gain on a sale of investments is subject to tax.

You're probably beginning to realize that you spend money every year on items you can use to reduce your taxes. And every little bit counts! With this in mind, in this tip we guide you through the nitty gritty of the Canadian tax system.

Understanding Where the Numbers Come From

If you live in Canada it's pretty easy to figure out what gets included in your *total income*. Why? Well, to keep things simple, the Canadian government requires you to include all of your world-wide income earned in a calendar year on your tax return. If you earned income, you can pretty much count on the fact that it's taxable. Of course some exceptions do exist, and we discuss these throughout this book.

The next step is to claim any deductions you're entitled to. *Net income* is the amount you arrive at when you subtract these deductions from your total income. You might think this net income figure is the amount on which you should pay tax. Well, no. The amount you pay tax on is your *taxable income*.

Determining what makes up taxable income

Here in Canada our income taxes are based on the amount of taxable income we earn in a year. Both the federal and provincial/territorial governments levy income taxes on your taxable income (we talk more about these taxes in Tip #2). Your base amount of tax owing is reduced by any tax credits available to you, and the net amount is your tax bill for the year. It stands to reason that if you can keep your taxable income to a minimum and your tax credits as high as possible, you will pay less tax. And with tax rates reaching as high as about 50 percent for some Canadians, this can mean a lot more money stays in your wallet.

Even though taxes are not based on net income, it's still an essential calculation that's used to calculate your entitlement to certain tax credits and programs — like the provincial/territorial tax credit (Tip #3), the GST/HST credit (Tip #23), the Canada Child Tax Benefit (Tip #49), and credits for charitable donations (Tip #9), medical expenses (Tip #59), and social benefits (Tip #64).

Taxable income has a different focus altogether. The types of deductions allowed under the taxable income category are not necessarily related to current-year activities. For instance, the calculation of taxable income includes deductions for prior-year losses. In fact, some of the deductions are permissive, meaning they allow for tax deductions based on your personal situation. For example, deductions are available for employee stock options, for residents in northern areas of Canada, and for certain non-taxable payments received in the year.

On many returns, net income and taxable income will be the same; therefore, you won't have to worry about these deductions at all. However, if you do have additional deductions, it's important to keep in mind that a difference exists between net income and taxable income — be sure to use the right figures in the right places!

Sometimes you will have so many deductions to claim you won't need them all to reduce your taxable income to the point where no taxes are owing. Use your available tax deductions to reduce your taxable income only to the point that it equals your total tax credits for the year. If you reduce your taxable income to zero, you won't owe any taxes, but you might be wasting some deductions. For example, most taxpayers are allowed to claim the basic personal credit amount — this means you would want to report at least that much income (about $10,000, but the amount changes yearly). To optimize your tax situation, you therefore don't want to waste tax deductions that you can carry forward to future years if it means reducing your taxable income below the amount of your tax credits. Zero taxable income is not the goal.

Tallying up your effective tax rate

Your *effective tax rate* is the percentage your tax is of your total taxable income. It's easy to calculate — it's simply your tax liability (after you've taken all the tax credits you're entitled to) over your taxable income:

$$\frac{\text{Tax liability}}{\text{Taxable income}} = \text{Effective tax rate}$$

Take a look at some figures from Micha's tax return. She lives in Thompson, Manitoba, and her taxable income is $53,000. She calculates the tax on the $53,000 and then reduces the amount for any tax credits she is entitled to. After these credits are deducted, her federal/Manitoba tax liability is $12,885. Her effective tax rate, then, is 24.3 percent ($12,885/$53,000).

The calculation of your effective tax rate takes into account that portions of your income are taxed in different tax brackets. The effective tax rate calculation "averages" the rates of tax paid in these brackets. The more income you have taxed in the highest tax bracket, the higher your effective tax rate.

Calculating your marginal tax rate

When tax geeks talk about *marginal tax rates,* we are referring to the tax rate that applies to your next dollar of taxable income.

Assume your taxable income is $130,000 and you are taxed in the top tax bracket. Further, assume you live in Alberta and that the highest tax rate is 39 percent. If you were to earn $1 of additional interest income, you would pay 39¢ in tax on this dollar. In other words, your marginal tax rate is 39 percent. On an after-tax basis, that extra dollar of income leaves you with only 61¢, or 61 percent. This is referred to as your after-tax rate of return. It can be calculated as:

1 – Your marginal tax rate = Your after-tax rate of return

The calculation of your marginal tax rate ignores that portions of your income are taxed in different tax brackets and subject to different tax rates. The marginal tax rate is focused on your next dollar of taxable income — not your overall taxable income.

The marginal tax rate is an easy way to assess the impact of a raise. With a marginal tax rate of 39 percent, you know that if you receive a $10,000 raise you will be taking home only an additional $6,100. When looking at investment returns from alternative investment opportunities, ensure you compare after-tax rates of return.

A marginal tax rate can also be used to calculate the tax savings that a deduction will provide. Again assume your taxable income is $130,000 and you live in Alberta. You are wondering what the impact would have been if you had contributed $5,000 to your RRSP and taken a deduction on your tax return. Your taxable income would have been reduced to $125,000 by the $5,000 RRSP deduction. You know your marginal tax rate on that $5,000 would have been 39 percent. The tax saving you would enjoy if you were able to deduct the $5,000 RRSP contribution is $1,950 ($5,000 multiplied by 39 percent)!

Knowing You Have the Right to Pay Less Tax

Canada's tax system is based on self-assessment. Each of us is responsible to ensure our tax return includes all necessary information for reporting income, claiming tax deductions and tax credits, and, finally, calculating our tax liability. In complying with the tax laws, we all have the right to pay as little tax as is legally possible. We stress legally.

Tax evasion occurs when you purposely understate the amount of income tax you should pay. This can occur when you don't report all your income, or when you overstate tax deductions and credits. At worst, tax evasion can result in a charge being laid under the *Criminal Code*.

Tax planning is a continuous process. With the ever-changing economy and tax legislation, and the investment vehicles available in the market, you can always be planning ways to minimize your taxes. Many opportunities for tax planning arise when you experience a significant change in your life.

Reducing Your Tax Bill with Tax Credits

Tax *credits* directly reduce the amount of income tax you owe — they do not reduce your taxable income. In this way they differ from tax deductions, which are subtracted in computing your taxable income.

Two kinds of credits are available: refundable and non-refundable. When a credit is referred to as *non-refundable,* it means that if it exceeds your tax you do not get a refund of the excess. Every Canadian is entitled to at least a basic personal credit (non-refundable) worth over $10,000, although this amount increases each year. This means you can earn at least $10,000 without paying any tax because the credit essentially wipes out the tax (see Tip #44).

Report all of your federal tax credits on schedule 1 of your tax return. Each province/territory also calculates its own tax credits to help offset provincial/territorial taxes. These credits are reported on your provincial/territorial tax calculation forms. It's a good idea to take a peek at these forms to see whether any of the credits sound like they might apply to your situation.

#2

Understand the Different Types of Taxes

*N*o doubt about it, Canada is a high-tax nation — which gives you all the more reason to minimize the taxes you pay. In this book we're primarily concerned with income taxes, but many different types of taxes might apply to your situation. It's your responsibility to understand what taxes you're accountable for and to ensure you're filing the proper returns.

A Tale of Two Income Taxes

Canada's constitution gives income taxing powers to both the federal and the provincial/territorial governments, which does make things a little more confusing. But on the bright side, individuals need to deal with only one tax collector — the CRA. The CRA administers the tax system for the federal government and all of the provinces and territories except Quebec.

Both the feds and the provinces/territories have "tax on income" systems: taxes are based on taxable income, and each province and territory has the right to set its own rates and policies.

When you file your tax return, you fill out federal tax forms and provincial/territorial tax forms. The rules are similar, but not identical, for both. And when it comes time to file your return, you send your whole tax package to the CRA (unless you file in Quebec, in which case your federal return goes to the CRA and your provincial return to the Ministère du Revenu du Québec).

Figuring out your federal taxes

Canada's income tax system is a *progressive tax rate system,* which means that the percentage of your income that goes to fund your tax liability increases as your income increases. Take a look at the four federal tax brackets for 2009 shown in Table 1-1. These brackets are set to increase to inflation annually; therefore, in years after

2009, each bracket will cover an additional amount of income. You can find current-year rates on the CRA Web site, or on the Web sites of major accounting firms (see Tip #8).

Table 1-1 2009 Federal Income Tax Brackets and Rates (provincial/territorial taxes not included)

Tax Bracket	Tax Rate
$0 to $40,726	15%
$40,727 to $81,452	22%
$81,453 to $126,264	26%
$126,265 and over	29%

As you can see, the greater your taxable income, the greater the percentage of tax applied to that additional income.

The tax rates in Table 1-1 are only the federal tax rates, and do not include provincial/territorial income taxes. When your taxable income falls into the top federal tax bracket (that is, greater than $126,265), your combined federal and provincial/territorial tax rate on the portion of your taxable income in the top tax bracket can be as high as the tax rates summarized in Table 1-2. However, the tax rates shown are before any tax credits (except the basic personal amount) that may be available to individuals. Your tax liability is based on your taxable income. After the liability is calculated, it's reduced by tax credits available to you.

Taking a look at provincial and territorial taxes

In additional to federal taxes, every province/territory in Canada levies taxes based on taxable income. Table 1-2 indicates the total tax rates you would pay if you were taxed at the highest rates in each province/territory. Note that different highest rates apply depending on the type of income you earn. Regular income such as salaries and interest income (among others such as foreign income and rental income) are taxed the highest. Capital gains are only one-half taxable; therefore, the tax rate on capital gains is always exactly half that of regular income. And Canadian dividends are taxed at lower rates as well, due to a dividend tax credit.

Table 1-2	2009 Top Tax Rates (federal and provincial/territorial taxes combined)			
Province/Territory	*Salary & Interest*	*Capital Gains*	*Dividends*	
			Non-Eligible	*Eligible*
Alberta	39.0	19.50	27.7	14.5
British Columbia	43.7	21.9	32.7	19.9
Manitoba	46.4	23.20	38.2	23.8
New Brunswick	47.0	23.5	35.4	23.2
Newfoundland and Labrador	44.5	22.3	32.7	27.4
Northwest Territories	43.1	21.5	29.6	18.2
Nova Scotia	48.3	24.1	33.1	28.3
Nunavut	40.5	20.3	29.0	22.2
Ontario	46.4	23.2	31.3	23.0
Prince Edward Island	47.4	23.7	33.6	24.4
Quebec	48.2	24.1	36.4	29.7
Saskatchewan	44.0	22.0	30.8	20.3
Yukon	42.4	21.2	30.5	17.2

Note: Figures are current to September 2009.

You probably noticed that two different tax rates apply to dividends. The actual rate that will apply depends on their source. Non-eligible dividends are generally dividends paid from small businesses in Canada. If you own your own company and receive dividends from it, these rates likely apply to you. Alternatively, eligible dividends are those paid by public corporations resident in Canada. It's these eligible dividends that most investors in Canada receive when they invest in a non-registered account.

GST/HST

The Goods and Services Tax/Harmonized Sales Tax is not an income tax, but rather a consumer tax. But you already know that; when you make a purchase of goods or services in Canada you usually find this tax added onto your final bill.

GST/HST also finds its way into our income tax system in many ways. If you run a business, you're generally required to charge GST on the goods and services you sell. You must remit the tax to the CRA, just like you remit income tax. Any GST/HST you pay on goods and services used in your business can be used to offset the GST/HST payable.

If you're an employee, you might pay GST/HST on expenditures you have made for business purposes. The expenses you incur might be eligible for a tax deduction. And the GST/HST paid on those expenses is eligible for a rebate. You claim the rebate when you file your income tax return; see Tip #23 for details.

Finally, the government offers GST/HST rebates to taxpayers who meet the criteria. All you have to do is tick the box on your income tax return stating that you would like to apply. The CRA does the calculations, and if you qualify the CRA will send you quarterly non-taxable payments. What could be easier!

Alternative Minimum Tax

What is alternative minimum tax, you ask? *Alternative minimum tax* (AMT) is designed to prevent taxpayers with significant tax deductions from skipping off without paying some tax — a minimum tax, at least.

Minimum tax is not something the average taxpayer will ever have to worry about. But if you have some less than common tax deductions, take a look at form T691. The types of deductions listed on T691 that may lead you to pay minimum tax are not everyday types of deductions but include:

✔ Limited-partnership losses including carrying charges related to the limited partnership units

✔ Resource expenses, depletion allowances, and carrying charges related to resource properties and flow-through shares. You would have these deductions if you purchased certain tax shelter investments

✔ Stock option and share deductions if your employer offers stock options and you chose to exercise those options

✔ The non-taxable portion of capital gains (50 percent of gains) reported in the year. This includes any capital gain on which the capital gains exemption is claimed. Capital gains occur when you sell an asset, like a stock, for more than you paid for it.

✔ Employee home relocation loan deduction if your employer loaned you funds at a low interest rate to help you pay for a move

If you owe AMT, don't fret. You can use that minimum tax to offset regular taxes payable in any of the next seven years. Assuming you pay regular tax during those years, you will get your money back. Consider it a prepayment of your future tax bill. Minimum tax is often more of a cash-flow issue than a true income tax.

International Taxes

Canada levies income taxes based on residency. If you are a resident of Canada, you're liable for tax on your worldwide income (see Tip #31). In addition, Canada has a right to tax Canadian-source income, even if you're not resident here. For example, if you sell a piece of Canadian real estate but live elsewhere in the world, Canada still has a right to tax the gain because the asset, the real estate, is located in Canada.

Other countries have similar tax laws. If you own assets such as investments on which you earn dividends or interest; real estate on which you earn rental income or gains upon sale; or if you earn income such as pensions or employment income in another country, those other countries have the right to tax that income according to the tax laws in those countries.

If you're paying attention, you'll notice that residents in Canada are taxed on their worldwide income, and that other countries may tax you on that same income. Isn't that double taxation? The good news is that Canada has tax treaties with many major countries in the world that are designed to avoid double taxation. If you pay tax to another country you can claim a foreign tax credit for the foreign taxes that will serve to offset the Canadian taxes paid on that same income. But be aware that if you earn income that comes from another country, you very well could have tax liabilities — and perhaps even tax filing requirements — in the other country. You may want to consult a tax pro.

Get Free Money from the Government

*E*ven though you may not be required to file a tax return this year, consider doing so anyway. You can gain a lot of benefits from filing — including free money! — that far outweigh the time and frustration spent preparing your return. (Did we mention "free money"?)

Claiming GST Credits

You might be entitled to a tax-free quarterly cheque from the government for the Goods and Services Tax (GST) or the Harmonized Sales Tax (HST). That's right; some of these dreaded sales taxes may actually be refunded to you via a tax credit. Not everyone is eligible for the GST/HST credit, but if you are eligible you can receive it only if you apply for it each year.

Applying is easy: When you file a tax return, tick the box that says you want to apply. The CRA will do the calculations and let you know if you qualify based on information such as your net income, the net income of your spouse, and the number of children under the age of 18 who live with you.

Even if you have no income, you need to file a tax return to apply for the GST/HST credit.

You're entitled to the GST/HST credit when you turn 19, so you'll need to file a tax return for at least the year prior to your 19th birthday to ensure you get your payments. If your birthday is in January, February, or March, file for the two years prior to your 19th birthday. If you forgot, you can always file after the fact.

Benefiting from Provincial Tax Credits

Many provinces and territories in Canada offer special tax credits to their residents. However, these credits do not come to you automatically. You must apply for them on your personal tax return. The tax credits vary by province/territory and some are very generous. They include credits such as sales tax credits and property tax credits.

Receiving Child Benefits

If you're responsible for the care of a child who is under age 18, you might be eligible to claim the Canada Child Tax Benefit (CCTB) for that child.

To apply for the CCTB, the first step is to complete Form RC66, Canada Child Benefits Application. However, because the benefits are based on net family income, you must file a tax return to substantiate your income. Even if your income is nil, file a tax return to ensure you don't miss out on these benefits.

Obtaining Refunds for CPP or EI Overpayments

Canada Pension Plan (CPP) and Employment Insurance (EI) premiums are deducted from your pay and reported on your personal tax return. If you've worked at only one job in the year, it's unlikely that your CPP or EI premiums were drastically wrong. However, if you have more than one employer in a year, each employer is required to deduct CPP and EI based on your earnings at that job alone. In this case it's very common that your total CPP and EI paid was too much. (By the way, this often has nothing to do with your employer's payroll skills; it's because of the way the calculation is done.)

You're entitled to receive a refund of CPP and EI overpayments in the year. The way to do this is to file an income tax return.

Knowing What to Do If You've Paid Too Much Tax

If you've earned employment income in the year, you should receive a T4 slip from your employer. Box 22 of that slip will note whether taxes were deducted from your pay. If you earn other types of income, such as investment income, you might be required to pay quarterly income tax instalments to the government. Either way, these taxes were based on a lot of assumptions, which may or may not reflect your tax reality at the end of the year. Depending on your personal circumstances, these taxes may be too high, which means you're entitled to a tax refund. And you guessed it — the only way to claim a tax refund is to file a tax return.

Anytime you've paid taxes in the year, file a tax return just in case you're entitled to a refund.

Claiming Other Benefits

Even if you don't owe tax or have free money to claim, there still may be reasons to file a tax return, including:

- ✔ **You want to maximize your RRSP contribution room for future years.** You're allowed to make RRSP contributions each year based on your RRSP contribution room, which is calculated using your earned income from prior years. In years when you have little income you may not need to file a return; however, even a little income may still be considered earned income, giving rise to RRSP room. Unused RRSP contribution room never expires, so you could use it to claim RRSP deductions — and save taxes — down the road.

- ✔ **You have deductions or credits to carry forward to future years.** You may have incurred some costs that would normally be a tax deduction or credit, which are of no use to you because of your income level. Certain of these amounts can be carried forward to help your tax situation in future years, including tuition, education, and textbook amounts, RRSP contributions, and moving expenses.

✔ **You received Working Income Tax Benefit (WITB) advance payments and you want to apply for WITB advance payments for the upcoming year.**

✔ **You have a non-capital loss, such as a loss on your unincorporated business, that you want to be able to apply in other years.** Although that loss is not going to attract tax this year, you might be able to benefit from it in other years. And the only way to document the loss is by filing a tax return. Non-capital losses can be carried forward for 20 years. However, consider carrying your losses back (up to three years), if possible, to receive a tax benefit from the loss sooner rather than later.

✔ **You want to continue to receive the Guaranteed Income Supplement or Allowance benefits under the Old Age Security Program.** You can usually renew your benefit simply by filing your return by April 30. If you choose not to file a return, you will have to complete a renewal application form. This form is available from a Service Canada office or from the agency's Web site.

Set Up a Good Recordkeeping System

● ●

Do you want to know the secret to making sure you claim every deduction you're entitled to? To saving money when you have a tax preparer do your tax return? To surviving a CRA audit unscathed? Sure you do! Luckily, we have the answer. *Keep good records*. That's all there is to it, really. In this tip we spell out just how you can keep records that'll turn even the harshest auditor into a softie.

When dealing with the CRA, the burden of proof is on you to support the deductions you have claimed. The CRA is by law considered correct unless you can prove otherwise. Keeping good tax records is imperative so you can support your numbers.

Keeping Good Books and Records

You may think that by filing a tax return for the year you've absolved yourself of any further CRA requirements. Unfortunately, that's not true. You see, the CRA requires every person who pays or collects taxes, or who is carrying on business in Canada, to keep books and records. This requirement means you have to keep information pertaining to your taxes in case the CRA asks to review it in the future. Your books and records must enable the CRA to determine your taxes payable for the year and must be supported by source documents to verify the amounts reported.

Make sure you keep all source documents pertaining to your tax return, which may include:

- ✔ Sales invoices
- ✔ Purchase invoices
- ✔ Cash-register receipts
- ✔ Written contracts
- ✔ Credit card receipts

- ✔ Delivery slips
- ✔ Deposit slips
- ✔ Cheques
- ✔ Bank statements
- ✔ General correspondence

When deciding what type of document to keep, consider this: What document will best verify your tax records? The stronger the evidence, the less likely it is that your tax records will be rejected by the CRA.

The original bill is best — the CRA will not always accept cancelled cheques and credit card statements as authentication of an expense.

Setting up your recordkeeping system

In our experience, the number-one reason why people end up paying more tax than they have to is that they keep lousy records. We know that taming the paper tiger is no mean feat. What follows are our best suggestions to make your tax organization and preparation tasks much easier.

Save all the receipts and records you think you might be able to use. It's much more difficult to recover receipts that have been thrown away than to toss out whatever unnecessary paper you have left after your tax return is complete.

Our favourite method of organizing tax information is in an accordion file — pick one up at any office supply store. (You could also use file folders or envelopes.) Label each section by expense category. Use the categories listed on the tax form you will be completing; for example, charitable donations, medical expenses, office supplies, parking, advertising, and so on. As you collect receipts throughout the year, sort them into the proper category. When it comes time to file your tax return, all you have to do is take out the receipts, add them up, and enter the total on the tax form.

Consider organizing your tax information by the tax schedules you have to file, such as Statement of Real Estate Rentals, Capital Gains and Losses, and Statement of Business Activities. If your tax return is uncomplicated, it might be sufficient to have one file for each year. As you receive your tax information throughout the year, just put it into the file.

Any of these storage methods will save you from tearing your house apart looking for that investment statement or charitable receipt you were using as a bookmark last June. Keep a copy of the tax return you filed for that year, and when you get your Notice of Assessment put it in the same folder.

Making use of your computer

Your computer can be a huge help in tracking your tax information each year. Many software packages exist — each with its own merits. Speak with a knowledgeable software salesperson before purchasing to make sure you get only what you need. Don't buy an expensive accounting package if you're going to use only one or two components.

We recommend the software packages Quicken and Microsoft Money for tracking personal and small business expenses, and QuickBooks for tracking the expenses of larger businesses. These packages will help you do everything from tracking your investment portfolio to balancing your chequebook to monitoring payroll.

Using a software package to enter your data means more of a time commitment up front, but when you need the records for tax time your figures will be added up and ready to go.

If you do use a computer for all your recordkeeping, or if you have other valuable documents, store a recent backup of your computer files and those valuable documents, or copies of them, off-site. That way, if you suffer a fire or other disaster, all will not be lost.

(For more about tax software, check out Tip #6.)

Watching out for recordkeeping time bombs

Look out for these special situations:

✔ **Automobile expenses:** If you're claiming automobile expenses for a vehicle used for both business and personal purposes, you must keep a logbook for a sample period of time to support the vehicle's business use. Include details on dates, number of kilometres driven, and destinations. Because you're allowed to claim only the business portion of your automobile expenses, it stands to reason that you need some sort of proof to show what percentage of your auto expenses are in fact business related. The logbook is the perfect solution. (See Tip #17 for more about automobile expenses.)

✔ **Charitable receipts:** An official receipt from a registered charity is the only document accepted by the CRA for a charitable donation. Many charities now send these electronically. Cancelled cheques and ticket stubs will not be accepted. And if you want to claim a tax credit, ensure you're donating to a registered charity — ask to see a registration number if you're not sure. The registration number must appear on the receipt.

(For more about charities and taxes, see Tips #9 to 11.)

Knowing How Long to Keep Your Tax Records

One of the questions clients most frequently ask us is, "How long do I have to keep my records and receipts?" The answer, according to the CRA, is six years. The books and records must be kept in Canada at your residence or place of business. These books and records must be made available to the CRA should it ask to see them.

Even though the CRA can't go back and audit your tax return after six years — unless it suspects fraud, in which case all tax years are fair game — you need to keep purchase receipts and investment statements for assets you still own. You may need those records as proof of ownership if you ever have to make an insurance claim or if you sell the asset. And you may need proof of an asset's cost in the future if the gain or loss must be reported on your tax return.

If a particular tax year is under objection or appeal, keep your books and records on hand until the objection or appeal has been resolved and the time for filing a further appeal has expired. It would be a shame to throw out your books and records only to have legitimate tax deductions denied down the road.

Dealing with Missing Information Slips and Receipts

For many types of income you earn, you will be sent information slips, commonly called T-slips, that document the income received and that must be reported on your income tax return. This includes slips such as T4s (reporting employment income), T5s (reporting investment income), and slips from the government (Old Age

Security, Canada Pension Plan, and Employment Insurance). You should receive these slips by the end of February in the year following the year in which you received the payment. However, T3 slips (reporting trust income, such as from mutual funds) are often not available until after March 31. For other types of income such as business income, or capital gains from the sale of investments or other assets, no slips will be sent to you; it's up to you to calculate your income and report it on your tax return.

Just because you don't have a slip doesn't mean you're absolved from reporting that income. If you know you earned income in the year you are required by law to report it on your tax return. If you are missing any slips, call the issuer for a new one. In the case of government-issued slips, you can request many of them online.

Giving the CRA your best estimate

If you've made a reasonable attempt to obtain your slip but you are still "slipless," you need to estimate your income and related tax credits and deductions.

If it's your T4 that's missing, use your pay stubs to assist you in reporting your employment income and any tax credits or deductions for your CPP contributions, EI premiums, and union dues. Finally, don't forget to report the income taxes withheld by your employer! Attach a note to your return stating you were unable to obtain your slip and have summarized the estimated amounts. Give the name and address of the person or organization that should have issued the slip.

You must still file your tax return by the April 30 filing deadline (or June 15, if you or your spouse are self-employed) even if you know information is missing. Attach a note to your return explaining what is missing, detail any estimated amounts, and get it in on time! This is especially important if you owe money, because you will be charged a late filing penalty if the return is late — and interest, if your balance owing is not paid by April 30.

Coping with missing receipts

Receipts for some deductions, such as RRSP contributions, charitable donations, and medical expenses, must be attached to your tax return when it is filed (assuming you're paper filing your return). If these receipts are not included with your return, processing will be delayed and your deductions may be disallowed. Remember, the onus is on you to support all the income, deductions, and credits reported on your tax return.

If a receipt is missing, call the person or organization responsible for issuing it to obtain another copy. Even if you cannot get another copy before the April 30 tax return filing deadline, file your return on time. You can forward the receipt to the CRA when it does finally arrive. Alternatively, you can simply leave the deduction off your tax return and file an adjustment when you receive the receipt. (See Tip #75 for details.)

You don't have to attach some types of receipts to your tax return. For example, if you have claims for union dues, tuition fees, or childcare expenses, you don't need to attach the receipts to your return when you file it. However, be aware that the CRA does regular "reviews" of these types of credits and deductions, so ensure you have the proper documentation on hand should the CRA ask to see it in the future.

Don't think you can get away from keeping receipts and other supporting documentation because you are EFILING, NETFILING, or TELEFILING your return. The CRA can and often does ask to see the documentation! (See Tip #7 for more about alternate modes of filing your return.)

Knowing what to do when the dog really did eat your tax records

Your worst nightmare has come to life — you're being audited! And to top it off, Sparky has eaten some of your tax receipts. Does this mean you'll lose out on all your legitimate tax deductions? Not necessarily. The CRA does understand that these situations can occur, and will give you the benefit of the doubt (sometimes) when you can show reasonable support for the income, deductions, and credits reported on your return.

If the CRA does come calling and you simply don't have the records you need to support your tax deductions, you can still prove your claims were legitimate. It may take you some time to reconstruct records, but when you consider the alternatives (additional tax, interest, and penalties on disallowed deductions from an audit), the time you spend will be well worth it.

The simplest way to reconstruct missing tax records is to ask for new ones. For example, if you know you bought a number of prescriptions this year but can't find your receipts, go back to your local pharmacy and ask for a printout of your expenditures for the year. You will be surprised at how many deductions you will be able to reconstruct simply by asking for duplicate receipts.

If you sold or gave away an asset but you do not have a record of its original cost, either because you lost the relevant documents or because it was a gift, you can establish a cost in one of several ways:

✔ Look in newspapers from the year you purchased or were given an asset to determine what similar assets were selling for.

✔ If you're trying to find information on a property, consult with the local real estate board. They usually keep historical data on property in the area. You could also go to the property tax collector's office in your municipality. Their assessed values for the property might be of use.

✔ If you inherited an asset, the easiest way to establish its tax cost to you is to check the deceased's final tax return to see at what price they were deemed to have disposed of the property to you. This disposal price is the same as your tax cost.

✔ Call your investment advisor for help. Your advisor should have historical records of your financial affairs and may be able to help you calculate the cost of your shares, mutual funds, or other assets he or she manages.

Why is the cost value important? You need to know the original cost of the asset to properly calculate the capital gain or loss when the asset is eventually sold or otherwise disposed of — see Tips #38 and #39 for more details.

If it's your business records that have been lost or destroyed, you can re-create many of your expenses using the following tactics:

✔ Get copies of your phone, utility, credit card, rent, and other bills from the companies that issued the bills. Getting an annual statement from a major vendor shouldn't be too difficult.

✔ Ask for duplicate bank statements and credit card statements that will help you to establish income and some of your expenses for the year.

✔ Keep separate personal and business bank accounts and credit cards so you can easily verify what is what.

✔ Reconstruct automobile expenses based on a reasonable estimation of what it costs to run your type of vehicle. The dealer from whom you bought your car might be helpful in estimating these costs.

✔ Look at your previous years' tax returns to establish your expenses in prior years and also your profit margins. If you have lost those, too, you can obtain copies of previous years' returns from the CRA on request.

#5

Know When Your Tax Return Is Due

*F*iling your tax return on time is critical. If you don't, and you owe money, you'll be charged a late filing penalty in addition to interest on the taxes outstanding. And even if you don't owe money, it's still a good idea to file on time so that you don't needlessly hold up your refund and benefit payments!

If your due date falls on a Saturday, Sunday, or public holiday, you have until the next business day to file and you will not be considered late.

Due Date for Regular Folk

Personal income tax returns for the previous calendar year are due by midnight, April 30. If you're electronically filing your return, ensure you get confirmation that your return went through before this time. And if you're mailing in your return, ensure it's postmarked as being mailed on or before April 30. If you just put your return in a regular mailbox and it's not picked up until the next day, it will be considered late-filed.

If you have a balance owing on your taxes and don't file on time, you will be charged an automatic 5 percent late filing penalty based on the amount owing. A further penalty of 1 percent of the unpaid tax will also be added for each full month the return is late, up to a maximum of 12 months (so, there's an additional 12 percent maximum penalty). If you're late a second time within three years of the first late filing, the penalty is bumped up to a maximum of 40 percent! And that's not all: you'll have to pay interest, too. Ouch! Even if you cannot pay your tax, make sure you file your return on time to avoid these penalties!

Due Date When You're Self-Employed

If you or your spouse carried on an unincorporated business and have self-employment income to claim, your return is not due until June 15. However, if you owe taxes, you must estimate your tax bill and pay it by April 30 to avoid interest charges.

Special Due Dates in the Year of Death

The due date for the return of a person who died in the year depends upon the date of death. If the death occurred between January 1 and October 31, the return is due on April 30 of the next year. However, in recognition that pulling together tax documents for an individual who has passed away can be challenging, when an individual has died between November 1 and December 31 the due date is extended to six months after the date of death, which will be some time after the normal April 30 deadline.

The tax return of the surviving spouse is due the same day as the deceased's return. However, if there will be a balance owing on the survivor's return, it's due on April 30 following the year of death.

If the deceased or the deceased's spouse had been self-employed, different due dates apply. In that case, if death occurred between January 1 and December 15, the due date for the return is June 15 of the following year. For deaths between December 16 and the end of the year, the return is due six months after the date of death.

If death occurs in January to April, it may be difficult to file the tax return for the immediately preceding tax year. In that case, the prior year's tax return and any taxes owing are due six months following death. For example, if John died on February 1 of this year, his last year's tax return is not due until August of this year (it normally would have been due April 30). Any tax liability from the final tax year (which will include only the month of January) is payable by April 30 of next year.

Although you're given the option to file the final tax return on these alternate dates, it can be filed at any time after the date of death and will generally be processed right away as a service to the estate, using legislation applicable to the most recent tax year. You can request a reassessment of the return later if the tax laws change.

#6

Choose the Preparation Option That's Best for You

S o many choices, so little time. You know you have to file a tax return, but do you prepare your return yourself the old fashioned way, or using your computer, or do you throw in the towel and hire someone to do it for you?

Using Your Computer vs a Pencil to Tally Your Taxes

Ever thought of preparing your tax return using your computer instead of the old pencil and calculator method? Think about it. No more adding machines or the dreaded smell of correction fluid. No more tearing through the paper when you've erased the amount on line 150 one too many times. Tax preparation software makes sense when you've already dived into the world of preparing your own return. And even for those of you still sitting on the fence, tax preparation software may provide the nudge you need. When choosing between preparing a return on paper or on the computer, we'd choose the computer every time.

We're not the only ones who would choose the computer. According to the government, more than half the tax returns filed in 2008 were filed electronically. That adds up to a whopping 13.1 million returns prepared and delivered via computer. This number has been growing, and is expected to continue.

Looking at the perks and perils of going the techno route

Using software to prepare your tax return has a number of advantages over paper-filing. The favourite, of course, is automatic recalculation: When one number on your return changes, the program updates all relevant forms and recalculates your final tax bill.

Another advantage is that most software packages are dummy-proof, set up so all you need to do is find the window that corresponds to the particular slip you have — be it a T4, T3, T5, or so on — and fill it in based on what appears in your boxes. This can save you a lot of time and frustration!

Most tax software programs allow you to NETFILE your tax return, which is fast, efficient, and ecologically friendly. NETFILING means you send your return using the Internet, instead of printing it and mailing it in. If you're anticipating a refund, you can expect to get it faster when you NETFILE, which is an added bonus!

Computers aren't people. They can't look at numbers to determine whether they're reasonable, or whether they're correct. No computer will tell you to think again before deducting your all-inclusive trip for two to Jamaica as a business expense.

Shopping for tax software

It's surprising to see how many software programs are available to prepare Canadian tax returns. If your return is simple and you don't print off a copy to mail in to the CRA, pretty much any program will do the trick. That being said, some programs don't prepare Quebec returns, so watch out for that. If your return is complicated and you're looking for guidance, it's worth it to pay a few extra bucks for the more sophisticated programs. Assuming you want to NETFILE your return, here are some CRA-certified options:

- **GenuTax:** Downloadable multiyear software — you don't pay for annual updates! The software is Windows-only and doesn't support Quebec returns. Visit www.genutax.ca.

- **H&R Block:** You can have H&R Block complete your return for you, or use their Windows or Online Tax Programs to do your own taxes. Go to www.hrblock.ca for more information.

- **myTaxExpress:** For Windows users only, this program boasts a free trial before purchase and can handle Quebec returns. See www.mytaxexpress.com for details.

- **QuickTax** (Windows; download or CD-ROM, or online via **Quick TaxWeb** from Intuit Canada): QuickTax is Canada's best-selling tax software. Gather your receipts and answer the simple questions posed by EasyStep Interview in English or French. The program takes your information and puts it where it belongs on the federal and Quebec forms. QuickTax reviews your return when you're finished, and even alerts you to any missed deductions or credits. You can NETFILE your return with both the desktop and online versions. Check out `www.quicktax.intuit.ca`.

✔ **Tax Chopper (formerly CuteTax):** Online software; no Quebec returns. Get more info at `www.cutetax.ca`.

✔ **TaxTron:** The software is available in Windows and Macintosh versions, comes in English and French and can handle Quebec returns. Support is available online or by phone in English, French, Chinese, Hindi, and Punjabi. For more details, visit `www.taxtron.ca`.

✔ **UFile:** UFile is another program with Quebec capabilities. You can either use the UFile.ca online version or buy UFile for Windows to install on your PC. Check it out at `www.ufile.ca`.

Getting the Most from Tax Pros

When your plumbing is broken, do you immediately call the plumber, or do you try to fix it yourself? For some, calling for help is the last resort — and preparing their own tax return is no exception. Sometimes, however, admitting defeat and hiring someone before you get into trouble is a good idea.

Dealing with a tax professional

Be sure you have accumulated all the information necessary before sending it to your preparer. When you have a business, your best bet is to summarize all your revenue and expenses ahead of time. You'll cut down on your fee, and ensure no relevant information is omitted.

Hiring someone may be a good idea if you need some tax-planning advice. Sometimes the additional fees you pay may actually be recovered in saved taxes! However, be careful whom you hire for tax planning, because some individuals are more competent than others. We tell you how to find that "special" person next.

Asking the right questions

The Yellow Pages has dozens of pages of accounting firms and businesses that specialize in tax. Finding a reputable tax professional is kind of like finding a mechanic — you've got to be careful. In your initial meeting, the tax professional should ask a lot of questions about your situation. Ask her some questions, too, to make sure you've found the right person.

Here's a list of questions to ask your tax professional to ensure he or she can handle your situation:

- **What services do you offer?** Some tax professionals only prepare tax returns; others will help you with other matters such as retirement planning or estate planning.

- **Have you worked in this area before?** When you have your own business, or are an avid investor, make sure your professional has worked with similar situations before. Many firms have specialists in particular areas, but some may be used to working with employees whose tax documentation consists of a T4 and RRSP slips.

- **Who will prepare my return?** Unless you're dealing with a sole practitioner, the person you're speaking to will not necessarily prepare your return. Don't be alarmed if a junior staff member prepares your return — this is common practice and can actually save you preparation fees. However, ensure that a senior tax professional reviews it for errors.

- **What is your fee structure?** Most tax professionals charge by the hour, so make sure you ask upfront for the hourly fee, as well as for an estimate of the time your project will take to complete.

- **What qualifications do you have?** Many tax professionals are chartered accountants, and many are also certified financial planners. Those who specialize in tax should also have completed a two-year, in-depth tax course offered by the Canadian Institute of Chartered Accountants.

#7

Figure Out How to File Your Return

After you prepare your tax return (refer to Tip #6 for a look at your preparation options), you have some choices for filing your return with the CRA. What's the best choice for you? Read on. . . .

Turn It In Online: Electronically File Your Return

Electronically filing your return is a great choice because it's relatively easy, you can get your refund faster, and you can save a tree and the cost of a stamp!

Electronic filing is just that; you use a computer to send your tax information to the CRA's computer. It's kind of like e-mailing versus sending a letter.

Understanding the difference between EFILING and NETFILING

There are two methods of electronically filing your return:

- EFILING is used only when you've hired someone to prepare your return for you. The government must approve tax preparers to EFILE, so if you hire someone to do your taxes you'll want to ask them whether they are EFILE-approved.

You can't EFILE your tax return yourself. You must first have your return prepared by an approved electronic filer. Most businesses that offer tax preparation services are registered to EFILE returns.

- If you've prepared yourself using approved software (see Tip #6), you have the option of NETFILING your return. At the end of the day, EFILE and NETFILE are essentially accomplishing the same thing.

To be able to NETFILE your return to the CRA, you must pre-pare it using certified tax preparation software. Basically, the software saves your return in a format the CRA can read. A list of approved software is available on the CRA's Web site at www.netfile.gc.ca/software-e.html. You can also take a look at Tip #6, where we discuss tax software and the pro-grams that are NETFILE-compatible.

If you're able to NETFILE, the CRA will send you a four-digit access code in your tax return information package. If you lose the number, go to the NETFILE Web site and apply for your code online, get it via MyAccount (see Tip #8), or call for help.

The CRA doesn't want professional tax preparers to use NETFILE; to prevent this, they've place a limit of 20 returns per computer per year that can be prepared with certified tax software. Keep that in mind if you love taxes and agree to do returns for more than 20 family members and friends each year (sigh).

Considering the benefits of filing online

Most people like EFILING their return because they get their assess-ments and refunds faster. In fact, the wait is cut to two weeks from the usual four to six if you're a procrastinator and file toward the end of April. If you're one of those who file in the middle of March, you may actually see your refund in just over a week!

Some other benefits of EFILE are that it

- ✔ Saves the CRA from having to manually input your data, reducing the likelihood of data entry errors

- ✔ Is secure

- ✔ Is fast

- ✔ Is environmentally friendly

- ✔ Provides confirmation right away that your return has been received — handy when you're filing at the last minute and are worried about potential late filing penalties

- ✔ Saves you money on stationery, printing, and mailing

Assessing your chances of an audit when you file online

The first thing to keep in mind is that there is a difference between having your tax return *audited* and having some of your deductions or credits *reviewed*. EFILED and NETFILED returns are selected for audit using the same criteria as paper-filed returns. So if you're worried about an audit, you're neither increasing nor decreasing your odds by filing online. On the other hand, because you're not sending supporting documentation such as donation or RRSP receipts to the CRA when you file online, the CRA will do regular reviews of these types of deductions to ensure you have support for your claims. Such reviews keep the integrity of the tax system in check.

If you don't like having any contact with the CRA after you file your return other than the report card called the Notice of Assessment, then we don't suggest you file online. You see, because no supporting documentation is sent to the CRA when you file online, a CRA representative may contact you asking for backup information for some of your claims. The most common requests are for childcare, medical, and donation receipts. The CRA tries to select only returns for which they anticipate a higher probability of non-compliance, but this is not always the case. Don't panic, however, if you receive a request to send more information. It doesn't mean you're being audited. Simply send in the information requested — assuming you've kept your documentation (see Tip #4), you have nothing to worry about.

Figuring out who can file online

The majority of Canadian taxpayers can have their return electronically filed. Individuals who can't EFILE or NETFILE include non-residents, taxpayers whose social insurance number begins with "0," individuals who came to or left Canada during the tax year, individuals who have declared bankruptcy, and people who have to pay income tax to more than one province or territory. Tax returns of deceased individuals cannot be filed online either. You can file electronically only for the current tax year. Past year's returns must be paper-filed.

Paper Filing: The Old-Fashioned Way

Although we're living in the techno age, we realize that not every-one embraces the computer. If you want to paper file your return you have two preparation options:

- ✔ You can go totally old school and fill out your tax forms by hand — you can ask the CRA to send you the forms, print them from the CRA Web site, or pick up a copy at your local post office or CRA office.

- ✔ You can go for a hybrid approach, preparing the return using your computer but then printing off a copy to mail.

After you've prepared the return, the paper-filing is easy. Just attach necessary information slips and receipts (T-slips, RRSP slips, and donation and medical receipts, among others), sign your return, and place it in the mail. Make sure you postmark it no later than midnight on April 30 to avoid late filing penalties. And don't forget a cheque, if you have a balance owing.

TELEFILE: By Invitation Only

With TELEFILE, you don't need to have someone else prepare and file your return. You can electronically file your own return. All you need is a touch-tone phone, your social insurance number, an invitation from the CRA to TELEFILE if you wish, and a personal access code. The system accepts income tax information such as employment income, pension income, interest income, RRSP contributions, and charitable donations. The more complex returns would take more telephone time, and often the CRA needs to see supporting documentation in order to process them.

Only those individuals who would ordinarily file the T1 Special return instead of the longer T1 "general" return are eligible for TELEFILE. The T1 Special, or T1S, is sent to individuals who are wage and salary earners only, students, seniors, and filers who file only to obtain tax credits. When individuals eligible to use TELEFILE receive their tax package from the CRA, they will also receive the TELEFILE invitation along with an access code and instructions on how to use the system.

Money in the Bank: Direct Deposit of Your Tax Refund

When you set up direct deposit with the CRA you get your tax refund a few days earlier than if it were mailed to you. You don't need to worry about your mail being lost or making a trip to your bank.

Complete form T1DD, "Direct Deposit Request," with your banking details. This form can be sent in to the CRA at any time. If you haven't sent it in before your tax return is completed, you can send it in with your return.

In addition to having your tax refund automatically deposited to your bank account, you can have your entitlement to other payments such as the GST/HST credit, working income tax benefit, Canada Child Tax Benefit, and Universal Child Care Benefit deposited to your bank account.

Form T1DD can also be used to change information you've previously sent to the CRA. You do not need to redo the form each year, however: After it is set up, the CRA will continue to deposit funds to the account. They will never forget!

Don't forget to tell the CRA when you close a bank account. Refunds sent to a closed bank account will eventually be returned to the CRA, which will then send a cheque to the taxpayer. However, there are delays (weeks or months) in making all this happen. Avoid the hassle and advise the CRA of new banking information immediately.

Know Where to Turn for Help

• •

*N*avigating the tax rules is not always an easy task. Even tax experts like us have to research the rules from time to time! You've taken the first step by buying this book — and when you need a little more help, we're here with some suggestions.

Surfing Your Way to Tax Help

So it's 11 p.m. on April 30, and you need help. What do you do? Well, you may find the answers to some of your questions via the Internet. Several Web sites provide handy, up-to-the-minute tax tips. Here are our top picks:

✓ **BDO Dunwoody:** www.bdo.ca. This site is chock-full of tax information ranging from tax facts and figures for each province to weekly tax tips.

✓ **Deloitte:** www.deloitte.ca. The weekly tax highlights on this site will ensure you don't miss any tax changes. Keep your eye open for "TaxBreaks" and guides on a variety of tax topics. You'll also find a handy automobile logbook to help you keep track of business kilometres for auto expense claims.

✓ **Ernst & Young:** www.ey.com/global/content.nsf/ Canada/Home. This Web site provides the latest tax changes, as well as tax calculators. Watch for E&Y tax publications "TaxMatters@EY" and "Tax Alert." You can download the booklet "Managing Your Personal Taxes."

✓ **KPMG:** www.kpmg.ca. Find out all the latest tax changes by visiting this site and reading "TaxNewsFlash Canada" and the "Canadian Tax Adviser."

✓ **PricewaterhouseCoopers:** www.pwc.com/ca. Visit the publications area of the site for PWC's tax newsletter "Tax Memo" and tax guides on specific subjects.

When and How to Get Help from the CRA Itself

Believe it or not, the CRA Web site (www.cra-arc.gc.ca) is an excellent source for information. Here, you can download a copy of the income tax package and request additional forms. The site also contains detailed information on the most frequently requested topics.

TIPS

If your question relates to your tax situation or you need general help, try the CRA's automated TIPS line (Tax Information Phone Service). Call 1-800-267-6999.

Personal info

To obtain specific information on your tax account, you need to provide your social insurance number, your month and year of birth, and the total income reported on line 150 of your last assessed return.

Here's a rundown of what TIPS can tell you:

- ✔ **Tax refund:** Find out the status of your refund.

- ✔ **Goods and Services Tax/Harmonized Sales Tax (GST/HST) credit:** See whether you're eligible to receive the credit and when you can expect to receive a payment.

- ✔ **Child Tax Benefit:** Find out whether you're eligible to receive the benefit and when you can expect to receive a payment.

- ✔ **Universal Child Care Benefit:** Find out when your next payment is coming. (Or, if you have a child under 6 and you're not already receiving the UCCB, find out how to apply.)

- ✔ **RRSP deduction limit:** Want to know your RRSP deduction contribution limit for the year? TIPS has your answer.

General info

TIPS also provides general recorded information:

- ✔ **Info-Tax:** General tax information on a number of tax topics.
- ✔ **Bulletin Board:** Recent tax and benefit information.

✓ **Business Information:** Tax and GST information for those who operate a business or are thinking of starting one up (for example, how to handle payroll tax, CPP, and EI deductions).

My Account

The CRA offers a service through its Web site called My Account, where you can access information about your personal tax and benefits 7 days a week, 21 hours a day.

My Account is quite an innovative service for the CRA. (We're impressed, at least!) It give you access to information about your:

- ✓ Tax refund or balance owing

- ✓ Tax instalment payments made or owing

- ✓ Direct deposit or preauthorized payment plan information

- ✓ RRSP, Home Buyers' Plan, and Lifelong Learning Plan eligibility and outstanding balances

- ✓ Child Tax Benefit entitlements

- ✓ Universal Child Care Benefit entitlements

- ✓ GST/HST Credit eligibility

- ✓ Disability Tax Credit eligibility

Sure beats trying to phone in the middle of tax season, when all you get is a busy signal! You can also use My Account to change your filed return, to change your address and/or phone number, and to dispute your Notice of Assessment.

To access My Account, you need to register for a Government of Canada epass. You can do this by going into My Account on the CRA Web site. After you've completed the registration process and chosen your password, CRA mails an activation code to you. Just key in the CRA activation code and your password to get full access to My Account for the first time. After that, you'll just need to enter your password.

When you don't have an epass but need immediate access to some of your tax information, you can go into the Quick Access section of My Account. Quick Access will tell you the status of your tax return and benefit payments and your RRSP deduction limit. To identify yourself, have your social insurance number, date of birth, and total income from line 150 of your last processed tax return handy.

Enquiring by phone

Agents are also available to answer your questions by phone, Monday to Friday (except holidays), 8:15 a.m. to 5:00 p.m. To accommodate the flood of calls during tax season, these hours are extended until 10:00 p.m. weekdays, and include weekends from 9:00 a.m. to 1:00 p.m. from mid-February to April 30 (excluding Easter). Contact the CRA by phone at 1-800-959-8281.

If your query is in regard to electronic services (NETFILE, TELEFILE, or My Account), call the e-service Helpdesk at 1-800-714-7257.

If you would like someone else to call the CRA on your behalf, be sure you've completed and mailed consent form T1013, "Authorizing or Cancelling a Representative." This form gives the CRA permission to discuss your tax affairs with someone other than you.

Visiting your local Tax Services Office

If you can't find the information you need on the Web site, through TIPS, or through My Account, try contacting your local Tax Services Office (TSO). (Note, though, that they really prefer you to call the toll-free number — we just want to give you some options!) The TSOs are open Monday to Friday (except holidays, of course), 8:15 a.m. to 4:30 p.m. (sometimes 5:00 p.m.). To find the location of your nearest TSO, visit the CRA's Web site and click "Contact us" from the main menu. Service is by appointment only.

Where to Get Forms and Other Information

The package that's sent by the CRA in mid-February contains only the most commonly used forms. If you didn't receive a package, or need an additional one, you have many options:

- Download forms from the CRA Web site
- Use the online order form on the CRA Web site to order forms and have them mailed to you
- Call **1-800-959-2221** and ask for forms to be mailed to you
- Pick up the T1 General Guide and Forms package from any postal outlet or Service Canada office

Reduce Your Tax by Giving to Registered Charities

*T*wo advantages arise from giving to registered charities. (Well, more than two likely apply, but we deal with two in this tip.) One, you're assisting those in need of your help — and two; this assistance can result in some tax savings. This tax savings can then be donated to charity, which results in additional tax savings, which . . . you get the picture. Charitable donations to registered charities (and other qualified donees such as charitable foundations) result in federal income tax savings as well as provincial or territorial income tax savings.

Make Donations That Qualify for Tax Savings

You're able to claim charitable donations made by either you or your spouse/common-law partner. (We talk about charitable donations made by your spouse/common-law partner a little more at the end of this tip.) Add up all the donations made during the year, and don't forget any donations you made through payroll deductions — these donations will be shown on your respective T4 slips.

Charitable donations don't need to be made in cash. In Tip #10 we discuss giving away assets and highlight the special tax treatment (read "tax savings") available when you make a donation of a publicly listed security.

To claim a tax credit for making a charitable donation you must receive an official receipt from the registered charity acknowledging your donation. (We comment on the information to be noted on the receipt in Tip #11.) An exception to the need for an official receipt occurs where donations have been made through the payroll at your work and the amount is noted on your T4.

Know the Tax Savings from Making Charitable Donations

The tax savings in claiming charitable donations is two-tiered:

✔ On the first $200 of donations the federal income tax credit is 15 percent

✔ On the remainder, the federal income tax credit is increased to 29 percent

If you claim $200 in donations you'll save $30 in federal income tax. If you contribute an extra $100, for a total of $300, you'll save an additional $29 in federal income tax. There is an obvious incentive to donate more than $200 in a year. The provinces/territories also offer two-tier tax credit amounts.

Review the Amount of Charitable Donations You Should Claim

The total of the donations being claimed in a year is reported on schedule 9 of your tax return and the federal tax savings is calculated on schedule 1 of your return. The provincial/territorial credit is calculated on the respective provincial/territorial forms.

Limit of donations you can claim

Generally, you can claim charitable donations up to the limit of 75 percent of your net income reported on line 236. (In Tip #10 we comment on a special rule dealing with donations made in the year of death.)

To the extent your charitable donations are restricted in a year to the 75 percent of net income limit, the excess amount can be carried forward for potential claim in the subsequent five years — again, subject to the 75 percent of net income limit test. If the charitable donations cannot be claimed by the end of the fifth carryforward year, then no claim for those charitable donations can be made.

Defer claiming charitable donations

You don't have to claim the donations you made in 2009 on your 2009 return. Claiming charitable donations in the year they're made is optional. It may be more beneficial not to claim them for 2009 but rather to carry forward the donation amount to claim on your return for one or the next five carryforward years. This would be to your benefit if

✔ You already have sufficient tax credits to eliminate your tax liability, or

✔ Your donations were less than $200 in 2009. By deferring claiming these you can combine them with your 2010 donations and claim them on your 2010 return. If the combined total was in excess of $200 then the increased 29% tax credit, not the 15% tax credit, would apply to the excess. If the total still did not exceed $200, you could combine your 2009, 2010, and 2011 donations and . . . well, you get the idea.

Bump Up Donations at the End of the Year

Okay, say it's nearing the end of December and you wish to make charitable donations. You want to receive an official receipt from a registered charity that notes your donation was made in the current year so you can have the tax savings for the year.

You can make your charitable donations using your credit card. As long as your donation transaction is processed by the end of the year, the receipt will be dated with the current year.

Combine Your Donations with Your Spouse/Common-Law Partner's Donations

As we note earlier in this tip, you're permitted to claim charitable donations made by you and your spouse/common-law partner. It's generally beneficial to claim charitable donations made by both you and your spouse/common-law partner on one tax return. With the two-tiered level of tax savings noted above you and your spouse/common-law partner are subject to the 15 percent limit on the first $200 only once — not twice — so you can maximize the amount of donations subject to the 29 percent federal tax credit.

#10

Take Advantage of Special Rules for Charitable Donations

*I*n Tip #9 we discuss the nuts and bolts (okay, mainly the dollars and percentages) of the tax savings available by making donations to registered charities. It turns out we have a lot more to say on how making charitable donations can reduce your tax bite.

Donate Assets Rather Than Cash

Rather than donating cash to a charity, you can choose to give other types of assets. When you "gift" an asset, in most cases you're considered to have sold the asset for a price equal to the market value at the time. This is what tax geeks refer to as a deemed disposition and it can trigger a capital gain on the asset, which in turn triggers a tax liability despite the fact that you did not receive any cash to fund the tax. However, there likely will not be any tax to pay, because you'll receive an official receipt to claim a charitable donation equal to the market value of the property.

Only 50 percent of a capital gain is subject to tax (see Tip #38), and the value of the gift noted on the official receipt from the registered charity will be 100 percent of the market value.

Publicly listed securities

Special tax treatment is provided when publicly listed securities, such as shares of public companies or mutual funds, are directly donated to a registered charity (or charitable foundation). The taxable capital gain is reduced to zero, while at the same time you're able to claim a charitable donation tax credit for the full market value of the securities donated.

Rather than selling securities and donating the cash, donate the securities. The charity is free to sell the securities, and charities do not pay tax! This way, you'll pay no tax and still get the same donation credit.

Cultural and ecological gifts

Unlike other donations, the donation claim for cultural and ecological gifts is not limited to a percentage of net income. (In Tip #9 we discuss how the amount you can claim in a year is generally restricted to 75 percent of your net income as reported on line 236 of your tax return.) If you don't want to claim the full amount — or don't need to because your tax liability is already nil — you can choose to claim a portion in the current year and carry forward the unused portion for up to five years.

Donations of cultural property and ecologically sensitive land also enjoy an exemption from capital gains tax. That's an added tax advantage!

Donate in the United States

You may want to donate some to our big neighbour to the south, but are hesitant because you're not sure if there are any tax benefits. Good news — donating to charities and universities in the land of the brave and the home of the free does yield some tax breaks. Here's how:

- ✔ **Donate to U.S. charities:** Generally, donations to foreign charities are not eligible for a credit on your Canadian tax return. However, you can claim donations to U.S. charities, subject to a limitation of 75 percent of your U.S. source income, as long as the charitable organization is recognized as such by U.S. law and would have qualified in Canada had it been a Canadian organization.

- ✔ **Donate to U.S. universities:** If you make a donation to a qualifying foreign university, the donation can be treated as though it were a Canadian donation; that is, you don't have to have U.S. source income to benefit from the donation. A qualified university is one where the student body normally includes students from Canada. A listing of these universities can be found in Schedule VIII of the Income Tax Regulations; most large U.S. universities are included.

#11

Be Wary of Charity Fraud and Charity Tax Shelters

*I*n making charitable donations you want to be sure your money is going to a good cause and that the tax savings you're expecting will in fact occur.

Sometimes things can look too good to be true. Each year, a number of charity tax shelters are "sold." (We comment on tax shelters later in this tip.) Many will provide an official charitable receipt for more than you actually donate. As you may expect, the CRA frowns on these structures and has overturned a number of them. The result? Taxpayers are out their money, and, in some cases, are provided with no tax relief at all. Many charities that have participated in these structures have lost their registered charity status.

Check the Charity's Registration

You can claim only amounts you gave to registered Canadian charities and qualified donees (such as a charitable foundation).

To see whether an organization is a legitimate charity, check its registration status on the CRA Web site (`www.cra-arc.gc.ca/charities`). If the name doesn't come up it's not registered and not authorized to give out official receipts.

Look at Your Official Receipt

A number of organizations give out receipts for your donation that are not "official" receipts. The amounts you give to these organizations cannot be claimed as a charitable donation. The question to ask is not whether you'll receive a receipt, but whether you'll receive an *official* receipt, with the charity's registration number noted on it.

The CRA requires the following to be noted on an official receipt:

✔ **Your name and address.**

✔ The charity's business number (BN), which is also known as its charitable registration number. This is a 9-digit number followed by "RR."

✔ The amount of the cash donated or the market value of a non-cash donation.

✔ The date of the donation. If the donation was in cash, then simply the year needs to be noted.

✔ The statement "official receipt for income tax purposes."

✔ A notation of the CRA's name and Web site (www.cra. gc.ca/charities).

✔ A unique serial number.

Take Care in Investing in Charity Tax Shelters

Generally, a tax shelter is considered to be an arrangement where a taxpayer can claim tax deductions or tax credits greater than the cost to the taxpayer within a four-year period.

The CRA has cracked down on charity tax shelters that they call "donation schemes." The CRA cautions taxpayers who are considering participating in charity tax shelter arrangements that they need to be apprised of the associated risk of the CRA not accepting it as legitimate.

The CRA notes that charity tax shelters can take the forms of

✔ Gifting trust arrangements,

✔ Leveraged cash donations, and

✔ "Buy low, donate high" arrangements.

Even if the tax shelter has been assigned a CRA tax shelter number, no guarantee exists the taxpayer will receive the proposed tax benefit.

In overturning many of these structures the CRA has reduced the eligible amount for the tax credit available to the taxpayer to no more than the cash donation — or less, or none at all.

#12

Respond Promptly to Requests from the CRA for Information

During the initial tax assessment, or as a result of the re-review of your return, the CRA may have questions. To obtain the information it needs to answer these questions, the CRA will send you a letter called a "Request for Additional Information" as part of a "pre-assessment review." This letter will usually ask for specific information and will include a mailing label where the information is to be sent, a CRA reference number, contact information from the person sending the request, and a date when the information must be received (usually 30 days from the date of the request). Is the letter the beginning of a full audit of your return? Should you seek professional advice? Should you run screaming into the hills? The answer is no.

CRA's Verification Process

A request for information is a normal part of the CRA's verification process. Don't worry! A request for information doesn't automatically mean you owe more tax.

Electronically filed tax returns

Requests for information are becoming increasingly common as more taxpayers choose to electronically file their returns by EFILE, TELEFILE, and NETFILE. Remember that returns filed electronically are sent without any supporting documentation (receipts, etc.). To maintain the integrity of our tax system, the CRA asks for proof that certain items on your tax return are accurate and verifiable.

Paper-filed tax returns

Even if you haven't electronically filed your return, you still may receive a request for information. One of the most common reasons is that a particular receipt or slip of paper was not included with your paper-filed return. Perhaps the information was unclear or incomplete, or the CRA is doing random compliance checks to test the accuracy of returns.

The latter request is usually the result of a "desk audit." Such audits are done at the Tax Services Office and are primarily intended to test a large number of returns and identify potential problems that may be forwarded for a full audit. As long as the information you've reported on your tax return is truthful, supportable, and within the tax laws, you should have nothing to worry about.

Figuring Out What the CRA Is Looking For

The following is our unofficial hit list of items the CRA reviews most often with requests to see supporting documentation:

- ✔ **RRSP contributions, including a review of past overcontributions.** Why? The CRA wants to be sure the amount you've deducted is correct. In addition, because RRSP assets can earn tax-sheltered income, the CRA wants to make sure all the money that has found its way into your RRSP is supposed to be there. In the past, this wasn't reviewed often and many Canadians were over their allowable maximum $2,000 RRSP overcontribution. A few years ago the CRA began a big push to get this problem under control.

- ✔ **Moving expenses.** Why? Because often they are large, and sometimes employers have reimbursed the employees but the employees still claim a tax deduction. Keep all your receipts when you're claiming moving expenses.

- ✔ **Interest expense.** Why? Because if you borrow to invest in a non-registered investment account, or for a business purpose, you can generally deduct the interest cost on your tax return. But the rules can be complex, and some taxpayers comingle personal and investment loans, making this an expense that is often misrepresented.

Keep all supporting documentation — and please, we beg you, keep personal and investment or business loans separate.

- ✔ **Childcare expenses.** The CRA usually wants verification that the amount claimed is supported by a receipt or T4 slip (say, when you have a nanny), and that the costs were in fact incurred for childcare (and not sports or other activities).

- ✔ **Medical expenses and charitable donations.** These are reviewed particularly when large. If you're reporting significant medical expenses or charitable donations, we recommend you don't EFILE or NETFILE your return so that processing will not be delayed by a request for information.

- ✔ **Disability tax credit claims.** This is a standard review item for the CRA each year. Why? Because very specific criteria must be met to claim this credit (see Tip #61). Some individuals may have some incapacity but don't meet the statutory definition of being disabled. If you're claiming the disability tax credit for the first time you need to paper-file your tax return and include form T2201, "Disability Tax Credit Certificate," signed by the appropriate heath care practitioner, attesting to your disability.

- ✔ **Tax shelters.** If you've made investments in flow-through shares, limited partnerships, or others that allow special tax deductions it's common to be asked to provide evidence of your investment.

If you can't get the information within the time limit, call the number on the request and ask for an extension. In most cases, a further 30 days will be granted. This extension is usually a one-shot deal, however, and will not be granted a second time.

The Consequences of Not Replying to the CRA

The worst thing to do if you receive a request for additional information is to ignore it. Ignoring the CRA will not make your problem magically disappear. If you don't provide the information in the time allowed, or if you do not make suitable arrangements for an extension, the auditor will simply conclude the information does not exist and have your tax return assessed without the respective item — no childcare expense deduction or no RRSP deduction, or no deduction for your tax-shelter investment . . . The assessment can result in tax owing, plus interest.

For more serious situations, where a substantial amount of money is involved or potential criminal activities are suspected, the CRA can invoke a requirement or a judicial authorization forcing you to provide information. The *Income Tax Act* gives it the authority to do so.

#13

Avoid Interest and Penalties

• •

*Y*ou know about the importance of April 30 on the calendar —
it's the due date for taxes to be paid. If you're late, interest —
and the dreaded interest-on-interest — starts to be added to your
tax bill.

The due date for tax to be paid is still April 30 when you or your
spouse are self-employed. Even though your return doesn't need
to be filed before June 15, the tax is owed on April 30. We discuss
due dates for tax returns in this tip under the (ominous-sounding)
heading "Late-filing penalty."

The CRA may have requested that you pay your taxes quarterly by
instalments. If your final tax bill is greater than the instalments you
made, the remaining amount is due April 30. See Tip #14 for more
on paying tax by instalments.

Penalties can be assessed in addition to the interest assessed on
late or deficient taxes. Interest is also assessed on unpaid penalties. So, you can have interest charged on outstanding taxes,
interest charged on outstanding interest, and interest charged
on outstanding penalties. Wow! Also, none of this interest is tax
deductible.

Interest and penalties are not the cheeriest topics to read about.
It's important that you know about them so you don't get caught
owing big bucks to the CRA.

Take Steps to Avoid Interest

Pay your tax by April 30 to avoid interest charges. Pay it by that
date even if you'll be filing your tax return late — make the best
estimate of your tax and send it in. If you don't have the money, it's
likely cheaper to borrow from a bank than to pay the high interest
rate the CRA will charge.

Tax payment deadlines for the deceased

If you're filing a tax return for an individual who has died during the year, any balance owing on his or her final personal tax return (sometimes referred to as a *terminal* tax return) is payable on April 30 of the year following death, except when the death occurred in November or December. In this case, the final tax liability — and the tax return — are not due until six months after death. If death occurs in January to April, payment for the prior year's return is due six months following death. For example, if George died on February 1, 2010, his 2009 tax bill would not be due until August 1, 2010. Any tax liability for 2010 would be due April 30, 2011.

The CRA assesses interest based on tax owing on April 30. If you don't owe any tax on April 30, whether or not you've filed your return, no interest will be assessed.

As we discuss in Tip #5, your tax bill is considered paid on the day it was mailed to the CRA if it's sent by first-class mail or by courier. If you're filing your tax return at the last minute, don't drop it in just any old mail box. Ensure your return is postmarked on April 30 so it will not be considered late. If the mail doesn't get picked up until the next day, you'll be stuck with a late-filed return! (Yes, penalties exist for filing late. We discuss penalties later in this tip.)

If you have unpaid taxes for the current year, the CRA charges compounded daily interest starting on April 30. This applies to taxes owing per a Notice of Assessment (and Notice(s) of Reassessment), no matter the date of the assessment.

If you're assessed or reassessed for additional 2009 taxes on, say, August 17, 2010, the interest would be calculated from the due date of April 30, 2010.

The CRA calculates interest using its *prescribed* rates of interest. These rates are released quarterly and can be found on CRA's Web site at www.cra-arc.gc.ca/tx/fq/ntrst_rts/menu-eng. html. The interest rate CRA charges on taxes owing to it is always two full percentage points above what CRA will pay on refunds it may owe to you.

Interest charged by the CRA on unpaid taxes is never tax deductible.

Don't Be Sent to the Penalty Box

As though paying interest on taxes owing if you're late weren't enough, the CRA has penalties in store for you if you're late in filing your tax return, or if you commit more serious tax offences. This section can scare anyone straight!

Late-filing penalty

If you file your return late — after April 30, or perhaps June 15 if you or your spouse are self-employed — a penalty of 5 percent of the tax owing will be added to your tax assessment. A further penalty of 1 percent of the unpaid tax will also be added for each full month the return is late, up to a maximum of 12 months, so, there can be an additional 12 percent penalty added. In total, a 17 percent penalty is possible!

If you're late a second time within three years of the first late penalty, the penalty is bumped to 10 percent of the unpaid tax plus 2 percent per month, to a maximum of 20 months so, there can be an additional 40 percent penalty. This can bring the total penalty to 50 percent of the unpaid tax! Pretty steep!

Waiving penalties goodbye

Paying tax penalties is not the best use of your hard-earned money. In addition to the comments above on avoiding penalties, you may be able to "get out of" some penalties.

Need to "come clean" with the CRA? If you have unreported income or unfiled tax returns a voluntary disclosure can help you. To avoid penalties and prosecution, you can voluntarily come forward to the CRA and provide *all* the missing information. The CRA will waive penalties if you tell it before it catches you. You remain responsible for the tax and the interest.

Where extenuating circumstances have led to a situation where you were assessed penalties, the CRA has the ability to waive the penalties under the Taxpayer Relief provisions of the *Income Tax Act*. To request a review of your circumstances note the details on form RC4288, "Request for Taxpayer Relief", and send it to the CRA. The form needs to include all the facts and reasons why the taxpayer relief provisions should be applied in your situation. Read Information Circular IC07-1 before making your taxpayer relief request!

Even if you cannot pay your tax on time, make sure you file your return on time to avoid the late-filing penalties. (You'll be assessed interest on the tax owing but no late-filing penalty.)

Repeated failure to report income

If you have failed to report income, and this has been reassessed by the CRA, any subsequent failure to report income within the next three years will earn you a penalty of 10 percent of the unreported income.

If you do have unreported income — and the CRA does not yet know about it — you may wish to make a *voluntary disclosure* to the CRA to avoid penalties being assessed. You're still on the hook for the tax and interest, however. (We talk about voluntary disclosures earlier.)

Failure to provide complete information

If you fail to provide complete information, you'll face a fine of $100 per occurrence. Some examples include not providing a social insurance number on your return or omitting information the CRA requires to correctly assess your return. Complete all the information asked for on your return and avoid the hassle — and the fine — from the CRA.

If the information you need had to be obtained from a third party and this person (or company) would not cooperate, the CRA can waive your penalty. Attach a note to your tax return outlining the steps you took to try to obtain the information.

Tax evasion, gross negligence, and false statements

For serious situations where taxpayers intentionally try to misstate or misrepresent their returns, a penalty of 50 percent of the tax avoided will be added to their tax liability.

Criminal prosecutions

Tax evasion usually involves a criminal prosecution in addition to the above penalties. The courts can impose fines of up to 200 percent of the tax evaded and sentence you to five years in prison.

In one case, an individual was fined $36,000 after pleading guilty to two counts of tax evasion. The fine represented 120 percent of the amount of federal tax the individual was trying to evade! In addition to the fines, the individual was required to pay (obviously) the full amount of taxes owing, plus interest and penalties for a total of $214,000.

Pay Your Tax by Instalments

• •

*M*ost us think of April 30 as the "drop dead" date to pay our taxes, but many individuals have the pleasure of paying their taxes year-round! Taxpayers who earn income that is not subject to a withholding tax, and who earn sufficient amounts of this income to regularly create a tax liability, are asked by the CRA to pay their taxes throughout the year instead of just at April 30. CRA will ask you to pay by instalments in the current year if your tax owing on the previous year's tax return, and in either of the two years prior to that, was greater than $3,000. (If you're a resident of Quebec, the amount is $1,800.)

The instalment due dates are quarterly — March 15, June 15, September 15, and December 15. Any tax still owed is due on April 30 of the following year.

Wait for an Instalment Request from the CRA

If you're to pay your tax by making instalments, the CRA will send you a request. The request will include a remittance form (with the dollar amount of the requested instalment indicated) and an envelope to send the form — and cheque — to the CRA. (The CRA is very efficient in asking for money!)

Don't worry about calculating and sending in tax instalments unless you receive a request from the CRA. If you don't receive an instalment request, your total tax liability is not due until April 30 of the following year.

The CRA calculates the instalment amounts based on a combination of your actual taxes payable in the two previous years. The March 15 and June 15 instalments are calculated as one-quarter of your total tax payable for the year before last. The September 15 and December 15 instalments, when added to the instalments already made, are set to equal your total taxes payable in the prior year. (Yes, it is a little cumbersome.)

You can save yourself some cheque writing time if you allow pre-authorized payment of the requested CRA instalments from your bank account. This can be done through My Account (Tip #8) or by sending the CRA a completed form T1162A, "Pre-Authorized Payment Plan (Personal Quarterly Instalment Payments)."

Usually the first time the CRA sends an instalment request to an individual the request is made in late August for instalments on September 15 and December 15. Note that the instalment amount requested for each date will be one-half (not one-quarter) of the previous year's tax bill.

Paying instalments that differ from amounts requested by the CRA

If you expect your tax liability for the current year to be lower than in the previous year you can calculate and make an instalment amount lower than that requested by the CRA. In fact, if you expect that no need to make tax instalments for the current year exists you can choose to simply ignore the CRA instalment requests.

Beware if any of your instalment estimates are too low, or if you do not make instalments when you should be — the CRA will charge interest on the amount the instalment was deficient calculated from the due date of the instalment to whenever the amount is paid. So, be conservative in making your instalment estimates.

You can estimate your instalment payments in two ways:

- Take the amount you think you will owe for the current year and pay one-quarter of that on each payment date.

- Take the balance of tax owed on the previous year's tax return and pay one-quarter of the amount on each of the quarterly instalment due dates. The CRA will not charge you interest should a tax liability still exist when your return is completed and you make you final payment no later than April 30 of the following year.

As noted above, you can have the CRA withdraw your instalments directly from your bank account. This can be done even if you're paying an amount different from what the CRA is requesting. Simply provide the CRA with the amounts.

Change Your Return After You Have Filed

*I*f you think you've forgotten or omitted information on your filed tax return, or if you discover new information that pertains to a previously assessed tax return, the CRA will allow you to submit this information late.

As you can imagine, this is a common problem. But don't worry — you can change or add information to both soon-to-be-assessed and already-assessed returns.

Changing Your Return Before It Has Been Assessed

We've found it's best to fix or change or correct a tax return after it has been assessed. Actually, if you attempt to change a tax return after it's filed (but not yet assessed), the return is still likely to be assessed first as it was filed without the changes you've requested.

If the change to your tax return will cause an increase to your tax liability, remit the estimated tax resulting from the change immediately to avoid (or at least minimize) any interest charges that may apply as a result of the change.

Changing Your Return After It Has Been Assessed

The process for making a change to a tax return is as follows

- ✔ Do not file another return
- ✔ Inform the CRA of your changes
    - by mail or
    - via the Internet

Making changes by mail: Using Form T1ADJ "T1 Adjustment Request"

The "T1" reference is to the form number for a personal tax return. Form T1 is an individual's "Income Tax and Benefit Return." We know you wanted to know that.

To tell the CRA of your changes by mail,

✔ Complete form T1ADJ, "T1 Adjustment Request," available at all the CRA Tax Services Offices (and on the CRA Web site, www. cra-arc.gc.ca), or write a letter detailing the changes including the years involved, the specific details, your address and social insurance number, and your home and daytime phone numbers. Sign and date the form or letter.

✔ Provide all supporting documents for the requested changes.

✔ Send the adjustment request to the CRA Tax Centre where you filed your return.

Making changes via the Internet

To make a change using the internet, set up My Account on the CRA Web site (see Tip #8), and choose the "Change my return" option. You can make changes online for this year's tax return or for the two previous years' returns. Otherwise, you'll have to follow the mail route.

CRA's response to your change request

After the CRA has reviewed your requested changes it will do one of three things:

✔ Accept your changes and send you a Notice of Reassessment (or Notice of Assessment if the return had not yet been assessed).

✔ Deny your request. A letter will explain the reasons.

✔ Request additional information.

Part II
Tips for Employees and Business Owners

The 5th Wave   By Rich Tennant

"Leveling, grading, and terracing the land is a deductible expense – for FARMERS Mr. Daniels, not for people with putting greens in their backyards."

In this part . . .

1 f you're like many Canadians, much of your time is spent at work. Among us are farmers and bankers and teachers and bus drivers and tax accountants, plus occupations that many of us have yet to imagine. But the one thing that we all have in common is that we work to get paid so that we have income to enjoy the rest of our lives. In this part, we offer tips to help you hold on to as much of that income as possible, whether you're an employee or a business owner.

Employees are very limited in the expenses they can deduct when calculating the tax they owe to the CRA and therefore much to the chagrin of many Canadians, employment income is where we pay the bulk of our taxes. But don't despair — with some planning and a better understanding of how the CRA views employment income, you just might end up with a few more dollars in your pocket after all is said and done.

As for you business owners, running a small business is no "small" feat. Issues arise continually that need your attention — customers, manufacturing, marketing, sales, labour relations, and so on. And then there are the taxes. As we delve into Tips #28–33 of this part, we tackle many tax issues that a small business owner must face. Tons of these issues can lead to positive tax planning opportunities in terms of maximizing after-tax income for you and your family.

Determine Whether You're Self-Employed or an Employee

*A*re you your own boss? Consider this yet another question from the CRA. Of course we'd all like to *think* we're our own boss, but the CRA wants to know specifically whether you're self-employed or an employee. For many people the answer is simple, but for others it's not so obvious. The CRA makes the distinction between self-employed and employed based on several factors or tests — and the distinction can make a huge difference in your taxable income. If you're an employee, the Income Tax Act restricts the expenses you can deduct from your employment income. Basically, if a deduction isn't specifically mentioned in the Act, it's not deductible. Self-employed individuals don't have these same restrictions.

The Ups and Downs of Self-Employment

In most situations it's advantageous to arrange your business relationships so that you're an independent contractor (self-employed) rather than an employee. This is because independent contractors are entitled to claim deductions for many expenses not deductible by an employee.

That all sounds nice, sure, but be aware that self-employment comes with its own pitfalls. As a self-employed person you'll be responsible for paying the employer's share of Canada Pension Plan (CPP) contributions, which doubles your overall contribution. As well, before leaping at the opportunity to become your own boss, remember this: If your business venture fails, there will be no Employment Insurance (EI) or severance waiting for you. And, of course, you won't be entitled to any employment benefits such as medical or dental coverage. You also may have difficulty getting credit, as your income stream likely won't be predictable, and you'll be responsible for all the recordkeeping and income and sales tax compliance for your business. Self-employment can be great, but it's not all sunshine and roses!

Determining Whether You're Self-Employed

Table 2-1 illustrates the factors the CRA considers in its determination of whether you're self-employed or an employee. The tests in this table don't necessarily yield automatic answers, but they do provide the framework for the taxman's assessments.

Table 2-1	Factors Determining Self-Employed versus Employee Status	
Employee	**Criteria**	**Self-Employed**
Employee is under the direction and control of the employer. Control may not necessarily be exercised but right to do so is.	Supervision or Control	No direct control or supervision exists.
Employee complies with instruction about when, where, and how work is to be performed.	Instructions	Works his own schedule and does the job his own way.
The individual continues to work for the same person year after year.	Relationships	Hired to do one job. No continuous relationship.
Hours and days are set by the employer.	Hours	Individual is master of his own time.
Must devote full time to employer's business; restricted from doing other work.	Exclusivity	Free to work when and for whom he chooses.
Paid in regular amounts at stated intervals.	Payment	Paid by the job on a straight predetermined basis.
Usually employer furnishes tools.	Materials	Furnishes his own tools.

Employee	Criteria	Self-Employed
Cannot realize a profit or loss by making good or bad decisions.	Profit or Loss	Can realize a profit or loss as a result of his services.
Can end his relationship with employer at any time.	Termination	Agree to complete a specific job. Is responsible for satisfactory completion or is legally obligated to make good.
Employed as part of a business; services are an indispensible, integral part of that business	Integration	Person may perform work that is integral.

Improving Your Chances of Being Considered Self-Employed

Keeping the tests from Table 2-1 in mind, you can do a number of things to improve the likelihood you'll be considered an independent contractor in the CRA's eyes. When you're self-employed, be sure to:

✔ Document your business arrangement with your client in a contract

✔ Use your own equipment

✔ Send invoices to your client

✔ Refuse to accept fringe benefits

✔ Work for more than one client

✔ Establish yourself as a business — register your business name, set up an office, get business cards, advertise, and get a separate phone line

The CRA's guide entitled Employee or Self-Employed? (RC4110) identifies the factors that determine your status. You can find the guide under "Forms and publications" on the CRA Web site (www.cra-arc.gc.ca).

#17

Save for Your Retirement

*W*e know, we know — you'd rather hear about Aunt Petunia's bunions than the importance of saving for retirement. Many Canadians avoid thinking about it for so long that when retirement looms they suddenly realize they won't have enough saved to maintain their current lifestyle. We don't want this to happen to you, so listen up!

For most people, making use of the retirement savings plans available to them is crucial to saving enough for retirement. In this tip we address the different types of plans available to employees.

Understanding Your Registered Pension Plan

Registered pension plans (RPPs) are set up by employers or unions to assist employees in saving for retirement; they're designed to minimize taxes now to provide for maximum amounts available when the funds are needed during retirement.

If you have an RPP, consider yourself lucky. In this day and age only about a third of employees are covered by such a plan. The best thing about RPPs is that your employer has to help you save for retirement by contributing to the plan. The contributions you make to an RPP are tax deductible and the income you earn on the money you invest accumulates tax free. You'll pay tax on the money saved in an RPP only when you begin receiving it as pension income in retirement. How great is that?

You can get money into your RPP by

- ✔ Contributing funds through deductions from your salary
- ✔ Your employer contributing funds
- ✔ Earning money on the savings in your RPP
- ✔ Transferring funds from another retirement account into your RPP

Two types of RPPs exist:

> ✔ *Defined benefit plans,* which are based on a formula that includes employment earnings and years of service.

> ✔ *Money purchase plans,* which depend on the amount you contribute and the earnings on those contributions.

Defined benefit plans

The majority of Canadians with an RPP are employed by large companies or the government. If you belong to this type of plan you're entitled to a fixed annual income from the plan on retirement. You'll continue receiving payments during your life, and your former employer must ensure the pension is sufficiently funded to make those payments to you.

With a defined benefit plan you can deduct all the contributions you've made for service to your employer after 1989. You can also deduct up to $3,500 in respect of past-service contributions for a year before 1990 in which you were not contributing to any RPP.

Money purchase plans

If you belong to this type of plan your pension benefit is determined by adding up the contributions you've made to the plan over the years and the income you've earned on those savings. Your employer must contribute at least one percent of your salary to your plan — more is better! The amount you're entitled to on retirement depends on the total amount you save by retirement. In this case your contribution is fixed but your payment is not. These are also known as *defined contribution plans.*

For a money purchase plan the 2009 combined contribution that both you and your employer can make is the lesser of 18 percent of your earned income from the previous year and $22,000. Beginning in 2010 the amount you can contribute will be indexed to inflation. You can't make past-service contributions to this type of RPP (we define past-service contributions under "Buying Back Service" in this Tip).

Many employers will match the contributions you make based on a formula. If your employer matches contributions, make sure you contribute the amount required to get the entire employer match — if your employer wants to share, we say let him!

Knowing What to Do with a Pension Adjustment

As the value of your RPP increases, the amount you can contribute to your *registered retirement savings plan* (RRSP) decreases. The *pension adjustment* (PA) is a component of the calculation of your RRSP deduction limit. The idea behind the PA is that an individual who is not a member of an RPP can use only the RRSP to save for retirement. To keep things fair for all Canadians, the amount an RPP member can contribute to an RRSP is reduced by his or her PA. The pension adjustment reported on your current-year T4 will reduce the next year's RRSP deduction limit on a dollar-for-dollar basis. (See Tip #42 for a detailed discussion on RRSPs.)

When you receive your notice of assessment from the CRA after filing your tax return, you'll see that the current year's PA amount you disclosed when filing your tax return is included in the formula to calculate the next year's RRSP deduction limit. This is an important piece of paper to have around when it comes time to make the next year's contribution, because you face penalties when you overcontribute to your RRSP by more than $2,000.

Knowing What to Do with a Pension Adjustment Reversal

A pension adjustment reversal (PAR) often arises when you leave an employer where you were a member of the company pension plan. The PAR is essentially a statement that shows that the pension adjustments (PA) reported on your T4s over the years were too high — this means your pension adjustments were overstated, so your RRSP deduction limits were understated. The PAR simply corrects the understatement in your RRSP deduction limit. In fact, a PAR indicates your RRSP deduction limit is being increased — this is good news!

Your employer must send you a T10 slip to report your PAR to you within 60 days after the end of the calendar-year quarter in which you left your job. (So, if you left your job in the final quarter, you should receive your T10 slip by January 30.)

Buying Back Service

Contributions to your pension plan for past services are considered *past-service contributions,* meaning the contributions were made for work you did in prior years. The contributions, made by you, are generally made to upgrade the pension benefits you'll be entitled to in the future. Past-service contributions are often made in a lump sum. You may hear people refer to past-service contributions as "buying back service," or buying increased pension benefits — paying some money now for an increased pension down the road.

 Ask your pension plan administrator whether you're entitled to buy back any service. Based on your age, your years to retirement, length of service, and the dollars involved, it can be beneficial in terms of your future pension entitlement to buy back service!

Contributions for 1990 and later years

Your total contributions for current service and past service for 1990 and later years can usually be found in box 20 of the T4 slips you received from your employer. The full amount is to be included on line 207 of your tax return.

Contributions for years before 1990

 If your current and past-service contributions for 1990 and later years exceed $3,500, you'll find that none of your past-service contribution for years before 1990 is deductible on your current-year tax return. However, all is not lost! Those contributions become eligible for deduction in 2009 and subsequent years. The maximum total deduction is $3,500 per year or part year of service you bought back. So, if it costs you more than $3,500 to make a past-service contribution for a particular pre-1990 year, you will not (ever) be entitled to deduct your full contribution. And if you buy back more than one year's worth of pre-1990 service, even within the $3,500 maximum, you'll have to spread the deduction over a number of years.

Knowing What to Do When You Leave Your Employer Before You Retire

Funds held in an RPP are *locked in,* meaning if you leave your employer before you retire you can't simply have them paid to you in a lump sum. These funds must be used to provide you with a lifetime retirement income.

You generally have three options when you leave:

✔ Roll your existing pension into your new employer's pension.

✔ Leave it where it is and take your pension from that company when you retire.

✔ Transfer your money into a *locked-in retirement account* (LIRA). You can't draw an income from your LIRA until you reach the age of 50. At that point you can convert your LIRA into a *locked-in retirement fund* (LRIF) or an annuity and begin receiving the pension income (see Tip #43 for more details).

Contributing to Your Employer's Profit-Sharing Plan

We offer one final word on saving for retirement when you're an employee: If your employer has a *deferred profit sharing plan,* otherwise known as a DPSP, you'll want to participate.

DPSPs are set up by employers for their employees, and employers contribute to them based on the profitability of the company. When you save money in a DPSP, it's tax sheltered in the same way it is in an RPP — the contributions made and income earned is sheltered from tax until you withdraw funds from the plan. On retirement you can transfer the funds to an RRSP or an RRIF, or you can use the funds to purchase an annuity (see Tip #43).

Take Advantage of Employee and Shareholder Loans

*1*n certain situations — say, when the 14 year old car that Aunt Mable gave you decides it doesn't want to start again (ever) , or maybe instead you decide you want to move closer to the office where houses are more expensive so you can spend more time working and less time commuting (yah right!) — you might be able to convince your employer to make you a loan interest free. A loan made by a corporation to an employee who is not a shareholder of the corporation (or related to a shareholder of the corporation) is not included in the employee's income.

Hold on, hold on, we can hear you cheering from here. The employee does not fully escape tax! She is considered to have received an *imputed interest benefit* — a rather stuffy term that we clarify for you later in this tip as we consider the tax implications of employee loans.

Working with Employee and Shareholder Loans

If you receive a no-interest or low-interest loan because you own shares or because of your past, present, or future employment (how's that for a catch-all!), and the loan was not included in your income by virtue of the exceptions detailed earlier, you'll be considered to have received a taxable benefit referred to as an imputed or deemed *interest benefit*. This benefit is equal to the difference between the interest paid in the year (or within 30 days after the year-end), if any, and the interest determined by the CRA using its prescribed rates of interest. Still sound scary? All this technical jargon means is you pay tax on the difference between the interest rate set by CRA (prescribed rate) and the rate that you are actually charged by your employer if your employer's rate is lower.

Exploring the controversy over employer loans

Employee loans have been the focus of numerous court challenges and legislative changes over the years. The primary concern the government has with these arrangements is that they could be used as a way for corporations to distribute all their profit and retained earnings to shareholders and employees on a totally tax-free basis. By extending no-interest indefinite loans, the corporations could give you all the money you wanted with no tax implications to you or the corporation.

Banning these loans altogether is not the answer. The government recognizes that, in certain situations, loans from a corporation to an employee or shareholder are necessary — so corporations are allowed to extend loans in certain situations, but with very restrictive rules.

CRA's prescribed interest rates are updated every three months and can be found on the CRA Web site at http://www.cra-arc.gc.ca/tx/fq/ntrst-rts/menu-eng.html?=slnk. The rate was 2 percent for the first quarter of 2009, and 1 percent for the last three quarters.

If the loan was made by virtue of your employment, the imputed interest benefit is considered employment income, and the amount is included in your T4.

Say Duncan receives a non-interest-bearing loan from his employer for $100,000 at the beginning of the year. Duncan is not a shareholder, and the loan is outstanding until the end of the year. Using a prescribed rate of 2 percent for the first quarter of the year and 1 percent for the other three quarters, what is Duncan's interest benefit? Duncan will be deemed to have an interest benefit of $1,250 ($100,000 times 2 percent × ¼ plus $100,000 times 1 percent × ¾). This amount will be added to Duncan's employment income for the year and included on his T4. Any interest Duncan paid on this loan during the year (or the first 30 days of the next year) would reduce the imputed interest benefit.

If you receive a loan from your employer and are required to pay interest on the loan, try to arrange to pay the interest portion on January 30 (not 31) of the following year. This will let you keep your cash as long as possible and still reduce or eliminate the deemed interest benefit for the current year.

Where possible, convince your employer to make your loan interest free. You will have an imputed interest benefit added to your employment income, but the tax cost of a benefit is cheaper than actually paying interest. For example, at a marginal tax rate of 40 percent, a 1 percent deemed interest benefit costs you only 0.4 percent (1 percent benefit times 40 percent tax rate = 0.4 percent in tax payable). Effectively, you have a 0.4 percent loan — cheaper than actually paying interest at 1 percent and certainly cheaper than what you would get from a bank!

When a shareholder or employee loan or debt is forgiven, the forgiven amount is a taxable benefit and is added to the income of the shareholder or employee.

Recognizing Special Circumstances

Employee loans for the purchase or relocation of a home are given special treatment when it comes to calculating the imputed interest benefit.

- ✔ **Home purchase loans:** Where the loan is made to you as an employee home purchase loan, the interest rate used to calculate the imputed interest benefit for the first five years will never be greater than the CRA-prescribed interest rate at the time the loan was made. (However, you can take advantage of a lower imputed interest benefit should the prescribed rates decrease!) When the five years are over, the continuation of the loan is considered a new loan, and the prescribed rate in effect on that day will be the maximum rate charged for the next five years. For example, Maureen receives an interest-free employee home purchase loan on September 9, 2009. On that date, the CRA-prescribed interest rate was 1 percent. Over the next five years, Maureen's taxable benefit will be calculated using a prescribed rate that could be less than 1 percent but will never be more.

- ✔ **Home relocation loans:** When the loan is an employee home relocation loan — that is, a loan to help you purchase a home that is at least 40 kilometres closer to a new work location — you receive a special deduction in the calculation of the interest benefit.

Consider renegotiating your home purchase loan with your employer when prescribed interests rates are low in order to minimize your taxable benefit in subsequent years.

Employee home relocation loan deductions

The home relocation deduction is one deduction that you'll know you're entitled to claim. Why? Because it shows up right on the T4 slip you receive from your employer. When an amount is entered in box 37 of your T4 slip, you can claim a deduction for your employee home relocation loan.

So what qualifies as a home relocation loan? Unfortunately, a loan to allow you to move down the street because you want a view of the lake does not qualify. A home relocation loan is a loan your employer gives you, usually at a zero or low interest rate, to help you move for business reasons. Generally, this means you're changing jobs and your new employer is helping you out with a loan, or your current employer is transferring you to a new location.

To qualify for the employee home relocation loan deduction, all the following must apply:

- ✔ The loan must be received by an employee (or the employee's spouse).
- ✔ The employee must be moving at least 40 kilometres from his old residence in Canada.
- ✔ The employee must commence work in a new location in Canada.
- ✔ The loan must be used to acquire a new residence.

When you receive a home relocation loan, the amount received is not included in your T4 slip. However, an amount representing the "interest benefit" you have enjoyed (by not paying the interest!) is included in your T4 slip. Your employer has to report the interest benefit on all loans given to you when the interest rate you are paying (if any) is less than the CRA's prescribed interest rate.

The rate that should be used to calculate your taxable benefit is the prescribed rate in effect when your employee loan was granted. However, if the rate subsequently drops, you can start using this new lower rate. If the rate increases, you can continue to use the rate in effect at the time the loan was received. In other words, you're protected from rate increases after you receive the loan, and you benefit from lower rates. This protection lasts for five years, as a new loan is considered to be granted every five years. So, let's say you received a $20,000 loan at the end of last year when the CRA's prescribed rate was 3 percent. If the rate subsequently increases to 4 percent again, provided you're paying 3 percent interest on the loan you won't have to report any interest benefit in your income. However, if your loan is still outstanding five years from the date the loan was granted and at that time the prescribed interest rate is 6 percent, you'll have to start paying 6 percent in order to avoid having any interest benefit included in your income.

If you're required to pay at least the CRA's prescribed interest rate on your employee loan, you don't need to calculate a taxable benefit.

Now for the good part: the deduction! When an interest benefit is included in your income for an employee home relocation loan, and you meet the criteria above, you can claim a full or partial deduction from your income.

Your deduction is the lesser of the following:

- ✔ The interest benefit (which is included in your income)
- ✔ The amount of interest benefit that would have been computed if the home relocation loan had been $25,000

In friendlier terms, imagine you received a $20,000 interest-free loan from your employer when the prescribed interest rate was 4 percent, and this loan meets the definition of a home relocation loan. So, your deduction will be the lesser of $800 ($20,000 × 4 percent) and $1,000 ($25,000 × 4 percent). In this case, your entire taxable benefit of $800 will be offset by the deduction. Just to keep it interesting, another rule applies to employee home relocation loans. You see, the deduction does not last forever. It's applicable only for a maximum of five years from the day the loan was originally granted, or until the loan is actually paid off, whichever is shorter.

In negotiating your compensation for a new job that will require moving at least 40 kilometres, ask for a $25,000 home relocation loan. Due to the deduction for the interest benefit on the first $25,000 of a home relocation loan, you effectively receive the loan tax free for five years.

Loans made to a shareholder who is not an employee of the corporation

Generally, all loans to shareholders or persons related to a shareholder are included in the income of the shareholder or the related person in the year the loan was made. The same rules apply when a shareholder (or person related to a shareholder) becomes indebted to a corporation in some manner — for example, when a shareholder buys a vehicle from the corporation and pays for it with a promissory note. Of course, this being a tax, exceptions apply to this general rule.

Shareholder loans are not included in income of the shareholder when

✔ The loan is made in the ordinary course of the business of loaning money, provided that bona fide repayment arrangements are made at the time of the loan. For example, banks and other financial institutions can make loans to shareholders without the shareholder being concerned that the loan will be included in their taxable income, because a bank is in the business of loaning money to begin with.

✔ The loan is repaid within one year from the end of the corporation's taxation year in which the loan was made. For example, if the loan is made in 2009 and the corporation's year-end is December 31, 2009, the loan must be repaid by December 31, 2010, to avoid the entire amount of the loan being included in the shareholder's 2009 income.

The loan cannot be part of a series of loans and repayments. This means you, as a shareholder, can't repay the loan, then take out another loan — in theory, you really haven't paid back the original amount. The tax laws state that when you use this strategy you're required to report the amount of the loan in income.

Loans made to a shareholder who is also an employee of the corporation

When a shareholder is also an employee of the corporation making the loan, further exceptions to the general income inclusion rules discussed earlier apply. The shareholder/employee can avoid an income inclusion if the loan was made in any of these specific circumstances:

✔ The loan is made to an employee who is not a "specified employee" — that is, an employee who owns fewer than 10 percent of the shares of the corporation.

✔ The loan was made to an employee to acquire a home for occupation.

✔ The loan was made to an employee to purchase shares of the employer corporation from the corporation itself — not from another shareholder.

✔ The loan was made to an employee to acquire an automobile needed to perform duties of employment.

For the shareholder/employee to take advantage of these exceptions, two additional conditions must also be met:

> ✔ The loan arose because of the employee's employment and not because of shareholdings. In simpler terms, the loan must be available to all employees, or at least all employees of a particular class (for example, management), not just shareholding employees.

> ✔ Bona fide repayment terms must be in place. An agreement must be in place for the loan to be repaid within a reasonable period of time.

For corporations where a significant shareholder is also the day-to-day manager of the corporation's activities, it can be difficult to prove that the loan was made because the person was an employee, not a shareholder. The CRA has said that loans made to a person will be considered as being made by virtue of his or her shareholdings where the shareholder can significantly influence business policy. Nevertheless, an employee/shareholder may be able to have the loan excluded from income if he or she can establish that other employees who perform similar duties and responsibilities for a similar-sized employer — but who are not shareholders in that employer-corporation — received loans or other indebtedness of similar amounts under similar conditions. It's a tough one, but not impossible depending on the circumstances.

#19

Understand Your Stock Options

*H*ave you been granted stock options by your employer? Then this tip is for you! Stock options are one of the most popular forms of non-monetary compensation offered by employers today. But make no mistake about it — they are a taxable benefit and should be included in your total employment income reported on box 14 of your T4 slip. In this tip we offer a brief synopsis of the rules.

Checking Out the General Rule

Special rules exist when a corporation agrees to sell or issue shares to an employee as part of a compensation package. Basically, the employee is given an option to buy stock (also referred to as shares) of a company for an agreed-upon price at a future point in time. When given this option, the employee has nothing to report in income.

The general rule is that the taxable benefit comes into play when the option is exercised — or when you state that "Yes, I would like to purchase the stock now." When the option is exercised, the benefit included in your income is the difference between the fair market value of the shares on the date you exercised your option and the price you paid for the option and the shares.

Investigating the Exceptions

The general rule we cover in the previous section was pretty straightforward, right? Of course, it wouldn't be a "general tax rule" without exceptions. Exceptions occur when the option is given to buy shares of a publicly traded company or shares of a Canadian-controlled private corporation. We take a closer look at these rules in this section.

Public-company shares

In the past, when you exercised your stock options, you were considered to have received a taxable benefit equal to the difference
between the market value of the shares on the day you exercised
your options and your actual cost. Simple enough, but luckily for
some this is no longer the case. You see, when you're taxed upon
exercise of the option, you haven't necessarily sold the underlying stock yet — and therefore may have no cash to pay tax on the
benefit! Fortunately, if you have a stock option in a publicly traded
company, you may now be able to postpone the taxation of qualifying employee stock options to when the shares are sold, instead of
when the option is exercised.

Unfortunately, the rules don't end there. Even if you don't sell your
shares in the same year you exercise your option, you may not be
allowed to postpone the entire income inclusion. To complicate
matters, the maximum benefit that can be deferred is $100,000 per
vesting year. (Vesting year just means the year you earned the
right to or are entitled to the options.) This $100,000 is based on
the value of the underlying shares when the option was granted to
you. The option price doesn't matter — it's the value of the underlying shares that's used to calculate the $100,000 limit.

For example, say you were granted the option to purchase 100,000
shares of your employer corporation, at a price of $2 per share,
in 2008. (Assume the shares were trading at $2 at the time the
option was granted to you.) At the time you exercise your option,
the shares are trading at $5. (If you're quick at math, you realize
you had a $3 benefit per share, so for 100,000 shares the benefit is
$300,000.) If you exercise all your options this year, you will receive
only a partial deferral of tax. At the time the options were granted
to you, they were worth $200,000 (100,000 × $2). This means you'll
manage to defer taxes on only one-half of your options ($200,000 –
 $100,000 ÷ $2 per share = 50,000 options). Your taxable benefit
this year will be $150,000 ($5 – $2 × 50,000 options), and the other
$150,000 will be taxed only when you sell the shares ($150,000 taxed
now, $150,000 taxed later, $300,000 taxed in total — as expected).

To take advantage of this deferral for options exercised in one year
you must make an "election" with your employer before January
15, of the following year. The election is simply a letter to your
employer that must contain the following:

- ✔ A request for the deferral to apply
- ✔ The amount of the stock option benefit being deferred
- ✔ Confirmation that you were a resident in Canada when you
  purchased the shares

✔ Confirmation that you have not exceeded the $100,000 annual limit

You need to inform your employer so that your T4 is prepared correctly. In addition to making this election, you must complete form T1212, "Statement of Deferred Stock Option Benefits," and file it with your return every year you continue to have a deferred stock option benefit.

 Wait until you want to sell your option shares before you go ahead and exercise your stock options. This will ensure you have the cash (from the sale of the shares) available to pay your tax bill. We've seen too many situations where Canadians exercised their stock options, accrued a huge tax bill, and then got stung because the shares dropped in value after the exercise date. Nothing in the Canadian tax laws remedies this situation, meaning you'll still owe tax on the stock option benefit as of the date of exercise, even if the shares are worthless when they are actually sold. What's more, the difference between the sale price and the exercise price is a capital loss (or a capital gain, if it goes up in value). Because capital losses can be used to offset only capital gains, and not any other type of income (such as the employment income a stock option benefit gives rise to), you may be stuck with a useless capital loss. Ouch!

Canadian-controlled private corporations

If your employer is a Canadian-controlled private corporation (CCPC), you're in luck. When you exercise your stock options, you can defer all your taxable benefit until you actually sell the shares. The taxable benefit for CCPCs is calculated the same way as that for public companies: the market value of the shares on the date you exercise your option less your cost. By the way, your cost includes your exercise price (the amount you must pay for the shares under your option agreement) and amounts you paid (if any) to acquire the option itself.

 The rules for CCPC stock options will apply provided your employer was a CCPC at the time the option was granted to you (not when the option is exercised). So, if your company goes public in the future, you can still benefit from the more favourable CCPC stock option rules.

 Develop a strategy for managing your stock options when exercising and selling that takes into account not only the tax consequences but also the cash flow requirements and investment risk.

Stock option deductions

Now to the part you really want to know about — the stock option deduction. This deduction is available because the taxable benefit you'll be charged when you exercise your stock options is taxed as employment income (either this year or in a future year when you sell the stock). In other words, 100 percent of the benefit is taxable in your hands. To many people this seems unfair because the benefit is from a stock, which is normally treated as a capital item. As we discuss in Tip #38, capital gains are only one-half taxable, so you're taxed a full one-half more by exercising an employee stock option rather than purchasing the share yourself on the open market and then selling it for a profit.

But don't fret. Our tax laws understand this difference and allow a deduction, known as the stock option and shares deduction. The deduction is equal to one-half of the taxable benefit you must report. This means your stock option benefit will effectively be taxed in the same way as a capital gain would be.

Additional deduction for donated shares

An additional stock option deduction of 50 percent is available when you exercise a stock option and then donate the shares to a registered charity. This applies to all such donations on or after May 2, 2008. Yep, that's right. You get a tax deduction for 100 percent of your taxable benefit. You'll also get a donation receipt for the full market value of your donation. To take advantage of this incentive, the shares must be donated to the charity within the year and within 30 days of the option being exercised. Note that when you donate such stocks to a registered charity, you report the disposition on form T1170, "Capital Gains on Gifts of Certain Capital Property," and not on schedule 3 of your tax return.

Shares qualifying for the deduction

Like most good things, the stock option and share deduction is not available in every case. In order to qualify, some criteria must be met. (You didn't think a tax law would exist without qualifications, did you?)

The stock option deduction is available when all the following conditions are met:

- ✔ Your employer corporation, or a corporation that does not deal at arm's length with the employer (a related company), must be the seller or issuer of the shares.
- ✔ The shares must be common shares of the corporation.

✔ The exercise price of the option (that is, the amount you must pay to receive the share of your employer corporation — it's sometimes called the strike price) must be at least equal to the market value of the share at the time the option was granted to you. If you've paid an amount to acquire the option itself, this amount can be added to the exercise price of the option. For example, if you've paid $2 to acquire the option to purchase a share of your employer, and subsequently pay $5 to exercise the option, you'll be eligible for the stock option deduction (assuming all other criteria are met) as long as the market value of the employer's shares on the date the option was granted to you was at least $7 ($2 plus $5).

✔ You must be dealing at arm's length with your employer. This means that if you control the corporation (that is, you own the majority of the voting shares), or are related to a person who controls the corporation, you won't be eligible for this deduction.

Regulation 6204 of the Income Tax Act covers the entire list of criteria (good reading for anyone with insomnia).

If the option was granted to you while the corporation was a CCPC, you don't necessarily have to worry about the above rules. You see, if you hold the shares you've acquired under your stock option agreement for at least two years, you'll automatically qualify for the stock option deduction. However, if you don't hold the shares for two years, but meet the above criteria, you'll still qualify. (CCPC options are more flexible than public-company options in terms of the respective tax rules.)

Although these rules might sound fairly complex, fear not — it's not up to you to determine whether you're eligible for the deduction. Your employer should make this determination (we know, they have all the fun!), and your T4 slip for the year will indicate that your taxable employment benefit is in fact eligible for the "110(1)(d) or 110(1)(d.1) deduction." (You guessed it — these are references to the Income Tax Act.) The amount eligible for the deduction is reported in either box 39 or box 41 of your T4 slip. If an amount shows up in these boxes, report it on line 249 of your tax return.

If you own shares of a CCPC under a stock option plan and the company is going public, you may be able to make a special election for a deemed disposition of the shares to take advantage of the $750,000 capital gains exemption. We recommend you get professional help if you think this may apply to you.

Don't Be Surprised by Other Taxable Benefits

*E*mployers — nice ones, anyway — sometimes provide other benefits for your work in addition to your paycheque. Generally, when you receive a benefit by virtue of your employment and it increases your net worth it will be taxable. In this tip, we cover what would be considered a taxable benefit, why they're good for you and which ones to chase that nice boss for.

In times like these it may be easier to negotiate with your employer for a smaller salary increase and additional benefits instead of that significant salary increase you were hoping for.

Understanding the Benefit of a Taxable Benefit

Even though you may not be pleased that some perks your employer offers are taxable, a taxable benefit will usually be more financially advantageous than if you had to pay for the benefit yourself.

For example, if your employer pays group term life insurance premiums of $4,000 for you annually, and you're taxed on the amount at 40 percent, you'll pay tax of only $1,600 — that's much less expensive than having to pay the $4,000 premium out of your after-tax income.

Looking at Common Taxable Benefits

After the interest benefit (Tip #18) and the stock option benefit (Tip #19), the following are some of the more common taxable benefits that may show up on your T4 slip. We've also got some tips for using these benefits to your best advantage.

✔ **Car allowances:** If your employer gives you an allowance to help defray the cost of your vehicle, ensure you receive a per-kilometre reimbursement. If you receive a lump-sum allowance that's not based on a per-kilometre rate, you'll find yourself with a taxable benefit. The good news is that even when the allowance is taxable, you may be entitled to deduct some of your auto expenses when you use your car for employment purposes. See Tip #22 for details.

✔ **Company cars:** If you're provided with a company-owned or -leased car, you'll pay tax on the benefit for having the car available for personal use (called a standby charge) — regardless of whether you use the car personally. In addition, if your employer pays for operating costs (such as gas, insurance, or maintenance), you'll pay tax on this benefit (referred to as an operating benefit) to the extent the car was used for personal purposes.

Think twice about accepting a company car as part of your compensation. You'll be required to pay tax on two separate benefits: the standby charge (which can be 24 percent of the cost of your car each year or two-thirds the annual lease costs!) and an operating benefit (24¢ per personal kilometre driven). Even though the value of your car is reduced as soon as you drive it off the lot, your standby charge stays the same. The car's depreciating value is ignored in calculating the standby charge.

You can reduce the standby charge if you drive at least 50 percent for employment use and your personal kilometres driven are less than 20,004 in a year. If you're employed principally in selling or leasing automobiles, you're entitled to a lower operating benefit and standby charge.

✔ **Club dues:** If your employer is willing to pay for your dues to a recreational, sporting, or dining club, ensure you can show the membership is primarily to your employer's advantage (think networking and sales prospecting!). When this is the case, the benefit is not taxable to you.

✔ **Employee profit-sharing plans:** Your employer should provide you with form T4PS, "Statement of Employee Profit-Sharing Plan Allocations and Payments," which details the amounts to include in your income. Amounts received by the plan from your employer and income earned in the plan during the year are included. However, a distribution actually made by the plan to you will generally be tax free because you've already paid tax on the amount received.

✔ **Employment-related insurance payments you receive:** Payments made to you for loss of income because of disability or sickness or accident or from an income maintenance plan are taxable if your employer paid your premiums.

Make sure your plan at work is set up so that you pay the premiums. That way any disability payments will be tax free if you ever have to collect.

- ✔ **Forgiveness of employee debt:** Do you have a nice employer who has lent you money? Do you have an even nicer employer who forgave some or all of this debt? In this case, your debt may be gone but the value of the forgiven amount is taxable. (Refer to Tip #18 for more about employee loans.)

- ✔ **Group term life insurance premiums:** These premiums, paid by your employer, are considered to be a taxable benefit received by you.

- ✔ **Reimbursements and awards:** Such items received because of your employment — for example, paid holidays or incentive awards from employer-related contests — are taxable to you.

- ✔ **Rent-free or low-rent housing:** If your employer provides you with rent-free or low-rent accommodations, the difference between the actual market value of that housing and the amount you're required to pay will be included in your employment income. An exception occurs when your duties are performed at a remote location or special work site. See Tip #21 for further details.

- ✔ Spouse's travelling expenses: If your spouse joins you on a business trip, you'll probably have a taxable benefit equal to your spouse's travelling expenses paid for by your employer, unless your spouse was primarily engaged in business activities on behalf of your employer.

No harm exists in extending your business trip to include a personal vacation. Because the initial trip was for business purposes, the costs paid by your employer will be tax-free benefits. Of course, this is provided you pick up all the additional costs for your extended trip (other than the trip home).

- ✔ **Surface transit passes provided to family members of transit employees:** Effective for 2010, the non-taxation of free or discounted surface transit passes applies only for passes provided to the transit employee and for the exclusive use of the employee (so, passes that can be used by family members will now be a taxable benefit).

#21

Negotiate Non-Taxable Benefits

Non-taxable benefits are benefits from your employer you can enjoy tax free. Keep them in mind when you're negotiating your way into a new job or simply at your next compensation review — you can load up on these perks with abandon, because they have no negative effect on your tax situation.

Big Wins

The following are some of the more common non-taxable benefits that may translate into major tax relief for you:

- ✔ **Computer and Internet services:** The CRA says that the provision of home computers and Internet services to an employee where the primary use is for work or for the employee to become more computer literate is not a taxable benefit. The CRA suggests the employee pay a nominal fee for personal use.

- ✔ **Death benefits:** If you pass away and your employer pays a death benefit to your family, they receive the first $10,000 of that benefit tax free.

- ✔ **Education costs:** When your employer picks up the tab for education, you won't have to pay additional taxes for taking a course provided you're benefiting your employer. If the course is of personal interest, it would result in a taxable benefit because it has nothing to do with your work. So, if your employer kindly agrees to pay for your Bee Keeping for Beginners course, just be prepared for the taxable benefit.

- ✔ **Food and lodging:** Food and lodging are not taxable benefits if you were required to work at a temporary site for more than 36 hours consecutively. To qualify, the temporary site must be in a remote place or be farther away than a reasonable daily commute from your residence, and you must keep your usual residence.

✔ **Moving costs:** When your employer pays for or reimburses you for moving costs where the move is for employment, no taxable benefit exists.

Ensure you negotiate this tax-free benefit when considering a new job where a move is necessary.

If your employer compensates you for the diminished value or loss on the sale of your home due to relocation, you're considered to have received a taxable benefit. However, the taxable amount is only half of the amount reimbursed over $15,000. Better than nothing, we say!

✔ **Parking space:** The fair market value of an employer-provided parking space, minus any amount you pay for the spot, must usually be included in your income. If your employer provides a parking space to you and you use your vehicle regularly during business hours to carry out your employment duties, it's not a taxable benefit. Of course, when the spot is in a location where free parking is readily accessible, then there will be no taxable benefit.

✔ **Personal counselling:** Not many people know this, but your employer can pay for counselling related to your or a relative's mental or physical health and you won't have to report a taxable benefit. The counselling may be related to tobacco, drug, or alcohol abuse; stress management; job placement; or retirement. Be sure to negotiate these payments with your employer if you find yourself or someone related to you in need of these services.

✔ **Scholarship:** If your employer has a scholarship plan to assist children of employees, the scholarship money can be received tax free by the child.

✔ **Transportation to the job:** Some employers provide their employees with transportation to and from work, for security or some other reason (think private limo with a driver, not city bus with an employer-provided bus pass). Whatever the reason, there will be no inclusion for the value of the benefit in the employee's income. Sit back and enjoy the ride without worrying about any tax hit.

Smaller Victories

The benefits we cover in this section may be slightly less impactful than some of those we discuss in the previous section over the long term, but they can translate into significant savings. After all, Rome wasn't built in a day. Try to negotiate for the following from your employer:

- ✓ Contributions to private health services plans
- ✓ Contributions to pension plans
- ✓ Contributions to a deferred profit sharing plan (DPSP)
- ✓ Merchandise discounts, if extended to all employees
- ✓ The cost of uniforms, and the cleaning of them
- ✓ In-house recreational and fitness facilities
- ✓ In-house daycare services (but not daycare provided by a third party and paid for by your employer)
- ✓ Supplemental unemployment benefit plan premiums

Subsidized meals

The CRA has relaxed the rules for overtime meals to reflect seasonal overtime and general market conditions. Employees now have to work only an additional 2 hours daily for a meal reimbursement or allowance of up to $17 to be tax-free.

Travel and meals within a municipality or metropolitan area

The CRA has announced it will accept that travel allowances (including meals) paid for travel within the employer's municipality or metropolitan area can be excluded from income if the allowance is paid primarily for the benefit of the employer. As long as you can demonstrate that the amount you received benefited your employer more than you it's a green light to exclude these amounts from income.

Loyalty programs

CRA used to take the position that a taxable benefit existed where employees incurred business expenses (using personal credit cards) that were later reimbursed by their employers and accrued reward points on these expenses that were used for personal purposes. This is obviously beneficial to an employee, but there was no way an employer could possibly track and report a benefit.

The CRA admitted this and made it clear there generally shouldn't be a benefit. Bring on the Air Miles!

Gifts and awards from your employer

You can receive two non-cash gifts per year, and if the combined cost to your employer is $500 or less the entire amount is non-taxable. But watch out: If the total amount of the gifts you receive cost your employer more than $500, the entire amount becomes taxable — not just the portion above $500. The CRA provides for a second $500 exemption where a long-term service award is provided.

Gifts that have been personalized with your name or corporate logo will have a reduced market value. When the award is a plaque, trophy, or other memento for which no market exists, there likely will be no taxable benefit.

A prize recognized by the public for certain achievements or services can be non-taxable!

For 2010 and subsequent years the CRA revised and simplified its policy such that the $500 exemptions can now be used as a deduction when calculating taxable benefits. For gifts and general rewards, there will be no limit to the number of gifts/awards that can be given during the year.

Cash and near-cash awards (think gift cards) are still excluded from this policy, as are those of you who own your business and are also employees of it. (We know, we know — life's not fair!)

#22

Deduct Employment Expenses

● ●

You may be one of many employees who are required to fund the costs of carrying out your employment duties. These costs can vary from taking prospective customers out to lunch to using your own car for sales calls to perhaps using space in your home or apartment for work purposes. If your employer doesn't directly reimburse you for these costs (usually via an expense report), one of two things likely happens:

- ✔ Your employer pays you an allowance to cover your expenses, but the allowance is included in your T4 employment income. In other words, you pay tax on the allowance.

- ✔ Your employer does not pay you an allowance. You're simply required to pay your own expenses.

If you fall into one of these categories, you should be able to claim a deduction for at least some, if not all, of the expenses you incur to do your job.

When you don't fall into one of these categories, try not to be overly jealous of those who do. Though it's nice to be able to deduct employment expenses, limits apply on what you can claim, and it's better when your employer simply reimburses the costs. The reimbursement is not a taxable benefit to you. With a reimbursement, you're not out any money; your employer returns to you every dollar you spend in doing your job. In deducting employment expenses, the best you can do is receive about a 46-cent refund for every dollar deducted — and this assumes you're in the top tax bracket.

Figuring Out Who Can Deduct

To deduct the expenses you incur to carry out your employment duties, the following must apply to you:

✔ You must be **required** to pay expenses to earn your employment income (in the CRA's words, you must be required to incur the expenses under the terms of your employment contract, whether or not you have a written contract).

✔ Your employer must provide you with a form detailing the expenses you're required to incur. The form is T2200, "Declarations of Conditions of Employment." It's completed and signed by your employer — not you.

Comparing Commissioned Salespeople and Regular Employees

CRA's rules governing what commission salespeople can deduct are somewhat more generous than the rules for salaried employees (see Table 2-1 for details). In addition to being allowed to deduct specific expenses, salespeople can deduct any reasonable expense incurred to earn income (such as commissions) that is based on the amount of sales they generate.

To be able to deduct expenses as a salesperson, you must pass the following tests:

✔ You must be required to pay your own expenses by virtue of your contract of employment;

✔ You must ordinarily be required to carry on the duties of your employment away from your employer's business location (e.g., at customer locations);

✔ Your remuneration must be wholly or partly based on commissions or other amounts, such as bonuses, which are calculated by reference to the volume of sales made or contracts negotiated; and

✔ You must not be in receipt of a tax-free travel allowance for your expenses.

If you're deducting expenses as a commission salesperson, you have a few things to remember. First, you can deduct expenses only to the extent of your commission income. If your expenses exceed this income, you cannot deduct the excess amount. And the excess can't be transferred to another year to deduct against income earned then. Second, you can always deduct certain expenses as a regular employee against your salary. You need to use the rules that allow you to deduct certain expenses as a commission salesperson only if you couldn't otherwise deduct them as a regular employee.

Always consider the rules for regular employees and then use the rules for commission salespeople only when expense deduction is higher, to reduce the likelihood that your expenses will exceed your commission income.

Table 2-2 compares the expenses that can be deducted by an employee earning a salary and those that can be deducted by an employee being paid on a commission basis.

Table 2-2	Can I Deduct It?	
Expense	Earning Salary	Earning Commissions
Legal fees to collect wages, salary, or commissions owed	Yes	Yes
Accounting fees for tax-return preparation	No[1]	Yes
Advertising and promotion	No	Yes
Entertainment for customers	No	Yes[2]
Food and beverage[3]	Yes[2]	Yes[2]
Lodging and travel	Yes[4]	Yes
Parking[5]	Yes	Yes
Automobile expense	Yes	Yes
Office supplies[6]	Yes	Yes
Uniforms	Yes	Yes
Clothing, dry cleaning, makeup, and hair-styling	No	No
Computer or fax purchase	No	No
Computer or fax lease	No	Yes
Cell phone purchase	No	No
Cell phone lease	No	Yes
Cell phone airtime[7]	Yes	Yes

Expense	Earning Salary	Earning Commissions
Long-distance calls[7]	Yes	Yes
Internet[8]	No	Yes
Licences[9]	No	Yes
Salaries to assistants[10]	Yes	Yes
Office rent[10]	Yes	Yes
Home office[10]	Yes	Yes

Notes

1. An alternative filing opportunity is to claim the accounting fee as a carrying charge on schedule 4. Refer to Tip #42, which deals with the deduction available for carrying charges and interest expenses.

2. Only 50 percent of entertainment, food, and beverage expenses can be deducted. This restriction also applies to gift certificates for these items.

3. Food, beverage, and lodging are deductible only if your employer requires you to be away from the municipality or metropolitan area where your employer is located for at least 12 hours.

4. You can deduct travel expenses if you were normally required to work away from your employer's business or in different places, and you did not receive a non-taxable allowance to cover travelling expenses.

5. The CRA's position is that parking costs at your employer's office are not deductible because they're considered a personal expense. However, if you need to go to the office before or after seeing a customer, or to work at a different location, we would argue that the parking in these circumstances should be deductible.

6. Supplies must be used directly in your work and for nothing else. The CRA takes the position that these supplies include "pens, pencils, paper clips, stationery, stamps, street maps, and directories." They do not include items such as briefcases or calculators. Tools are not deductible unless you're a tradesperson. (We discuss tools later in this tip.)

7. Restricted to work-related cost of calls and airtime.

8. The CRA's guide Employment Expenses now specifically states that Internet charges are not deductible by an employee. However, it remains silent on Internet charges for a commissioned employee. We expect that they would be deductible, to be consistent with the treatment of cell phone charges and leasing costs.

9. Annual licence fees are deductible if needed to carry out work (for example, real estate and insurance licences).

10. Your employer must specifically indicate on form T2200 that you're required to incur these costs.

The benefit of leasing tools and computer equipment

Consider renting or leasing tools and computer equipment from a third party. Generally no deduction can be claimed by employees for capital assets, but the cost of renting or leasing these assets can be deducted. You could also consider having a family member such as your spouse purchase the assets and rent them to you. You would then be entitled to a deduction against your employment income. Your spouse would report the rental payments received from you as income but would be entitled to deduct capital cost allowance (CCA) on the assets, interest expense, and other related costs against the income.

We recommend you get professional help before implementing this strategy to make sure it makes financial sense for you and that you do not run afoul of the tax man.

Consider an example that illustrates some of the points in Table 2-2. Charlie took an industrial sales job with Pinegrove Products Inc. of Oakville, Ontario, on February 1, 2009. His conditions of employment were that he was to be paid on a commission basis and that he was required to do the following:

- ✔ Pay for his own office supplies (paper, toner, postage, and so on)

- ✔ Pay the salary of his part-time assistant, Buffy

- ✔ Provide a home office for himself and Buffy (Charlie was not provided with a workspace at Pinegrove.)

- ✔ Provide his own car because the job involved significant travel in southern Ontario

During 2009, Charlie made commissions of $90,000. He paid 5 percent GST on his expenses when applicable. (All his expenses were incurred in Ontario, so he did not pay any HST in 2009.) In this example, assuming Charlie spent $5,300 on office supplies and $4,000 for Buffy's salary, he'd be entitled to a full deduction of $9,300 against his commission income.

The distinction that Charlie is being paid on a commission basis is an important one. The expenses that may be deducted by commission employee versus a regular employee are different.

Let the CRA's Forms Help You

The CRA publishes form T777, "Statement of Employment Expenses," to assist you in gathering and summarizing your employment expenses. This is the form used by the majority of employees.

A second employee expense form, TL2, "Claim for Meals and Lodging Expenses," is used by employees involved in air, rail, bus, and trucking industries. Another form that can come into play is form GST 370, "Employee and Partner GST/HST Rebate Application." Most employees like this form because it works only one way: It assists you in calculating the amount of GST/HST you can recover from the government!

The employment expenses you deduct are to include the GST, HST, and provincial and territorial sales taxes you paid. Do not separate the GST/HST or provincial/territorial sales taxes from the non-tax portion of your expenses. If you lived in Alberta (no provincial sales tax) and purchased $100 of deductible supplies to do your job, you would actually pay $105 when the GST is added. It's the $105 that is included in your employment expenses on the T777.

If you're eligible to claim a deduction for employment expenses, recordkeeping is vital for a number of reasons. One, you don't want to miss out on claiming a legitimate expense. If you do, you overstate your tax liability! Two, the CRA can request employees to provide support for the expenses claimed on their tax return. The CRA is usually happy to accept the deduction for employment expenses, provided the support (receipts, invoices, ticket stubs, kilometre log, and so on) is organized and available for inspection should it be requested. Third, you simplify your tax return preparation. Don't even think of bringing a shopping bag (or the infamous shoebox) full of receipts and stuff to an accountant in late April and expect to be pleasantly welcomed!

Deals on Wheels — Claiming Your Automobile Expenses

If you pay your own automobile expenses and are required to use your car to carry out your employment duties, you can deduct a portion of your costs in completing your income tax return. As noted above, your employer would indicate on form T2200 that you need to supply your own car and incur expenses to keep it on the road. Here are some types of automobile expenses that can be deducted:

✔ Capital cost allowance (CCA or tax depreciation)

✔ Fuel

✔ Insurance

✔ Interest incurred on a loan to purchase a car

✔ Leasing costs

✔ Licence and registration fees

✔ Repairs and maintenance

It's only the "employment use" portion of automobile expenses that is included in your deductible employment expenses. The CRA states that driving only to and from work is personal use — not employment use. However, if you need to go out in your car in the middle of the day (say, to see a potential customer), or perhaps on your way to or from work, the whole trip can be considered employment use.

Recall our friend Charlie, who started working at Pinegrove on February 1, 2009 and was required to provide his own car. Charlie used his Honda Civic, which he had leased a few years back. His lease costs for the period were $3,300 ($300 per month for 11 months). From February to December 2009, Charlie drove the Civic a total of 20,000 kilometres — 15,000 were work related.

Charlie, being ever fearful of a CRA query, kept a log in his glove compartment that detailed his work trips and kilometres driven. He updated the log daily. Based on the kilometres, it's clear that Charlie used his car 75 percent of the time for work and 25 percent for personal use. Charlie can deduct 75 percent of his automobile expenses in calculating his deductible employment expenses.

Let's calculate Charlie's automobile expenses:

Expenses	*Dollar Value*
Fuel	$2,000
Maintenance and repairs	$1,500
Insurance	$1,100
Licence and registration	$125
Lease	$3,300
Other — car washes	$100
Total expenses	$8,125
Employment use portion	75 percent
Allowable amount of automobile expenses that Charlie can deduct on his tax return	$6,094

Do you really need to keep a log of your kilometres driven for employment use? Yes, kind of. If the CRA asks you to support your automobile expenses, it will want to see your log of kilometres. So get in the habit of keeping the log in the car. Every time you get in the car, make an entry of where you're going, and later where you have been and the kilometres travelled.

Starting in 2009 you have to keep this log only for a time that is considered representative of your normal auto use. We recommend you do this — you'll thank us if the CRA comes knocking!

Capital cost allowance (CCA) when an automobile is owned rather than leased

Because your car is expected to last more than a year, its cost cannot be completely deducted in computing your employment expenses. However, a percentage of the car's capital cost allowance (CCA for short) can. CCA is the tax term for depreciation (see Tip #32). The first step in determining the amount of CCA you can deduct is to decide whether your automobile is "class 10" or "class 10.1" for CCA purposes. Both CCA classes 10 and 10.1 calculate the maximum CCA that can be claimed, at a rate of 30 percent calculated on the declining-balance method of depreciation, which involves applying the depreciation rate against the non-depreciated balance. Instead of spreading the cost of the asset evenly over its life, this system expenses the asset at a constant rate, which results in declining depreciation charges each successive period.

Note: Use class 10.1 if your car cost $30,000 or more (before PST and GST or HST) and class 10 if it cost less than $30,000.

In the year you purchase an automobile, the "half-year" rule applies — meaning you can take only 50 percent of the CCA you would otherwise be entitled to. This results in a CCA calculation at 15 percent (30 percent × ½ = 15 percent). The determination of whether your car is considered a "class 10" or a "class 10.1" automobile is important, as the CCA on class 10.1 automobiles is restricted to a maximum amount. We discuss the restrictions on CCA and other automobile expenses shortly.

Assume that rather than leasing his Honda Civic, Charlie purchased the Civic in 2009 for $23,000, taxes included. (By the way, this car qualifies as class 10 — therefore, no restrictions apply in calculating CCA.) Let's take a look at how Charlie would calculate CCA for 2009 and 2010.

Before calculating CCA, Charlie would calculate his employee expense deduction for the operating expenses of his car in the same way as above. He would add up the amounts he spent for fuel, repairs, licensing, insurance, and so on. (Of course there would be no leasing costs, as we are assuming here that he owns the car!) He would then multiply the total amount of expenses by the employment-use portion. In our preceding example, 75 percent was used for the 2009 year; we'll assume the appropriate employment usage figure is also 75 percent for 2010.

Table 2-3 summarizes how Charlie would calculate CCA for 2009 and 2010.

Table 2-3   Charlie's Capital Cost Allowance (CCA) Schedule for 2009 and 2010

Year: 2009	
Undepreciated capital cost (UCC)	$0 at January 1, 2009
Acquisitions in year	$23,000
Subtract one-half[1]	($11,500)
Base for 2009 CCA calculation	$11,500
CCA at 30 percent[2]	($3,450)
Add back one-half subtracted above	$11,500
UCC at December 31, 2009	$19,550
Year: 2010	
UCC at January 1, 2010 (as above)	$19,550
CCA at 30 percent[2]	($5,865)
UCC at December 31, 2010	$13,685

1. This part of the calculation results in only half of the capital cost of the acquisitions in 2009 being depreciated. While the CCA rate is 30 percent, the subtracted amount results in the CCA being only 15 percent — half of 30 percent. This calculation is referred to as the "half-year" rule.

2. Remember that Charlie used his car only 75 percent of the time to carry out his employment duties. Therefore, his tax deduction is 75 percent of the CCA calculated. In 2009 — $3,450 × 75% = $2,587.50. In 2010 — $5,965 × 75% = $4,398.75.

Claiming CCA, whether for an automobile or any asset on which CCA can be claimed, is optional. A taxpayer (whether employed or self-employed, or perhaps a corporation) may decide to claim less than the maximum CCA, or no CCA at all! Although at first it may seem odd that a taxpayer would not take maximum advantage of a tax deduction available, some logical reasons for this do exist. For example, perhaps the taxpayer will be in a higher tax bracket next year. This will result in a greater tax reduction than if the CCA is taken this year.

Restrictions on certain automobile expenses

If you're entitled to deduct a portion of your automobile as employment expenses, you deduct only the "business use" portion of the expenses you actually paid. This is true for most of your expenses. The amount you pay is the starting point in determining what you can deduct. Three exceptions apply:

✔ **Automobile leasing costs** (see Table 2-4)

✔ **Interest on car loans** (see Table 2-4)

✔ **Capital cost on which CCA will begin to be calculated** (see Table 2-5)

Table 2-4   Maximum Amounts Deductiblefor Lease and Interest Costs

	Leased/Purchased In	
	2001–2009	*2000*
Monthly lease cost	$800	$700
Monthly interest cost	$300	$250

1. The government reviews these limits annually and announces any changes prior to the end of the year so that taxpayers are aware of the rules in advance of the year in which they apply. The rates are set by the Department of Finance Canada and released by press release.

2. All limits are before sales tax. The limits are actually slightly higher when provincial and territorial retail sales tax and GST/HST are added.

Table 2-5	Maximum Amounts on Which CCA Can Be Claimed on Automobiles	
	Automobiles Purchased In	
	2001–2009	*2000*
Maximum capital cost amount for purposes of claiming CCA on an automobile	$30,000	$26,000

The above limits are before provincial/territorial retail sales tax and GST/HST. If you purchased a car in Ontario, for example, you would pay an 8 percent Ontario sales tax and the 5 percent GST — a total of 13 percent. The deemed maximum capital cost for claiming CCA on your car purchase in 2009 would be $33,900 ($30,000 × 113 percent = $33,900).

When these exceptions apply, you'll find that the amounts you use to begin calculating your deductible automobile expenses are less than you actually paid. And remember, these maximums apply before you prorate your automobile expenses between employment use and business use.

Let's look at Finlay's situation. Finlay is a salesman. On January 1, 2009, he leased a Mercedes. His monthly lease cost is $850 (including taxes). Finlay uses his car 60 percent for work. He expects that his monthly effective tax deduction will be $510 ($850 × 60 percent), or $6,120 per year. He's not worried about the lease cost restriction because he understands the maximum cost for leases commenced in 2009 is $800 (see Table 2-4). Finlay is wrong! The effective tax deduction he will have is the $800 per month maximum multiplied by his 60 percent employment use, which results in a tax deduction equal to $480 per month, or $5,760 for all of 2009.

Home Is Where the Office Is — Claiming Home Office Expenses

If your employer requires you to provide space in your home or apartment to carry out your employment duties, your employer must indicate this on form T2200 and provide it to you. If you do maintain a home office, you can deduct a portion of the expenses related to maintaining the workspace. This includes a portion of the expenses that you incur anyway, such as monthly utilities and rent.

For the costs to be deductible, you must ensure your workspace meets one of two tests — you don't have to meet both! Under the first test, the workspace must be the primary place where your employment duties are carried out. A sales representative employed by a company may work from home and rarely "go to the office." A part-time night school teacher may not have an office at a school and must plan lessons and mark exams at home.

Under the second test, your workspace must be used exclusively to carry out your employment duties and you must use the space on a "regular and continuous" basis for meeting customers or clients or others associated with carrying out your duties. Infrequent meetings or frequent meetings at irregular intervals won't cut it.

Deductible home office expenses

As Table 2-5 details, an employee paid on a commission basis is able to deduct more home office expenses than an employee paid by salary.

Table 2-6	Home Office Expenses Deductions	
	Earning Salary	*Earning Commissions*
Electricity, heat, and water	Yes	Yes
Maintenance	Yes	Yes
Rent	Yes	Yes
Property tax	No	Yes
Home insurance	No	Yes
Mortgage interest	No	No
Mortgage principal	No	No

Telephone expenses are not mentioned here. Though you may think of these as a home office expense, they can be deducted as "supplies" in completing form T777. The CRA's position is that long-distance charges for calls made to carry out your employment duties can be deducted, but that the monthly charges for your residential phone line cannot — not even a portion of them. However, if you have a separate phone line for your employment, the full costs associated with this phone can be deducted.

Deductions for Special Employment Situations

Many of us have truly unique employment circumstances, and some of them call for uncommon expenses. Happily, the CRA recognizes this, and allows for a wide range of deductions. Here's a look at some of the occupations that have deductions of their own — be sure to claim everything that fits:

- **Artists:** If you're an employed artist, you'll enjoy some deductions in addition to the "regular" employee expenses. The CRA considers you an artist if you do any of the following:

  - Create (but don't reproduce) paintings, prints, etchings, drawings, sculptures, or similar works of art

  - Compose dramatic, musical, or literary works

  - Perform dramatic or musical work, as an actor, singer, or musician

  - Belong to a professional artists' association that is certified by the Minister of Canadian Heritage

  An artist who earns income from any of the above activities may deduct related expenses incurred to earn this income. Again, these "related" expenses are in addition to the regular employment expenses deductible by all types of employees who are required to incur these expenses as part of their job.

- **Mechanics' apprentices:** A mechanic's apprentice can deduct a portion of the cost of tools acquired in a year on his or her personal tax return. Those of you with a "vehicle mechanic in training" in the family will know what a significant investment these tools are in relation to income.

  Unfortunately, a deduction for the full cost of the tools is not allowed. The allowable deduction amount is the total cost of new tools acquired in a taxation year, less the greater of $1,000 or 5 percent of the individual's apprenticeship income for the year.

  Any part of the eligible deduction that is not taken in the year in which the tools are purchased can be carried forward and deducted in subsequent taxation years. You can also claim a GST/HST tax credit for the sales taxes paid on the deductible portion of the tools.

- **Musicians:** In addition to the costs noted above for employees, if you're a musician you may be entitled to deduct capital cost allowance on your instrument (class 8 — 20 percent declining basis), as well as any amounts paid for the maintenance, rental, and insurance of the instrument. To claim these amounts, you must be required, as a term of your employment, to provide your own musical instrument.

✔ **Tradespeople:** Tradespersons who acquire eligible tools for employment can deduct the cost exceeding $1,000 each year up to a maximum of $500 per year.

✔ **Transport employees:** If you're employed in the transport industry (air, rail, and bus travel, and trucking), you and your employer are required to complete form TL2, "Claim for Meals and Lodging Expenses." The total of the amount deductible is to be included on line 229 of your tax return. Like non–transport industry employees, you may be eligible for a GST/HST rebate.

#23

Get Your GST Rebate

• •

The Goods and Services Tax (GST) and Harmonized Sales Tax (HST) are consumer taxes. This means that when you incur GST or HST in carrying out your employment duties, you're really incurring it on behalf of your employer's business — not as a consumer. Therefore, the GST or HST should be refunded or rebated to you because it was not incurred for a consumer purchase. In this tip, we outline when you're eligible to claim a GST/HST rebate, what purchases are eligible for the rebate, and how to get your money back.

 No rebate applies for provincial and territorial sales taxes. They simply remain part of the costs you incurred in carrying out your employment responsibilities.

Assessing Your Eligibility for the GST/HST Rebate

If you have to pay your own expenses to carry out your employment duties, you're probably able to claim a rebate for the GST and HST included in your expenses.

You're **not** eligible to claim the GST/HST if either of the following applies to your situation:

✔ Your employer is not a GST/HST registrant

✔ Your employer carries on a GST/HST–exempt activity, which includes one of the following:

   • Health care (for example, a medical or dental practice)

   • Financial services (for example, banking, insurance, and investing)

Determining Which Expenses Qualify for the GST/HST Rebate

You can claim the GST/HST rebate on any expenses you paid GST/HST on and deducted on form T777, plus the GST/HST component of the union or professional dues deducted on line 212 of your tax return.

Naturally, you can't claim GST/HST on purchases that didn't attract the tax, such as the following:

- ✔ Goods or services that are GST exempt, such as some membership fees and dues, insurance, licences, and salaries to assistants.

- ✔ Employment expenses where no GST/HST was paid because the vendor of the goods or provider of the services was not registered for GST and, therefore, did not charge GST.

Additionally, you can't claim the rebate on the personal-use portion of your automobile and home office expenses. Remember, the rebate is for business expenses, not consumer purchases.

Calculating and Claiming Your GST/HST Rebate

In order to claim your GST/HST rebate you need to tally up your employment expenses you've deducted in the year, subtract the non-eligible ones (which we discussed in Tip #22) and then back out the GST to figure out what your rebate should be.

Now you say, "HOLD IT!" You've just realized that you receive two benefits doing the calculation this way:

- ✔ You got a tax saving from being able to deduct the GST component of your employment expenses.

- ✔ You received back the GST you paid.

Isn't this double dipping on a tax/GST break?!

Congratulations on being so observant. You will indeed have received a double benefit. In fact, the government purposely designed the system this way! (Who else could?) However, when you prepare your tax return for next year, the double benefit will be taken away. The GST/HST rebate you recieve will be included on line 104 of your tax return and will be fully subject to tax. So, in one year you have the benefit of deducting the GST/HST portion of your employment expenses. After two years, the only double dipping you will do is at Dairy Queen.

The rebate you're entitled to is calculated on form GST 370, "Employee and Partner GST/HST Rebate Application."

#24

Give Yourself Credit: More Tips for Employees

• •

*E*mployees are very limited in the expenses they can deduct when calculating the tax they owe to the CRA — therefore, much to the chagrin of many Canadians, employment income is where we pay the bulk of our taxes. But don't despair. In this tip we provide a few more strategies to help you keep your taxes to a minimum.

Get a Refund When You Overpay CPP Premiums

As you may know, your employer has to take CPP premiums off your pay. However, it's possible that you paid too much! This most commonly happens when you held more than one job during the year — because each employer is obligated to withhold CPP without regard to your other employers, you may have maxed out your annual payments. See the CRA Web site (www.cra-arc.gc.ca/tx/bsnss/tpcs/pyrll/clcltng/cpp-rpc/cnt-chrt-pf-eng.html) for the current year's maximum contribution.

If you were not a resident of Quebec and you contributed more than you were required to, enter the difference on line 448 of your tax return. The CRA will refund the excess contributions to you, or will apply them to reduce your balance owing. If you were a resident of Quebec, this line does not apply to you; claim the excess amount on your Quebec provincial tax return.

Don't worry if you don't realize you made a CPP overpayment. The CRA will catch it when assessing your return.

Get a Refund When You Overpay EI Premiums

As with the CPP overpayment, you may have had too much EI deducted from your pay in the year. If you contributed more than you had to, enter the difference on line 450. The CRA will refund the excess amount to you or use it to reduce your balance owing. See the CRA Web site (`www.cra-arc.gc.ca/tx/bsnss/tpcs/pyrll/clcltng/ei/hstrc-eng.html#chart`) for the current year's maximum contribution.

If you repaid some of the EI benefits you received, don't claim the repayment on this line. If the repayment was in connection with EI received in 2008 or later years, you need to include the amount on line 235.

Again, if you fail to calculate that you have overpaid EI premiums, the CRA will catch it on assessing your return.

Claim the Canada Employment Tax Credit

This credit is designed to help offset some of the work-related expenses incurred by employees. For 2009, the credit amount is calculated as the lesser of $1,044 and the individual's employment income for the year.

You don't have to actually incur expenses in order to claim this credit. And no receipts are required. This is a gimme, so be sure to claim it — and save $157 in federal tax ($1,044 × 15 percent)!

Deduct Your Union or Professional Dues

Because you're taxed on pretty much all your income, it's logical that costs incurred to earn the income are deductible. It is logical — but no one ever said the Income Tax Act was logical. One of the deductions permitted is the cost of belonging to a union or to a professional body, or the cost of carrying professional or malpractice insurance. Union dues paid are noted in box 44 of your T4. Fees paid to professional organizations are usually receipted. If your employer pays the fees for your professional memberships or insurance, the employer gets the tax deduction — you don't, even if the receipt is in your name.

If you paid GST or HST on your union or professional dues, you may be able to have the GST refunded to you. See Tip #23 for the details on making the claim.

Get Credit for Your Commuting Costs — Public Transit Expenses

If you use public transportation, you may be able to offset the cost of your transit pass with this non-refundable credit. The federal tax credit, or federal tax savings, is the eligible amount you spent multiplied by 15 percent.

The credit applies when you

- ✔ Purchase public transit passes with a duration of a month or longer

- ✔ Purchase four consecutive weekly passes and each pass entitles you to unlimited use for at least five days each week.

- ✔ Purchase via electronic payment cards if you use the card for at least 32 one-way trips during an interrupted period of no more than 31 days.

Public transit includes transit by local bus, streetcar, subway, commuter train, commuter bus, and local ferry. The credit can be claimed by you or your spouse for eligible transit costs incurred by you, your spouse, or dependent children under the age of 19.

If this credit applies to you, be sure to keep your receipts and passes in case the CRA asks for proof — we know from experience they like to review the support for this credit.

Plan for a Loss of Employment

•••

*L*osing your job is a dramatic and stressful life event that can have a profound effect on your finances. If you're faced with the loss of employment, a good financial plan and being familiar with the following tax strategies could be invaluable.

Deduct Your Legal Costs

If you lose your job, any legal fees you pay to collect a severance or retirement allowance or a pension benefit are tax deductible on line 232 of your return. You can claim fees only up to the amount of the payment received in the year — minus any amount transferred to your RRSP. If you cannot claim all your legal fees in the year paid, they may be able to be claimed over the next seven years.

Ensure your lawyer details the bill such that fees for tax-deductible services are highlighted!

Roll Over Your Pension

The funds in your Registered Pension Plan (See Tip #17 for more details on pensions) are locked in so they will be there to provide you with an income on retirement. If you leave your employer you can't simply receive a cheque for the value of your pension savings. You will need to choose one of the following three options:

- ✔ Roll your existing pension into your new employer's pension.
- ✔ Leave it where it is and take your pension from that company when you retire.
- ✔ Transfer your money into a *locked in retirement account* (LIRA).

We recommend you consult with a qualified and experienced financial professional to help you decide which of these options is for you. Your future financial security could depend on you making a good decision.

Shelter Your Retiring Allowance

Don't be confused by the term retiring allowance — it doesn't apply only to payments you receive when you retire. In fact, it also includes what people normally refer to as "severance" or "termination" pay, as well as to a court award or settlement for wrongful dismissal.

Portion of retiring allowance eligible for RRSPs

Retiring allowances are taxable. However, when you leave your employer and receive a retiring allowance, you might be able to pay a portion of your payment into your RRSP. This portion is called your "eligible" retiring allowance. If you choose to do this, you include the full amount of the allowance on line 130 of your tax return, but a deduction is given on line 208 for the amount paid to your RRSP. If those two amounts are the same, you will effectively receive the retiring allowance tax free — or at least tax-free (yes that's right — we said tax-free) until the time you make withdrawals out of your RRSP.

Not all retiring allowances are eligible for transfer into your RRSP. In fact, the Income Tax Act sets limits on the amount of retiring allowance you can have paid into your RRSP. The limit is calculated as follows:

- ✔ $2,000 per year or part year of employment service prior to 1996, plus

- ✔ $1,500 per year or part year of employment service prior to 1989 in which you had no vested interest in any employer's contributions to a registered pension plan or deferred profit-sharing plan.

So, if you worked for an employer from, say, 1997 to 2009, any retiring allowance paid to you would not be eligible for the special transfer into your RRSP. Too bad!

Let's suppose Alex left her employer in 2009 and received a $50,000 termination payment. She had started working there in 1985 and joined the pension plan in 1987.

The amount she can have paid to her RRSP is calculated this way:

$2,000 × 11 years (1985 to 1995)	$22,000
$1,500 × 2 years (1985 to 1987)	$3,000
Eligible portion of retiring allowance that can be paid to her RRSP	$25,000

The amount of a retiring allowance that can be paid to your RRSP and deducted on your personal tax return is over and above your regular RRSP contribution (or "deduction") limit. You can still make your regular RRSP contribution in addition to this special contribution. It's not critical that the retiring allowance be paid directly to your RRSP. However, you must contribute the funds to your RRSP within 60 days following the end of the year in which you receive the payment. For allowances received in 2009, this means the contribution must be made by March 1, 2010, or you lose your right to this special contribution.

The eligible portion of a retiring allowance can be rolled into an RRSP of which only you are the annuitant. It cannot go into a spousal RRSP.

Ineligible portion of retiring allowance

Any allowance received in excess of the amount you can have paid to your RRSP under the rules outlined above is considered an ineligible retiring allowance. In other words, the ineligible retiring allowance is any portion paid to you that relates to your employment from 1997 on. This amount is reported in box 27 of your T4A, and must be reported on line 130 of your income tax return. The ineligible portion of a retiring allowance does not open up new RRSP room for you.

Here are a couple of tips that may help ease the tax burden on any ineligible portion of a retiring allowance:

- ✔ If you have regular unused RRSP contribution room, consider making an RRSP contribution with your ineligible retiring allowance. In fact, you can have your employer send the portion that you are going to contribute directly to your RRSP and avoid any withholding tax. To do this you must show your employer that you have the RRSP contribution room available.

- ✔ Ask to receive the retiring allowance payment over a number of years. You don't have to pay tax on a retiring allowance until it's received, so this can help to defer tax to a year when you may be in a lower tax bracket.

#26

Claim Your Moving Expenses

• •

*1*f you moved at least 40 kilometres to start a job (even just a summer job), to start a business, or for full-time post-secondary education, you may be eligible to deduct at least a portion of your moving expenses. In this tip, we spell out ways to determine just how much of your move is eligible, and how to deduct the cost of your move.

 The eligible moving expenses may be deducted only from your employment or self-employment income earned at the new location. If your current year's eligible moving expenses exceeded your current year's income at the new location, the excess can be carried forward for deduction on the next year's tax return.

Eligible Moving Expenses

Most moving expenses are eligible for a tax deduction. You must pay for the expenses by December 31 of the year you're claiming them as deductions. Specifically, they are as follows:

- ✔ Travelling expenses, including automobile expenses for you and your family

- ✔ Meals and accommodations on the way to the new residence

- ✔ Costs of moving your stuff (moving van, storage, insurance, and so on)

- ✔ Costs for up to 15 days for you and your family for meals and temporary stay

- ✔ Costs of cancelling your lease on the old residence

- ✔ Costs of selling your old residence (advertising, legal fees, real estate commission, and mortgage prepayment penalty if applicable)

- ✔ Costs of maintaining your old residence when vacant (including mortgage interest and property taxes) to a maximum of $5,000

- ✔ Legal fees and land transfer fees paid in acquiring the new residence, provided you sold the prior residence as a result of the move

✔ Fees for utility disconnection and hook-ups

✔ Incidental costs related to the move (for example, costs of changing your address, and costs of acquiring new auto and driver's licences)

With respect to automobile and meal costs incurred while moving, the CRA permits you to either claim the actual costs or use a flat rate. The CRA refers to the flat rate system as the "simplified method" — appropriately named, we say. Where you use the flat rate, you don't need to retain receipts.

The flat rate for automobile travel varies by province or territory. If you don't use the flat rate, you need to track all the costs of operating the car for a year (gas, maintenance, insurance, interest on car loans, depreciation, and so on). You then prorate the total of these costs by taking the number of kilometres driven for the move over the total number of kilometres driven for the complete year. (Ugh — that's a lot of math.)

The flat rates for automobile and meal costs change every year and are posted on the CRA's Web site at www.cra-arc.gc.ca/travelcosts.

Employer-paid or -reimbursed Moving Expenses

You can deduct moving expenses only to the extent that the expenses were incurred by you. You cannot deduct expenses that were paid for by your employer, or that you incurred and were later reimbursed for by your employer. On the other hand, if your employer provided you with an allowance, this amount must be included in your income. Make sure you then claim any eligible moving expenses as a deduction.

When possible, always get your new employer to reimburse you for your moving expenses. This is advantageous for a number of reasons:

✔ You won't be out any money. Even in the top tax bracket, a tax deduction is worth less than 50 cents on the dollar. This means that for each dollar you deduct, you save less than 50 cents in tax. Isn't it better to have your employer give you back the full dollar? (The employer can claim a deduction for amounts reimbursed to you.)

Coming to or leaving Canada?

In most situations, moving expenses are not deductible if you're moving to or from Canada. (In this situation, you definitely want to have your employer reimburse your moving expenses!) However, if you leave Canada to study full time, your moving expenses may be deductible if you have taxable income and you continue to be a Canadian resident for tax purposes. If you're a full-time student and you came to Canada, you can deduct your moving expenses against your taxable income earned in Canada. (See Tip #51 for more details.)

✔ Some moving costs are not tax deductible. You definitely want to be reimbursed for these.

✔ You avoid the hassle of detailing all your moving expenses on your tax return, plus you are far less likely to have the CRA question your return.

✔ You do not need to wait for a tax refund to get your money back.

 The CRA has stated that your employer can provide you with a non-accountable allowance of up to $650 as a reimbursement of moving expenses. The allowance will not be considered income provided you certify in writing that you incurred moving expenses of an amount at least equal to the allowance you received.

Claiming Moving Expenses on Your Tax Return

To claim moving expenses, complete form T1M, "Moving Expenses Deduction." On this form you report where you moved from and to, why you moved, and the specific details and dollar amounts of your moving costs.

Oddly, you're not required to file either the T1M or any moving receipts with your tax return. However, you are required to keep these on hand in case of a CRA query. And trust us, queries happen.

Take Advantage of Special Employment Situations

*C*anadians who are sent abroad by their employers for six months or longer and those who live in the northern regions get special treatment when it comes to tax time. In this tip, we look at the credits and deductions you may qualify for if you fall into one of those categories.

Over the Seas and Far Away: Claim the Overseas Employment Tax Credit

The overseas employment tax credit may be available to you if you're a Canadian resident but worked abroad for six months or longer in connection with a resource, construction, installation, agricultural, or engineering project. Your employer must complete and sign form T626, "Overseas Employment Tax Credit." If you qualify, you'll find that some (and maybe most!) of your overseas income is exempt from tax in Canada.

Calculate the credit amount on form T626 and then carry it to line 426 of schedule 1.

 If you have severed your ties with Canada and become a non-resident, you will not be eligible for the credit because your income as a non-resident generally will not be taxable in Canada.

True North Strong and Free: Claim the Northern Residents Deduction

Rainy Hollow, B.C.; Belcher, Manitoba; Flin Flon, Saskatchewan; Pickle Crow, Ontario. What do these places have in common (other than their intriguing names)? Well, their residents can claim a northern residents deduction. In recognition of additional costs of living incurred by those who live in remote areas of Canada, the CRA allows special tax deductions to help with the extra burden.

Living in a remote area does not mean the nearest McDonald's is an hour away. In fact, the CRA has a very detailed (and very long) list of specific areas of Canada where you have to live to claim the deduction.

The actual deductions you can claim depend on where you live. The CRA has set up two different "zones":

- ✔ **Northern zone:** You are allowed the full northern residents deduction.
- ✔ **Intermediate zone:** You can deduct half the potential amount.

If you think you may live in a northern zone or an intermediate zone, check out the CRA's publication T4039, Northern Residents Deductions — Places in Prescribed Zones. (You can find it on the CRA Web site at www.cra-arc.gc.ca.)

Two types of northern residents deductions are available:

- ✔ Residency deductions
- ✔ Travel deductions

If you qualify for the northern residents deduction, you must fill out form T2222, "Northern Residents Deduction," and file it with your personal tax return. Keep any supporting receipts in case the CRA asks to see them.

Claim your residency deduction

To claim the residency deduction, you need to live exclusively in one of the prescribed zones. Stopping by for a visit won't do. In fact, to qualify, you must have lived, on a permanent basis, in one of the zones for at least six consecutive months beginning or ending in the current year.

You may be able to claim two separate types of residency deductions:

- ✔ **Basic residency amount:** This is a credit for simply living in a zone. The credit is now $8.25 per day for living in a northern zone, and one-half of this, or $4.13, for living in an intermediate zone.

✔ **Additional residency amount:** You can claim an additional credit of $8.25/$4.13 per day if the following situations apply:

- You maintained and lived in a dwelling during your time up north (generally a house or apartment — sorry, a hotel room or bunkhouse won't qualify).

- You're the only person claiming the basic residency amount for living in that dwelling for that time.

You're considered to have maintained and lived in a dwelling even when your employer or another person paid for your accommodations and other costs relating to the dwelling.

 If more than one taxpayer lived in the same dwelling at the same time during the year, either each taxpayer can claim the basic residency amount deduction ($8.25 or $4.13 per day), or one taxpayer can claim both the basic residency amount deduction and the additional residency deduction.

 If you're considered to receive a non-taxable benefit for board and lodging at a special work site in a northern or intermediate zone, the non-taxable benefit (as reported on your T4 or T4A slip) is to be deducted in calculating your residency deduction.

 If you received non-taxable board and lodging benefits but the special work site is more than 30 kilometres away from an urban area having a population of at least 40,000, you do not have to reduce your residency deduction.

Take your travel deductions

The second type of northern residents deduction you may be eligible to claim is the travel deduction. Generally, whenever your employer pays for something on your behalf, you're considered to have received a taxable benefit. This means that some travel benefits that your employer offers to you and your family may be taxable. When you live in a remote northern area, the fact that your employer will pay for some trips for you and your family could be a popular employment perk. Unfortunately, it could also lead to a tax bill. In recognition of the costs involved in travelling in remote areas, some relief from the taxable benefit rules is available. You can claim an additional northern residents tax deduction under these conditions:

✔ You qualify to claim a northern residents deduction (although you don't have to claim it to meet this criterion — *qualify* is the key word).

✔ You were an employee.

✔ You received taxable travel benefits in connection with your employment in a northern and/or intermediate zone.

✔ The travel benefits have been included in your employment income.

Box 32 of your T4 slip, or box 28 of your T4A slip, will report the taxable travel benefits you received in the year. If you received non-taxable benefits, such benefits will not show up on your slips and you're not eligible to claim the travel benefits deduction.

You must claim the travel benefits deduction in the same year that you report the taxable benefit received from your employer.

Types of travel qualifying for deduction

Different rules apply depending on your reasons for travelling. If you're travelling for medical services that are not available where you live, no limit applies on the number of trips you can make in the year. However, if you're travelling for any other reason, you can claim a deduction for only two trips a year for each member of your household.

If you're claiming a travel deduction for trips made for medical reasons, no one else can claim the expenditures as medical expenses as well.

If you're travelling for medical reasons, ensure your employer notes this fact on your T4 or T4A slip.

If you're travelling for medical reasons and cannot travel alone, you can claim a deduction for your travel expenses as well as those of another member of your household who will act as your attendant (assuming the other conditions for the deduction are met).

Amount of deduction available

Can you take a first-class, whirlwind trip and hope it qualifies as a travel deduction? Let's not be greedy. As with many of our tax rules, maximum amounts that can be claimed do apply. In this case, the maximum deduction that can be claimed for each eligible trip in the year is the **lowest** of the following:

✔ The taxable employment benefit you received from your employer for the trip.

✔ The cost of the lowest return airfare available at the time of the trip between the airport closest to your residence and the nearest designated city, even if you did not travel by air, or to that city.

✔ The total travel expenses for the trip. These travel expenses include such items as:

- Air, train, and bus fares.

- Meals. Actual cost (keep your receipts) or claim a flat rate of $17 per meal to a maximum of $51 per day per person for 2008. Rates for 2009 and later years can be found on the CRA's Web site at `http://www.cra-arc.gc.ca/travelcosts/`.

- Motor vehicle expenses. You can claim motor vehicle expenses based on actual costs incurred, or on a fixed per-kilometre amount. The per-kilometre amounts are published in a CRA fact sheet titled *Travel Expenses for Northern Residents Deductions, Medical, and Moving Expenses.* You can find it on the CRA Web site at www.cra-arc.gc.ca/travelcosts/.

- Hotel and motel accommodations.

- Other incidental expenses, such as taxis, road tolls, and ferry costs.

So, if you're travelling from a northern or intermediate zone to Cape Breton, Nova Scotia, you'll have to determine the airfare from the closest airport to your remote location to Halifax, Nova Scotia (which is the closest designated city to Cape Breton). This is the case even if you didn't fly between these two locations, and even though you're not planning on visiting Halifax! A list of designated cities can be found in the CRA guide entitled *General Income Tax and Benefit Guide.*

If you don't know the actual cost of the trip taken (for example, when you're given free airline tickets), include the market value of a similar trip as the actual cost. You could determine the market value of such a trip by getting a quote for return airfare for a regularly scheduled commercial flight on the date of your actual trip.

#28

Cover the Self-Employment Essentials

*W*hen you decide to go it alone, you need to make many decisions and handle many tasks that may have been handled for you by an employer in the past. Many of these decisions and actions will have an effect on your taxes. In this section, we look at two critical aspects of self-employment: selecting a taxation year-end, and setting aside Canada or Quebec Pension Plan contributions. (In Tip #29, we look at another important decision with tax ramifications: determining your business's ownership structure.)

Choose a Taxation Year-End

Choosing a year-end for tax purposes for your small business is an important decision. The selection of your first year-end is governed by the date you first commence business. The business year cannot exceed 12 months for a proprietorship or partnership.

The majority of self-employed individuals are now required to have a December 31 year-end. However, self-employed individuals, as well as partnerships that only have individuals as partners, have the option of selecting an off-calendar year-end provided they use the "alternative method" when calculating income for tax purposes. (See Tip #29 for more about partnerships.)

If you are self employed or an individual partner, consider whether the timing of your year-end can defer or save income taxes or can be used to coincide with a cyclical slow period in your business.

Here's an example of how to use the "alternative method" when the timing of your taxation year can save taxes.

Imagine that you, as a self-employed person, started your business on February 1, 2006. Because you chose to have an off-calendar year-end of January 31, 2007,

> ✔ In 2006, you wouldn't have an income inclusion because your fiscal period ended in 2007.

✔ In 2007, you would have to include income for the period February 1, 2006 to January 31, 2007, as well as an estimate of income for the period February 1, 2007 to December 31, 2007. The estimate is based on a proration of your income for the year ending January 31, 2007.

✔ In 2008, in addition to reporting your actual income for the fiscal year ending January 31, 2008, you would also have to include a new estimate to December 31, 2008. You will be able to deduct the previous year's estimate of income to December 31, 2007.

Note that you can elect to include some income from the January 31, 2007 fiscal year in the 2006 taxation year to maximize your RRSP contribution or to even out your tax burden. Any amount included in 2006 would be deducted on your 2007 tax return.

After you start using the calendar year-end method you can't change to the alternative method. However, you can switch to the calendar-year method at any time.

Pay CPP on Self-Employment Earnings

You will often hear employees grumble about seeing how much money they "lose" to CPP/QPP contributions, but it's self-employed people who really understand the true cost.

If you're self-employed, you're required to pay both the employer and employee portion of CPP/QPP contributions to a maximum. For 2009, that maximum was $4,237 ($2,118 × 2). Ouch! (As an employee you only pay half ($2,118) and the company you work for pays the other half.)

If you think of your contribution to CPP as forced savings for retirement rather than just another tax making the payment is somewhat less painful. Trying to make you feel better here!

The maximum CPP contribution increases each year. See the CRA Web site at `www.cra-arc.gc.ca/tx/bsnss/tpcs/pyrll/clcltng/cpp-rpc/cnt-chrt-pf-eng.html` for the current year's maximum contribution.

If you have employment and self-employment earnings, the amount of CPP or QPP contributions that you have to make on your self-employment earnings will depend on how much you've already contributed to the CPP or QPP as an employee. Schedule 8 of the T1 return will help you with these calculations.

Self-employed individuals can claim a deduction on line 222 of the T1 for the portion of CPP or QPP contributions that represents the employer's share (that is, one-half of the contributions made). Only the portion of the CPP or QPP contributions that represent the employee's portion qualify for the 15 percent federal non-refundable tax credit.

Choose the Right Business Ownership Structure

Businesses can be operated through one of three main types of ownership structures: sole proprietorship, partnership, or corporation. The structure you choose at the start of your business, and as the business grows, will be a key factor in the business's future growth, profitability, tax minimization, and cash flow. In this tip, we take a look at each of the options so you can choose the ownership structure that works best for you.

No matter what the form of your business ownership, you'll want to purchase some type of liability insurance — in many industries it's mandatory.

Operate a Sole Proprietorship

A *sole proprietorship* is a common business ownership structure when there is one owner. Unlike a partnership or a corporation, a sole proprietorship is not a separate legal entity — it's simply treated as an extension of the owner, or the "proprietor."

A sole proprietorship is generally the way to start any business. An exception may be where the business may incur significant liabilities — not only actual liabilities for money owed (say from financing start-up activities) but also potential litigation liabilities. The reason? When you own a sole proprietorship, you own all the *assets* of the business but you're also responsible for all its *liabilities*. In other words, the amount of liabilities you're responsible for is "unlimited." (Operating a business through a corporation may be a way to limit your liability; see Tip #30.)

The advantage of starting as a sole proprietorship is that any start-up losses are claimed on your personal tax return. These losses are deducted from your other sources of income in the year. Therefore, your net income and taxable income will be lower — meaning the taxes you pay will also be lower! Losses are generally bad from a cash flow point of view, but good from a tax savings point of view. (For more about losses, see "Claiming losses" in this section.)

Checking out the advantages

A sole proprietorship has a number of advantages. These advantages stem from the simplicity and low cost of setting up a sole proprietorship to the uncomplicated requirements of reporting the results for tax purposes. Here's a detailed look at the advantages of a sole proprietorship:

- ✓ **Ease of operation.** It's the easiest of the three business ownership structures.

- ✓ **Simplicity of recordkeeping.** However, the CRA still requires that you maintain a set of books separate from your personal affairs.

- ✓ **Simplicity of income tax filing.** No separate tax return is required. If you need an accountant to assist you with your personal tax return, the fees will be minimal.

- ✓ **Low cost to begin business.** There's no incorporation fee. Depending on where you live and the name of the business you choose, you may need to register the business's name.

- ✓ **Opportunity to apply losses against other sources of personal income in the year the loss was incurred and the previous three years.** Where a loss is carried back, you can recover some of the taxes paid in those years. (See "Claiming losses" in this section for more.)

- ✓ **Ease of changing to an incorporated business.** The income tax rules permit a sole proprietor to convert the business to an incorporated business without tax being triggered, provided the correct tax election is made, documented as required, and filed with the CRA within statutory time limits. It often makes sense to defer the conversion of a sole proprietorship to an incorporated business until the business is profitable.

Dealing with the drawbacks

With every bit of sunshine comes a little rain. With the many advantages of a sole proprietorship come a few disadvantages:

- ✓ **Your liability is unlimited.** All your personal assets (your home, car, jewellery, and so on) are exposed to creditors, even though these assets are not used in the business.

- ✓ **You can't take advantage of the low corporate tax rate available on the first $500,000 of a corporation's business (non-investment) income provided by the tax credit referred to as the "small business deduction."** When compared to a corporate business ownership structure, fewer after-tax funds are available to the business owner to reinvest in the business. We discuss the small business deduction in detail in Tip #30.

✔ **You can't take advantage of the $750,000 capital gains exemption.** To make use of the exemption the business must operate through a corporation. We explain the exemption below in our comments dealing with corporations. The exemption is also discussed in Tip #30.

You can avoid these disadvantages fairly easily. Remember that one of the advantages of a sole proprietorship is the ease of changing to a corporate ownership structure. So, to avoid the disadvantages of a sole proprietorship, simply convert your proprietorship to a corporation!

Reporting income

The owner uses the following lines of the personal tax return to report revenues and expenses of a business operated through a sole proprietorship:

✔ Line 135 — Business income (complete form T2125, "Statement of Business or Professional Activities")

✔ Line 137 — Professional income (complete form T2125)

✔ Line 139 — Commission income (again, complete form T2125)

✔ Line 141 — Farming income (complete form T2042, "Statement of Farming Activities")

✔ Line 143 — Fishing income (complete form T2121, "Statement of Fishing Activities").

Claiming losses

In this section we cover how to report any business losses you may realize in a year. Losses obviously aren't ideal but if you have them making sure you use it to your best advantage can mean significant tax savings for current or other tax years. The story of Susie and her flower shop demonstrates someone making the most of losses.

Susie opened up her very own florist shop in Edmonton on January 2, 2009. Prior to opening, she went to see an accountant for advice on which business ownership structure she should use. She decided that a sole proprietorship made the most sense. Previously, Susie was employed by a florist shop in Red Deer, Alberta. Over the past five years, she has reported about $30,000 of taxable income each year on her personal tax returns. Susie expects to lose money in the first two years — $15,000 in 2009 and $8,000 in 2010, due to start-up costs and low revenues while she builds her customer base. If Susie had incorporated her florist shop when she started her business, the losses would be "trapped" in the corporation until she made a profit — three years from now, in 2012! At that time, the $23,000 in losses incurred in 2009 and 2010 could be used to offset the profits in 2012.

A loss from a business, whether incorporated or not, can be used to offset business profits of the subsequent seven years or prior three years. Note that a business loss, referred to as a non-capital loss, can be used to offset any other type of income, including capital gains. This is in contrast to a capital loss, which can be applied only against capital gains. A capital loss can also be carried back to the three previous years. However, a capital loss carryforward period is indefinite. Refer to Tip #39 for comments on claiming losses of prior years on your tax return.

Because she has operated her business as a sole proprietorship from its commencement, Susie's losses in 2009 and 2010 can be carried back and applied against the taxable income she reported in the past three years (2006, 2007, and 2008) on her personal tax returns. The result: She can immediately recover some of the taxes she paid in those years. Obviously, Susie prefers to recover some of the taxes now than to wait for the tax savings three years from now. Also let's say Susie had, in addition to her business loss of $15,000 in 2009, investment income of $10,000 in 2009. Before carrying the loss back to 2006, Susie would first claim a portion of the loss against the $10,000 in investment income so no tax would be payable in 2009. The excess loss remaining would then be carried back to 2006.

To request a loss be carried back to a prior year, complete form T1A "Request for Loss Carryback" when you're preparing your personal income tax return. To ensure speedy processing of your loss carryback request, mail your T1A to the CRA separately from your tax return. (If you e-file your return, you still mail a paper copy of the T1A to the CRA.) After a T1A is processed by CRA you'll receive a Notice of Reassessment for the year in which the loss was carried back to. You'll also receive a cheque!

Enter into a Partnership

A partnership is similar to a sole proprietorship, except that more than one owner exists; there are at least two owners, and they're referred to as "partners." Partnerships and partners comply with the same tax rules we all do.

A *partnership* is a separate legal entity. This contrasts with a *sole proprietorship,* which is considered merely an extension of the business owner. The partners determine how they will split the profit (or loss) of the partnership. The partnership does not pay any income tax. Its profit (or loss) is allocated out to the partners, who then become responsible for paying income tax on their share — or, where a loss has been allocated to them, making the best use of the loss in minimizing taxes.

Figuring out which type of partnership is for you

Three forms of partnerships exist: a general partnership, a limited liability partnership (LLP), and a limited partnership (LP). Each form has slightly different characteristics. The type of partnership you use will depend on the business or investment undertaking, your faith in the business or investment, and your faith in your partner's capabilities.

General partnerships

General partnership is the most common partnership, where the partners are actively involved in running the business. The partners share the ownership of the assets and the liabilities.

Just as with a sole proprietorship, general partners have unlimited liability with respect to debts of the partnership. Even worse, they have "joint and several liability." This means that if one of the partners can't fund his share of the liability, creditors can still come after the other partners for the full debt. So, if a partner in a law practice messes up really badly and litigation is commenced against the law firm, all the other partners are on the hook for the potential debt even though they had nothing to do with the mess! This quite obvious negative characteristic of a general partnership has been somewhat softened by the introduction of limited liability partnership (LLPs).

Limited liability partnerships (LLPs)

A *limited liability partnership* works to limit the liability of the partners in a partnership who were not responsible for the liability. In other words, it's the partner(s) responsible for the liability that is (are) exposed to creditors.

The "joint and several" liability characteristic of a general partnership does not exist in an LLP. Due to fairly recent changes in many provincial partnership laws over the past few years, many accounting and law firms have converted from a general partnership to an LLP.

Limited partnerships (LPs)

In a *limited partnership,* each partner's liability is limited to the investment each has made in the LP and any financial commitments to which they have agreed. LPs are generally used for investments.

By definition, a limited partner cannot be active in the day-to-day running of the partnership. Each LP has one general partner. The general partner, usually the operator of the LP, assumes all the responsibilities for the LP's debts in excess of the limited partners' investments and financial commitments.

Understanding the tax implications of a partnership

The partnership itself does not file an income tax return. The income or loss of the partnership is allocated to the partners based on their agreement for sharing income and losses.

Common items claimed by partners on their tax returns include promotional costs such as meals and entertainment expenses, and automobile expenses. The partner's "net" income or loss (partnership share of income or loss, less expenses incurred personally by the partner) is then reported on one of lines 135, 137, 139, 141, or 143 of their tax return.

The amount of partnership income is usually reported on the T2125 self-employment form that we discuss in the section "Operate a Sole Proprietorship." Then the partner will deduct any expenses incurred by the partner personally in carrying out partnership duties. These expenses would be for any expense a partner incurred to earn his or her partnership income. A partner's expense that has been paid for or reimbursed by the partnership cannot be claimed because it has already been taken into account in determining the partnership income.

Hearing the good news about partnerships

Using a partnership as your form of business organization offers many of the same advantages provided by a sole proprietorship:

- ✔ They are relatively easy to set up
- ✔ Minimal government regulations are imposed on partnerships (a limited liability partnership and a limited partnership have a few more regulations than does a general partnership)

✔ Income tax filing is simple — no separate tax return required. (However, form T5013, "Partnership Information Return," and T5013 slips for each partner may be needed.)

✔ Skills of others are available to help run the business

✔ Risks of the business can be shared with other partners

✔ You can use your share of the partnership loss to shelter other sources of personal income from tax

✔ Like a sole proprietorship, it's fairly easy to convert a partnership into a corporation.

Looking into the not-so-good partnership news

Disadvantages of owning a business through a partnership are similar to the disadvantages faced by sole proprietors:

✔ With a general partnership, your liability is unlimited. As in a sole proprietorship, your personal assets are exposed to creditors, even if you had nothing to do with the liability. (An LLP works to minimize this disadvantage.)

✔ If relationships between partners deteriorate, it may be necessary for a partner to leave the partnership — potentially a very unpleasant task to deal with. To minimize the unpleasantness, your partnership agreement should deal with how partner departures will be handled.

✔ If you're operating your business through a partnership, you can't take advantage of the low corporate tax rate available on the first $500,000 of a corporation's business (non-investment) income. When compared to a corporate business ownership structure, fewer after-tax funds may be available to reinvest in the partnership's business.

✔ If you're operating your business through a partnership you can't take advantage of the $750,000 capital gains exemption. To take advantage of the exemption a corporation must be used for the business ownership structure.

Partnerships with more than five partners are required to file financial statements and a form T5013, "Partnership Information Return," with the CRA. Also, each partner's share of the partnership's income or loss needs to be documented on a T5013 slip prepared for each partner. The T5013 slip is included with the partner's personal tax return.

Decide to Incorporate

A *corporation* is a legal entity separate and distinct from its owner(s) — the shareholder(s) of the corporation. A corporation is created under federal or provincial law. The income tax rules applied to federally incorporated business are identical to those that are incorporated under provincial legislation. Because a corporation has a separate existence, it owns all the assets and is responsible for all liabilities of the corporation.

Are you currently operating your business through a sole proprietorship or a partnership? Because the $750,000 capital gains exemption (which we discuss in Tip #30) is available only on the sale of shares of a corporation, consider converting your business to a corporation only if it makes sense considering the advice we've given previously.

Both a sole proprietorship and a partnership can be converted to a corporate ownership structure without you incurring any immediate income tax on the accrued capital gain of the assets of the proprietorship or partnership. You must make a tax election, and document that election by completing and filing a specific tax form with the CRA.

Make the Most of Incorporation

• •

*I*f you're here because you think incorporation is for you but are fuzzy on some of the details then this tip is for you. Read on to learn all about the strategies that will help you to maximize the tax and other benefits that incorporation can offer.

Sidestep Personal Guarantees

This first benefit isn't a tax benefit, but it's one of the primary reasons people incorporate. When a shareholder provides a creditor with a personal guarantee of a corporate liability, the shareholder's assets are exposed, but just in connection with the specific debt of the corporation. Often shareholders will be required to provide personal guarantees on corporate obligations such as bank debt, and on rental and leasing agreements for premises and equipment.

A request for your personal guarantee is a standard request of a creditor — especially when your business is a start-up or has very little in tangible assets. Just because you're asked for the guarantee doesn't mean you always have to comply! Here are the steps in avoiding a personal guarantee:

- ✔ Get out your best negotiating skills.

- ✔ Focus your creditors on your track record.

- ✔ Highlight the successes you've had.

- ✔ Ensure your creditors know you've put a lot of money into the corporation, too. (The creditors won't care about the blood, sweat, and tears you've put in — only the money.)

- ✔ Make sure your business plan contains specific, measurable, reachable, realistic goals.

- ✔ Let your creditors know that you have a network of savvy businesspeople to call on as needed — lawyers, accountants, information system specialists, corporate communication advisors, and so on.

> ✔ Promise your creditors monthly cash flow statements and accounts receivable listings.
>
> ✔ Perhaps pledge the receivables.
>
> ✔ Do anything you can to avoid a personal guarantee.

What are the other ways your creditor can secure his loan? In your mind, does the alternative security give the creditor sufficient collateral? If so, tell the creditor!

Where no personal guarantees are provided, the shareholders of the corporation generally have limited their liability to their investment in the business. Our lawyer friends tell us that when a shareholder is also an officer of the corporation (officers include the president, vice-president, and secretary-treasurer) and acts in a "grossly negligent" manner, the shareholder, due to his or her role as an officer, can have some personal exposure to creditors.

Become a Secured Creditor of Your Own Corporation

Here's another non-tax benefit to incorporation. Even with limited liability, you still want to protect your investment in the incorporated business. Where you have put a significant amount of cash into a corporation, we recommend the following strategy to protect your investment as much as possible.

In return for the money you've invested in the corporation, classify a minimal amount as your purchase of shares of the corporation — say, make the first $100 of your investment represent your purchase of 100 common shares of the corporation.

Treat the remainder of your investment as a loan you've made to the corporation. This loan should be documented with a promissory note between you and the corporation. No requirement exists for you to charge interest on the loan to the corporation.

Have your lawyer register the note under your province's personal security act.

You will now have made yourself a secured creditor of the corporation. When things turn sour, it's the secured creditors who get paid first. Unsecured creditors fight over the dregs.

Take Advantage of the $750,000 Capital Gains Exemption

A big advantage of owning shares of a corporation is evident when the shares are sold. One purpose of our income tax rules is to offer taxpayers incentives when they spend their money in ways the government likes. The government wants to encourage all of us to invest in shares of private Canadian-owned incorporated businesses. When shareholders sell shares of these businesses, they may be eligible to claim a capital gains exemption in respect of the gain incurred on the sale. This means that all or a portion of the gain is exempt from regular income tax. This is the incentive the government is offering to you to make these desired investments in Canadian business.

When shares qualify, a shareholder may find that he or she can receive the first $750,000 of capital gains free of regular income tax. (Refer to Tip #31 where we review how to claim the capital gains exemption.)

Take Advantage of the Small Business Deduction

In addition to accessing the $750,000 capital gains exemption, a second major advantage of operating your business through a corporation is the tax savings provided by the small business deduction. The word *deduction* here means a deduction in corporate income tax. (It's the same as saying a "tax credit.")

Like the capital gains exemption, the small business deduction works as an incentive to become an entrepreneur — start a business, hire employees, rent a warehouse, lease a fleet of trucks, and so on. These are all things the government wants you to do because they are beneficial to the Canadian economy. Also like the capital gains exemption, to take advantage of the small business deduction the business must be operated through a corporation.

The net income of a sole proprietorship or a partnership is taxed directly in the hands of the business owners — the proprietor or the partner. In Tip #2, which summarizes the top federal/provincial/territorial tax rates, you can see that the top tax rate a business owner could pay on sole proprietorship or partnership income varies from 39 percent (Alberta) to 48.25 percent (Nova Scotia). Taking Nova Scotia as an example, on an after-tax basis the business owner is left with only 51.75 cents to put back into the business to fund operations. However, in most provinces and territories the combined federal and provincial/territorial tax rate applied to the first $500,000 of business income (non-investment income) is about 16 percent. This is referred to as the *small business deduction*. The corporate tax rate on business income in excess of $500,000 is about 33 percent. The rate climbs to about 49 percent where the corporation's income is investment income.

If your business is a corporation, you're required to prepare and file a corporate tax return and pay corporate income taxes. It's the after-tax corporate funds that are available for reinvestment in the business or for the payment of dividends to shareholders or additional salary (a bonus) to the employees. (Who, in many cases for those reading this book, will be the same individuals as the shareholders.)

Obviously, with a 16 percent tax rate on the first $500,000 of business income, 84 cents on the dollar is available for reinvestment in the business — far more than the 51.75 cents remaining in the Nova Scotia sole proprietor's hands.

Choose between Salary and Dividends

If the operators of the corporation do not wish to reinvest the after-corporate-tax funds in the business, the funds can be paid out to the operators as a bonus (which is simply treated as additional salary) or as a dividend payment to the shareholders. Either way, the receipt will trigger *personal* income tax in the recipient's hands.

You may be thinking that when faced with the choice of taking a salary or a dividend from a corporation, you should always choose the dividend because it's taxed at a lower rate. You're correct that the *personal* tax is lower — confirm this by referring to the table in Tip #2, which summarizes top tax rates.

However, the corporation is not entitled to deduct a dividend payment in computing its taxable income. A dividend is not considered a deductible expense incurred in the process of earning corporate income. The payment of a dividend is considered an after-corporate-tax distribution of profits — therefore, no tax deduction to the corporation applies. A salary payment is considered a deductible expense incurred to earn income of the corporation. A salary payment is deductible in computing a corporation's taxable income. A tax deduction results in a tax saving to the corporation — a dividend does not.

In summary, when looking at the dividend scenario you must add the corporate and personal tax. It's this aggregate tax number you must use to compare to the personal tax on salary. In many cases, you'll find the tax numbers will be almost the same. Again, this is referred to as the integration of the corporate and personal tax systems. Integration is designed to ensure business owners receive no tax savings or incur extra tax on funds taken out of a business for personal use just because they decided to use one form of business ownership over another.

To maximize your retirement savings contribution room

Salary is considered earned income for the purposes of making RRSP contributions, but dividends are not. To be eligible to make the maximum RRSP contribution of $22,000 in 2010, an individual needs at least $122,222 in 2009 salary. (*Note:* From 2010 onward the RRSP contribution maximum will be indexed — see the CRA Web site at http://www.cra-arc.gc.ca/tx/ndvdls/tpcs/rrsp-reer/cntrbtng/lmts-eng.html.) This is because one of the calculations in the formula to determine your maximum RRSP contribution limit is 18 percent of your earned income: $122,222 \times 18$ percent equals $22,000. If you received only dividends in 2009, your 2010 RRSP contribution limit would be zero! We cover these aspects of RRSPs in Tips #42 and #43.

To minimize your personal tax

If you don't want to pay any personal tax, don't take money out of the corporation! Okay, okay — we understand that you need some money to live on. But to maximize the tax deferral of your personal tax, you should minimize your withdrawals from the corporation. The period of deferral is potentially unlimited. Where a business is run through a corporate ownership structure, opportunity exists to defer tax. As we have seen, no personal tax is payable unless money is taken out by the owners (shareholders) of the corporation. The personal tax part of the overall tax rate is *deferred* until money is taken out of the corporation. A corporation offers you flexibility in determining when your personal tax liability is triggered. If personal tax rates are expected to go down, you'll want to minimize the withdrawals you make from the corporation until the year when personal tax rates are the lowest.

If you decide to leave the after-corporate-tax funds in a corporation so your personal tax is deferred as long as possible, carefully consider the following three tax repercussions:

1. **If the funds exceed the amount needed to operate the business of the corporation, you may be tainting your access to the $750,000 capital gains exemption.** For the shares of the corporation to be QSBCS *at the time of their sale,* the corporation must have at least 90 percent of the market value of its assets invested in assets used to earn business income (that is, non-investment-type assets such as trucks, machinery, computers, office equipment, and so on). Excess cash and short-term and long-term portfolio investments are not considered to be used to earn business income. Should the value of these "tainted assets" exceed 10 percent of the corporation's assets at the time you sell the shares, those shares will *not* qualify for the $750,000 capital gains exemption. It's imperative that the level of "non-business" assets of the corporation be monitored on an ongoing basis. For the 24 months prior to the sale, the tainted assets (the investment or non-business assets of the corporation) cannot exceed 50 percent of the corporation's total asset value.

2. **If you invest the excess funds, the investment income earned by the corporation will be taxed at the full corporate tax rate applied to investment income — not at the small business deduction tax rate.** This tax rate may be higher than the personal marginal tax rates of the shareholders. If so, you will want to increase the shareholders' incomes so that the lower tax brackets of these shareholders are not "wasted." A shareholder's income can be increased if the corporation pays them more dividends. No tax saving from the small business deduction applies because investment income is not considered to be "earned" from operating a business. However, the first $500,000 of business income continues to qualify for the small business deduction tax rate.

3. **You're exposing high-quality assets to creditors.** If this is a concern, another company can be incorporated that would serve as a holding corporation for the shares of your operating corporation. The active corporation can pay up excess funds as tax-free dividends to the holding corporation. Because the funds are not being paid to an individual, no personal tax liability arises. The funds remain in a corporation.

Sell Your Business in a Tax-Savvy Way

*I*f you're the owner of a small business, your company is likely your most valuable asset. You may have dreams of selling the business one day and using the proceeds to travel or invest in another business. Or you may be considering selling part of your business to a partner to reduce the amount of time you have to spend at the office.

Minimizing the taxes you will pay on a sale requires careful planning — especially when the economy is volatile. Even if you don't intend to sell your business immediately, having a strategy in place gives you control so you realize the most value for all your hard work.

Evaluate Your Options

Two models typically exist for selling a business: the asset sale, and the share sale. Which model you use depends on the type of business and the needs of seller and buyer. Each model has different tax consequences. Here's a closer look at the two models:

- ✓ **An asset sale,** common for unincorporated businesses and businesses in capital-intensive industries such as transportation, is often preferred by the buyer. In an *asset sale,* the buyer purchases only the assets of a business. In so doing, the buyer can avoid taking on any potential corporate liabilities that come with purchasing shares and may benefit from increased tax deductions that would not be available in a share deal (for example, increased capital cost allowance; see Tip #32).

- ✓ **A share sale** is often favoured by the seller. In a *share sale,* the seller sells the shares (well, duh) and reports whatever capital gains are realized. The great appeal of this strategy is that the seller may be able to take advantage of a capital gains tax exemption (yes, that's right, we said tax exemption) that is not available in an asset deal. In the next section we look at the potential capital gains exemptions you need to know about.

Take Advantage of Qualified Small Business Corporation Share Status

If you own shares of a small business corporation you won't want to miss this one — arguably the best tax break in Canada. In 2007 the government increased the capital gains exemption from the disposition of *qualified small business corporation* (QSBC) shares from $500,000 to $750,000. This $250,000 increase was also extended to the sale of qualified farm and fishing property. If you made use of the previous $500,000 capital gains exemption, you now have another $250,000 to use should you own qualified small business corporation shares or qualified farm or fishing property.

Just to be clear — when you sell shares of a QSBC, the first $750,000 of proceeds you receive on the sale of your business may be exempt from tax. Check with your tax professional.

Understand the term "qualified small business corporation"

We won't go into excruciating detail, but note that a share of a corporation will be considered to be a QSBC share if the following criteria are met:

- At the time of sale, it was a share of the capital stock of a Canadian controlled private corporation (CCPC), and it was owned by you, your spouse, or a partnership of which you were a member.

- At least 90 percent of the corporation's assets at market value were used by the corporation in an active (for example, non-rental, non-investment) business.

- Throughout the 24 months immediately before you disposed of the share, it was a share of a CCPC and more than 50 percent of the market value of the assets of the corporation were used mainly in an active business carried on primarily in Canada.

- Throughout the 24 months immediately before you disposed of the share, no one other than you, a partnership of which you were a member, or a person related to you owned the share.

Know how to report a tax-exempt gain

You report the capital gain or loss realized on the sale of QSBC shares in section 1 of schedule 3, "Qualified small business corporation shares." A $750,000 capital gain would become a $375,000 taxable capital gain and be reported on line 127 of your return. If the full $750,000 capital gain qualifies for the $750,000 capital gains exemption, you would be able to claim a $375,000 capital gains deduction. Claim it on line 254 of your return and include form T657, "Calculation of Capital Gains Deduction." The line 254 deduction in computing taxable income would offset the line 127 inclusion in taxable income.

Be sure to visit a tax professional if you think your shares may qualify for the capital gains exemption. Even if they don't currently qualify, it's possible to "purify" the corporation of assets not considered to be active business assets, such as cash or investments, so that you will be eligible for this exemption when the time arises to sell the shares. This is one not to miss — get the help you need to make sure you take advantage of this strategy!

If you own QSBC shares, consider *crystallizing* — or locking in — your qualified small business corporation capital gains exemption now. You never know when the government might repeal the exemption, or when the rules listed above may no longer apply to your corporation.

If you operate your business as a sole proprietorship or partnership, you can't access the capital gains exemption when you sell. You may be able to transfer your unincorporated business into an incorporated entity prior to a sale in order to make possible a sale of shares and in doing so be able to use the QSBC share exemption. Again — you'll need professional help for this one.

Determine whether you may owe alternative minimum tax

When using the capital gains exemption, be wary of the implications of *alternative minimum tax* (AMT). The capital gain may be tax-free for "regular" tax but could result in AMT. What is AMT, you ask? It's a special tax that's charged when someone has a high amount of gross income but many favourable tax deductions, or "tax preferences" (in the eyes of the CRA, that is), resulting in a significantly reduced (again, in the eyes of the CRA) tax liability for the year.

The types of deductions that may lead you to pay minimum tax include limited-partnership losses, resource expenses, and stock option deductions. If you have these types of deductions on your tax return, fill out form T691, "Alternative Minimum Tax," to see whether the minimum tax will apply to you. If it does, don't fret. You can use that minimum tax to offset regular taxes payable in any of the next seven years. Assuming you pay regular tax during those years, you will get your money back — consider it a prepayment of your future tax bill. Minimum tax is often more of a cash-flow issue than a true income tax.

Shelter Capital Gains If You're a Farmer

The special $750,000 capital gains exemption is also available if you sell qualified farm property. The property will qualify when it meets either of these tests:

- The property must be used by you, your spouse, child, or grandparents in the 24 months immediately before you sell, and your gross revenue from the farming business must exceed your income from all other sources for a minimum of two years.

- The property must be used by a corporation or partnership where the principal business is farming for a minimum of 24 months prior to the sale.

Qualified farm property includes the following:

- An interest in a family-farm partnership that you or your spouse owns

- A share of the capital stock of a family-farm corporation that you or your spouse owns

- Real property, such as land and buildings, and eligible capital property, such as milk and egg quotas

You, your spouse, or a family-farm partnership must own the farm property. If a corporation or partnership carries on the farming business, the property will qualify if you, your spouse, or your child is an active participant in the business and more than 50 percent of the market value of the property is used in the business of farming. Generally, when you dispose of qualified farm property, you report any capital gain or loss realized in the special section of part 2 of schedule 3, "Qualified farm property and qualified fishing property." If you dispose of farm property other than qualified farm property, report any capital gain or loss in part 4 of schedule 3, "Real estate, depreciable property and other properties."

 If you transfer farm property to a child, it may be possible to completely avoid tax on the disposition. Consult a tax professional, who can determine whether you can take advantage of a "tax-free intergenerational transfer."

Determining whether your farm property qualifies for the $750,000 capital gains exemption is not a do-it-yourself project. The tax rules surrounding farm property are quite complex (definitely not bedtime reading material), so a visit to a tax professional is a must.

 Be cautious of the AMT implications whenever you make use of the capital gains exemption.

Shelter Capital Gains If You're a Fisher

The $750,000 lifetime capital gains exemption we discuss in this tip is also available for dispositions of qualified fishing property. In addition, a tax-deferred intergenerational rollover is also available for transfers of qualified fishing property to a child or grandchild.

 Be wary of the AMT implications when claiming the capital gains exemption.

 If you own shares of a qualified small business corporation, qualified farm property, or qualified fishing property with accrued gains, you can trigger the gain by means of an actual sale to a third party or by transferring the asset to your spouse (if you transact at fair market value) or to a corporation you control. And we know we've said it before, but we feel strongly that taking proper advantage of these potentially huge tax breaks means getting professional advice.

Defer Capital Gains on Eligible Small Business Investments

Have you sold shares of a small business corporation during the year? If so, then read on. Even if you've used up the $750,000 capital gains exemption, it's still possible to defer tax if you sell certain share investments and then replace those investments with new eligible small business investments.

To be eligible for this deferral, the shares you dispose of or repurchase must be of a Canadian-controlled private corporation (CCPC) that used at least 90 percent of the market value of its assets in an active business in Canada.

Time limits apply to this tax deferral. First, you must have held the original shares for more than 185 days. In addition, you must acquire the replacement shares at any time in the year of disposition or within 120 days after the year-end.

If you manage to defer your capital gain because of this rule, you must remember to decrease the adjusted cost base (ACB) of the "new" investment. You must do a number of calculations to come up with the exact ACB reduction. Take a look at the CRA's guide Capital Gains (T4037).

The rules for calculating the actual amount of gain you can defer are quite complex (trust us, you don't want us to go into them here). If you need to use this deferral, we strongly recommend getting a professional accountant involved.

Maximize Your Capital Cost Allowance (CCA) Claim

*T*he money you spend in operating your business can be classified in one of two ways:

- **Day-to-day expenditures of running the business:** These expenditures are not considered to have a future value and are therefore "expenses" of your business. Most of these expenses are noted on lines 8521 to 9270 on form T2125. Examples of day-to-day expenditures include salaries paid to employees, office rent, lease payments, bank charges, travel, and telephone.

- **Capital expenditures:** Capital expenditures are made when you purchase a capital asset — an asset that has an expected useful life that will extend beyond the end of your business's taxation year. Common examples of capital assets are computers, office equipment (photocopiers, printers), office furniture, buildings, and machinery.

Because the value provided by these assets is expected to extend past the end of your business taxation year, you cannot take a full deduction for these expenditures in one year. However, you're allowed to deduct a portion of the cost of a capital asset for each taxation year it is used in your business. The calculation of the portion that can be deducted on your tax return is called *capital cost allowance* (CCA).

In this tip, we get up close and personal with the CCA, giving you the scoop you need to know to make it work for you.

Understanding Capital Cost Allowance

Capital cost allowance, or CCA, is simply tax lingo for "depreciation" and "amortization." These are terms often used by accountants. Remember this the next time you are at a party and want to impress someone with your vast knowledge!

Your business can claim CCA on almost all capital assets purchased (one exception is land). And, of course, the asset must have been acquired for use in your business — not for personal use.

Eligible capital property (ECP) describes assets that do not physically exist. They are referred to as intangible assets and include such items as the purchase of goodwill, a customer or patient list, a marketing quota or government right, and an unlimited franchise, concession, or licence. Technically, you don't claim CCA on ECP, but a special deduction similar to CCA is allowed. The starting point for the deduction is 75 percent of the cost of ECP. The deduction you are allowed is 7 percent of this amount, on a declining basis each year.

Calculating CCA — the Declining Balance Method

For most types of assets, you calculate CCA using the declining balance method of depreciation. The costs of specific types of assets (generally the purchase price, but can also include freight costs, duty and customs fees, retail sales taxes, and even GST/HST when your business is not a GST/HST registrant) are grouped together in CCA classes to calculate the CCA deduction. The government dictates which "class" specific types of assets go into and the percentage rates used to calculate the CCA for each class.

For example, say your business purchased a meeting room table and a bunch of chairs. The table and chairs, both being "office furniture," would be treated as one asset, or "class." CCA is then calculated on the class balance using a legislated percentage rate. The remaining "class balance" (referred to as the undepreciated capital cost or UCC, discussed below) is carried to the next year, where again the same percentage is applied to calculate the CCA. Because the class balance on which the CCA claim is based declines each year, the method is referred to as the *declining balance method*. This method results in higher CCA deductions in the early years of a capital asset purchase and lower amounts as the asset ages.

If your business incurs costs to make rented premises more workable, such costs are referred to as *leasehold improvements*. Leasehold improvements are not depreciated using a percentage and the declining balance method. Instead, CCA is calculated as the lesser of the following:

$$\frac{\text{cost of leasehold improvements}}{5}$$

$$\frac{\text{cost of leasehold improvements}}{\text{\# of years in lease}} + \text{\# years in first renewal period}$$

To maximize the speed at which CCA is claimed on your leasehold improvements, negotiate your lease to be a maximum of four years with a renewal period of one year.

CCA is calculated on the balance of the CCA class as of the last day of your business's taxation year. You do not need to separate CCA calculations for capital assets owned for only part of a taxation year (although the "half-year rule," which we discuss later, does take care of assets purchased during the year). However, if you were not in business for the full year (say you just started up on September 1), you do need to prorate your CCA for your shorter-than-365-day year. In this case, you would take your total CCA times 122 days/365 days. (For more about taxation years, check out Tip #28.)

Common CCA classes and rates

For simplicity, the government has assigned CCA class numbers to similar groups of assets (CCA classes):

- **Buildings:** Class 1:
    - 4 percent (general rate)
    - 6 percent (if non-residential)
    - 10 percent (if used in manufacturing or processing in Canada)
- **Fences:** Class 6: 10 percent
- **Office equipment and furniture:** Class 8: 20 percent
  All capital assets eligible for CCA are included in class 8 if they do not fall into any of the other CCA classes.
- **Cars (less than $30,000) and trucks:** Class 10: 30 percent
- **Cars ($30,000 and more):** Class 10.1: 30 percent (Refer to the section "Restriction on the maximum capital cost of a class 10.1 automobile" in this tip.)
- **Computer hardware and systems software acquired before March 23, 2004:** Class 10: 30 percent

✔ **Computer hardware and systems software acquired after March 22, 2004:** Class 45: 45 percent

✔ **Computer hardware and systems software acquired after March 18, 2007:** Class 50: 55 percent

✔ **Computer hardware and systems software acquired after January 27, 2009 and before February 2011:** The January 27, 2009 budget provided for a temporary increase from 55 to 100 percent. This 100 percent CCA rate will not be subject to the half-year rule. As a result of this measure, a business will be able to fully deduct the cost of an eligible computer (including the systems software for that computer) in the first year that CCA deductions are available.

✔ **Computer application software, uniforms, linens, dies, jigs, moulds, and rental videos with a cost of under $200 and tools with a cost of less than $500:** Class 12: 100 percent

✔ **Manufacturing and processing equipment:** Class 43: 30 percent (however, if the equipment is purchased after March 19, 2007, and before 2009 it is considered class 29, with a 50 percent rate calculated on a straight-line-depreciation basis, not the regular declining-balance basis.)

A CCA example

CCA can best be explained through an example. Imagine your business purchased a meeting room table and chairs. The total cost of the furniture was $1,200. In preparing your tax return you know that you cannot deduct the full $1,200 on form T2125 in determining your net income from self-employment. The meeting room table and chairs are good quality and probably can be used in your business for several years. In fact, the chairs have a 10-year warranty!

Office furniture is considered a CCA class 8 capital asset with a CCA rate of 20 percent. (You're forced to accept the 20 percent rate whether the chairs are expected to last 5 years, 10 years, or 30 years.)

You would think you could calculate CCA as simply 20 percent of $1,200, or $240. However, there's a catch — a special rule called the "half-year rule," which dictates that when calculating CCA for the year in which the asset is purchased, only one-half (or 50 percent) of the CCA can be claimed. So, the correct way to calculate the 2008 CCA claim on the office furniture is $1,200 × 20% × 50% = $120.

Undepreciated capital cost (UCC)

Undepreciated capital cost is the term used to describe the amount of the capital cost at the end of a taxation year to which CCA has not yet been applied. In our CCA class 8 office furniture example from the previous section, the UCC at December 31, 2009, would be $1,080. It is calculated as follows:

Undepreciated capital cost (UCC) at

January 1, 2009 (assumed)	$nil
Capital cost of additions in 2009	$1,200
Capital cost allowance (CCA) claimed in 2009	$120/1,200 × 20% × 50%
Undepreciated capital cost (UCC) at December 31, 2009	$1,080

In 2010, assuming no further purchases or sales are made, CCA of $216 ($1,080 × 20%) can be claimed. The half-year rule applied only to assets of a CCA class purchased in a year. Because we are assuming no CCA class 8 assets were acquired in 2010, the half-year rule does not come into play!

Let's imagine now that your business hits the big time and you have money to burn. Naturally your first step (well maybe not first) is to upgrade your office furniture. Say you decide to upgrade the meeting room table and chairs in 2010. Your new table and chairs cost $1,700. The old table and chairs were sold to a used office furniture retailer for $750. We'll stick with our CCA class 8 office furniture example to show what happens when an asset used in your business is sold.

Sale of capital assets

When a capital asset is sold, the UCC is reduced by the lower of the following:

- ✔ The original capital cost of the assets sold (remember, this was $1,200)
- ✔ The sale price — the $750 noted above

When an asset is sold, the half-year rule comes into play once again.

UCC at January 1, 2010 (same as at December 31, 2009) $1,080

Add: Additions		$1,700
Sale of chairs		
Lesser of:		
Original cost:	$1,200	
Proceeds:	$750	($750)
CCA claim for 2010:		
$1,080 × 20% = $216		
($1,700 − $750) × 20% × 50% = $95		($311)
Closing UCC		<u>$1,719</u> (UCC at December 31, 2010)

When you purchase and dispose of an asset in the same CCA class during the year, you must net the addition and disposal together before applying the half-year rule.

Recapture and terminal loss

As long as assets are purchased for a higher cost than the sale price of previously purchased assets, the UCC will never reduce to nil. However, what if your business sells all the assets in a CCA class and does not replace them? Well, two things can happen, which we consider in this section.

Let's imagine now that you decide not to upgrade your meeting room table and chairs. You admit to yourself that you don't like meeting clients, so the best way not to meet clients is to get rid of your meeting room furniture. (Perhaps not a good career move, but it works with the example.)

Selling all the assets in a class for less than the UCC balance

Remember, the table and chairs originally cost $1,200. Again, assume you sell the whole set for $750. In this case, the following would happen:

Opening UCC at January 1, 2010 (same as UCC at December 31, 2009) $1,080

Sale of chairs:

Lesser of:

Original cost:	$1,200	
Proceeds:		$750
Lesser:	($750)	
UCC balance after sale	$330	

Because you sold all the assets in this class, you shouldn't have any UCC left — nothing is left to depreciate. However, you have $330 remaining. What this means is that you didn't depreciate the assets fast enough. Therefore, the taxman lets you make this up by allowing you to claim the full amount remaining as a deduction. After all, you were only using the rate they set — why shouldn't you get the deduction? The $330 is referred to as the terminal loss and is fully tax deductible as part of your total CCA claim.

Next up in the ongoing saga of the office furniture? Well it turns out that the designer of the furniture you bought wins a prestigious award and her furniture, even used, becomes all the rage. What happens if you sell it for more than you paid for it? (Nice move by the way!)

Selling the assets for more than the UCC balance

What happens if you sell the table and chairs for $1,800? Sounds good, but a downfall does exist. Let's look at the calculation again:

UCC at January 1, 2010 (same as UCC at December 31, 2009) $1,080

Sale of chairs:

Lesser of:

Original cost:	$1,200	
Proceeds:		$1,800
Lesser:		($1,200)
UCC balance after sale		($120)

See what's happened? Again, you sold everything in the asset pool, so your UCC balance should clear to zero. However, you have a negative UCC balance. This means you've taken too much CCA — the assets did not depreciate as fast as the taxman thought they would. Obviously, the CRA won't let you have too much of a good thing, so it will ask for the extra CCA that you took back (hence the term "recapture") by adding the negative UCC to your income in the year the asset is disposed.

If you sell an asset for more than its original cost, you may also have a capital gain to report. See Tip #46 for more details.

Restriction on the maximum capital cost of a class 10.1 automobile

The government does not want you driving an expensive car and being able to write off a significant portion in CCA in determining your self-employment income. Therefore, the amount of CCA that can be claimed on an automobile is restricted in certain situations. If you buy a car where the cost exceeds a certain threshold amount, that car cannot go in the regular class 10 for CCA purposes. Instead, it must go into a special class — namely class 10.1 — where special rules apply. The threshold amounts are shown in Table 22-4 in Tip #22.

As you can see, if you buy a car in 2009 that costs more than $30,000, you'll be allowed to use only $30,000 as your capital cost. The excess can never be written off for tax purposes. The CRA periodically adjusts the maximum amount to take into account rising car prices.

Special rules in calculating CCA on class 10.1 automobiles

Keep in mind a few special rules when you're tallying up CCA on your class 10.1 automobile. Have a look to see whether any of these circumstances apply to you:

✔ Calculate CCA on each car on its own. If your business used two cars and they both had an actual capital cost above the limits, your business would have two CCA class 10.1 calculations to make. The purchase or sale of one class 10.1 automobile does not impact the CCA calculation of another CCA class 10.1 automobile.

✔ Unlike other capital assets, when you sell a class 10.1 automobile, you don't have to calculate recapture or terminal loss. (We discuss how recapture and terminal loss are calculated under "Recapture and terminal loss" in this tip.)

✔ Normally, when you sell an asset you're not allowed to claim CCA on that asset. However, for a class 10.1 asset, a special rule allows you to claim one-half of the CCA you would have otherwise been allowed to deduct had you continued to own the asset.

#33

Be a Tax Winner Even When You Realize a Loss

*F*iling a tax return is one time when being a loser is to your advantage. If you've incurred losses (including limited partnership losses, non-capital losses, and net capital losses) in prior years, and were unable to use those losses on your prior years' tax returns, you are allowed to carry those losses forward to offset some of your current income.

If you've had losses in the past, you may be able to use those losses on your current year's tax return to offset your taxable income and reduce your tax bill! If you're unsure what your unclaimed loss balance is, give the CRA a call. If you forget to claim an amount, the CRA will not apply your unused losses to your current income, because these are optional deductions.

Depending on the type of loss you've incurred, limitations may exist on the amount of loss you can carry forward, and on the number of years it can be carried forward.

It's generally most beneficial to apply a prior year's loss to income that's taxed at a high rate. For example, if your income is low this year but is expected to increase in future years, you may want to forgo claiming the loss carried forward this year. Instead, you can save the loss for a future year when you know you'll be subject to a higher tax rate. Of course, because certain types of losses have a limited carryforward period (we discuss this in a moment), you'll want to be absolutely certain you'll be able to use the loss in future years. If there's any doubt, claim the loss this year — use it, don't lose it — even if you're in a low tax bracket.

Never claim losses to bring your taxable income to zero. Although you'll have no tax to pay with taxable income of zero, you'd also have no tax to pay if you report income equal to your non-refundable tax credits.

Limited-Partnership Losses

Limited partnerships are most commonly purchased as tax shelters. A limited partner, as opposed to a general partner, has limited liability with respect to the partnership's liabilities. The main reason (but perhaps not the best reason) for investing in a limited partnership is often the up-front tax losses allocated to partners. (For more about limited partnerships, see Tip #29.)

Although some of these partnerships eventually make a profit, often huge losses occur in the first years. These losses are passed on to investors (the partners), to be deducted on their personal tax returns. The tax authorities are not fans of limited partnerships in general, and the tax laws limit the amount of losses you can claim. Specifically, investors can deduct cumulative losses only up to the investor's "at-risk amount."

Your at-risk amount is the amount you paid to purchase the limited partnership, plus any further capital contributions you made to the partnership (in other words, your tax cost of the limited-partnership investment). Put more succinctly, you can deduct losses on your tax return only up to the amount that you paid (including any loans you've incurred) for your partnership interest.

If you've received form T5013, "Statement of Partnership Income," from your limited partnership in the year, your at-risk amount should be reported in box 45. If not, contact the partnership and ask them for details of this amount — this is something the partnership should track.

If your cumulative limited-partnership losses exceed your at-risk amount, you can carry the remaining losses forward for possible future use. You can deduct the additional losses to offset income produced by the partnership or to offset any additional capital you contributed to the partnership. Limited-partnership losses can be carried forward indefinitely. No expiry applies.

Your limited-partnership losses available for carryover will be reported in box 31 of your T5013 slip. This is the amount that can't be deducted on your current year's tax return, but can be carried forward to offset limited partnership income in the future.

If you have a limited-partnership loss that does not exceed your at-risk amount, this loss can be used to offset income from any source in the current year. In fact, the loss must be used this year if it can be. If not, it becomes part of your non–capital loss balance and can be carried back for up to three years to offset a prior year's taxable income, or carried forward for 20 years. But don't forget — if any portion of the loss can't be used because of the at-risk rules, it can only be carried forward to offset against limited-partnership income in the future, unless you increase the at-risk amount of your limited-partnership investment.

Non-capital Losses

In general, any business, employment, or property transaction is considered non-capital. (See Tip #39 for a discussion of net capital losses.) So, if you have your own business and it generates a loss, this is considered to be a non-capital loss. In addition, if you've incurred an allowable business investment loss, otherwise known as an ABIL (see the next section for further details), this is also considered to be a non-capital loss.

The amount of non-capital loss that is generated in a particular tax year is calculated on form T1A, "Request for Loss Carryback." This is also the form that allows you to carry back any current-year losses to prior tax years, and that reports the amount of the loss that can be carried forward to future years.

Form T1A is important because not all items on your tax return are figured into the calculation of your non-capital loss. Therefore, if you have a negative net income or taxable income amount (which is actually reported as a zero balance on lines 236 and 260 of your tax return), fill out form T1A so you know how much of the losses can be carried over to other tax years.

After the CRA receives and processes your form T1A, it will reassess the year to which you carried the loss back . . . and send you a tax refund cheque!

Items included in non-capital losses

The items included in the calculation of non-capital losses on your tax return are as follows:

- ✔ **Employment income/loss:** This includes lines 101 and 104, less any amounts reported on lines 207, 212, 229, and 231.

- ✔ **Investment income/loss:** Add together lines 120 and 121 and deduct any amount reported on line 221.

- ✔ **Partnership income/loss:** This includes any amounts reported on line 122. Note that only the allowable loss (not the restricted portion of the limited partnership loss) is included on this line.

✔ **Rental income/loss:** This is reported on line 126.

✔ **Business, professional, or commission income or losses:** These are reported on lines 135, 137, and 139.

✔ **Farming or fishing income or losses:** These are reported on lines 141 and 143. The amount of farming losses you can claim may be restricted if farming is not your chief source of income for the year (see Tip #29).

✔ **Taxable capital gains:** This is reported on line 127.

✔ **Non-taxable income:** This is reported on line 147.

✔ **Net capital losses of other years:** This is reported on line 253.

✔ **Certain other deductions:** These include the capital gains deduction, deduction for business investment losses, employee home-relocation loan deduction, stock option and shares deductions, other payments deduction, and income exempt under a tax treaty. Amounts are reported on lines 254, 217, 248, 249, and 250.

Form T1A requires you to separate the income and loss items on your tax return. For example, any deductions claimed would be placed in the "loss" column. You must then total all the income and loss items separately.

If you've claimed any amounts on lines 208, 209, 214, 215, 219, 220, 232, or 235 of your tax return, these amounts are deducted from your total income. It's possible that these deductions will cause you to have negative income; however, these amounts do not result in a non-capital loss. If the deductions claimed on these lines result in negative income (before taking into account allowable deductions in the loss column), your total income is deemed to be nil. You then take your total income, less the total amount reported in the loss column, to calculate the net loss for the year. You must then deduct any farming or fishing losses incurred in the year to come up with your total non-capital loss available for carryover. This amount can be carried back to offset taxable income in any of the previous three taxation years, or carried forward.

Calculate non-capital losses

Here's an example to help you understand how to calculate noncapital losses. Pam had more tax deductions than income in the 2008 tax year. She would like to know if she can take advantage of her losses on her 2009 tax return. Here is a summary of items claimed on her 2008 tax return:

Interest income	1,200
Business income (loss)	($9,000)
RRSP deduction	$2,000

Pam's 2008 non-capital loss is calculated as follows. Note that "personal" streams of income and deductions are handled separately from the business loss.

	Current-Year Income (A)	Current Year Loss (B)	2008 Non-capital Loss (A – B)
Interest income	$1,200		
Business loss			$9,000
Subtotal	$1,200		$9,000
Subtract: RRSP	($2,000)		n/a
Subtotal (if negative = 0)	0	$9,000	$9,000

Pam can carry forward the 2008 $9,000 non-capital loss to 2009 to reduce her 2009 taxable income.

Non-capital losses can be carried forward for 20 years. However, consider carrying your losses back (up to three years back), if possible, to receive a tax benefit from the loss sooner rather than later.

If you're certain you will have taxable income in the future, you may want to forgo a loss carryback and instead carry the losses forward to offset your future income. It's always most beneficial to claim the losses against income taxed at the highest marginal tax rate. So, if you're expecting to generate significant income in the future that will be taxed at a higher marginal tax rate than you're subject to this year, you may want to keep the losses intact until you're in that higher tax bracket.

Use Business Investment Losses (BIL) to Your Advantage

A capital loss occurs when you sell an investment for less than you paid for it. A capital loss can be used only to shelter or offset capital gains from tax — it cannot be used to shelter other types of income (say, employment income, pension income, interest, or dividends) from tax.

A business investment loss (BIL) is a special type of capital loss. A business investment loss, or a portion of that loss, can be deducted in the year incurred to shelter any type of income — not just capital gains — from tax.

A BIL occurs when you sell your shares or debt in a small business corporation at a loss. (Refer to Tip #31 for a discussion of small business corporation shares.) A BIL will also arise if you were deemed to dispose of the shares or debt when the corporation became bankrupt, insolvent, or no longer carried on business and the fair market value of the shares became nil.

Calculating the deductible portion of the BIL

Report your true loss on line 228 of your return. This is the difference between your proceeds of disposition (which may be nil!) and the tax cost of the investment (which is normally what you paid for the investment). However, as with capital losses, only 50 percent of a BIL is tax deductible. This is logical because only 50 percent of the gain on the sale of an investment is taxable. The deductible portion of a BIL is referred to as an allowable business investment loss (ABIL).

Reducing your BIL for past capital gains deductions

If you've used any portion of your capital gains deduction (see Tips #30 and #31), this will reduce the amount of the BIL that you can deduct. After any necessary reductions in the amount of the loss are calculated, the remaining loss to be deducted on your current year's tax return is reported on line 217.

Although you can carry a non-capital loss back 3 years and forward 20 years (see previous section), these rules do not apply to a non-capital loss resulting from an ABIL. Instead, an ABIL that has not been used within **10 tax years** will in the 11th year become a net capital loss that can be carried forward indefinitely against taxable capital gains.

Part III
Tips for Investors

The 5th Wave   By Rich Tennant

"That? That's schedule X. We've never had to use it. But, if anyone actually discovers how to grow money on trees, the CRA's got a form to get its fair share of the leaves."

In this part . . .

*I*t's often said that it doesn't matter what your investments return; it's the after-tax returns that matter most. The problem is that taxes can seem overwhelming when you are an investor. First, the tax rules are different depending on the type of investment account you choose. You could have a registered account, a non-registered account, a tax-free savings account, or maybe you invest in insurance products or in property or other assets. Furthermore, investment income is taxed differently depending on the type of income you are generating. Think about it. You might have a rental property and earn rental income as well as incur rental expenses. Maybe you like the stock markets and buy stocks that pay you dividends and generate capital gains and losses. Perhaps you like to play it safe and earn interest income on bonds and cash like investments. And don't even start on the rules for foreign investments!

Take a deep breath — help is on the way in the form of Part III. We give you tips broken down by the different types of investment accounts, and investment types so you can stick to the facts for your personal situation. So highlight, bookmark, and tag these pages! Do anything you have to do to remind yourself of the many ways to save tax as an investor!

Minimize Tax on Your Investment Income

*W*e often hear people say, "My taxes are too high. What can I do to reduce them?" Although we don't have the magical solution that will make your tax bill disappear, we can suggest some things you can do to reduce the amount you pay, particularly if you're an investor.

Tax efficiency doesn't matter when you own only registered investments (Tips #42 and #43) or have a Tax-Free Savings Account (Tip #41). Why? Earnings in these accounts accumulate tax free regardless of the type of return. You're taxed on your registered accounts only when you make withdrawals, and even then the type of underlying investment doesn't matter. The full withdrawal is taxed at your full marginal tax rate (Tip #1). Withdrawals from Tax-Free Savings Account are tax free.

Investment returns in a non-registered account are not created equal in the eyes of the taxman. In fact, the amount of tax you pay depends on the type of income your investment is earning, whether that's dividends, capital gains, or interest.

Always weigh your investment and tax objectives before making any investment decision. Even though a particular investment suits you tax-wise, it may not fit your investment-risk profile. In this tip, we show you that when you use registered, tax-free, and non-registered investment accounts you can decide where to hold your different investments for the ultimate tax efficiency.

Choose the Best Location for Your Investments

You may be lucky enough to have accumulated, over time, investment assets in registered, non-registered, and Tax Free Savings accounts. Some Canadians also have investment holding companies. After you have more than one "location" in which to make investment choices, consider where it makes the most sense, tax-wise, to make each investment.

First, determine your optimal asset allocation. Most people do this with the help of an investment advisor. It requires determining what percentage of your overall holdings you wish to invest in different types of assets, including cash, fixed-income investments like bonds, and equities. Decide, too, what percentage of each asset class you wish to hold in different geographic locations, such as Canada, the U.S., and globally.

After you figure out what you want to hold, you can choose the best location for each type of investment. If you want to hold some fixed-income investments, you would generally want those inside your registered accounts (see Tips #42 and #43) or your Tax-Free Savings Account (see Tip #41) where that highly taxed interest income can be earned tax-sheltered. If you want to hold Canadian equities, those are great in a non-registered account so you can take advantage of the dividend tax credit. Depending on how much money you have to work with in each account, there will likely be some overlap as well. That's okay. This is just a starting point.

Also consider the risk of each investment when choosing its location. For example, say you want to buy one stock that is more "speculative" in nature. It could make you lots of money, or it could bust. You may want to buy that stock in your non-registered account. Why? If it does go bust, you would create a capital loss, which could be used to offset capital gains. If that stock goes bust in your registered account, the loss is useless to you.

Choose Tax-Smart Investments

It pays to pay attention to how your various forms of investment income are taxed — like all things in taxland, each scenario has its pros and cons. In this section we look at tax-effectively managing your income from dividends, capital gains, and interest.

Canadian dividends have their advantages

A dividend is a distribution of a corporation's profits to its shareholders after all expenses and income taxes have been paid. Investors receive dividends on the stocks they purchase in their investment portfolios. If you're looking to generate dividend income, you want to invest in Canadian equities (either directly or via a mutual fund) that pay dividends annually.

Canadian dividends are a tax-efficient source of investment income because they qualify for a special dividend tax credit, which keeps the tax burden low. Canadian dividends are always taxed at a lower rate than interest income and are usually taxed at lower rates than capital gains. Dividends are only taxed at higher rates than capital gains in a few provinces at the higher tax brackets (we're talking $80,000 plus of taxable income).

 Dividends from public corporations resident in Canada — which is what you would normally hold in an investment portfolio — are called *eligible dividends,* and these must be included in your taxable income and grossed up by 45 percent (that is, multiplied by 1.45, or 145 percent). So, if you receive $10,000 in eligible dividends this year you'll have to include $14,500 in your income. The grossed-up dividend represents an estimate of what the dividend would have been had the corporation not been subject to tax.

Now for the good stuff. A dividend tax credit exists that's designed to reflect the tax paid by the corporation. Put another way, you as a shareholder receive a tax credit for the tax the corporation paid on your behalf. The federal dividend tax credit is 13.33 percent of the grossed-up non-eligible dividend, and 19 percent of the grossed-up eligible dividend paid. (Don't you just love all the math?)

Say Tom receives a $10,000 eligible dividend from IM Canadian Corporation, a publicly listed Canadian corporation he holds in his non-registered investment account. Assume Tom has a high taxable income and therefore will pay federal tax of 29 percent on the dividend. Further, assume Tom is subject to a provincial tax rate of 14 percent, and a provincial dividend tax credit 6.5 percent of the eligible dividend (refer to Table 3-1). How is tax calculated on the dividend that Tom receives?

Table 3-1   Taxation of Eligible Dividends

	Eligible Dividend
Actual dividend received	$10,000
Taxable dividend (grossed-up dividend)	$14,500
Federal tax (at 29%)	$4,205
Less federal dividend tax credit	($2,755)
Net federal tax payable	$1,450

(continued)

Table 3-1 *(continued)*	
	Eligible Dividend
Provincial tax (at 14%)	$2,030
Less provincial dividend tax credit	($942)
Total tax	$2,538

As you can see, the net result of this calculation is that Tom pays about 25 percent tax on the eligible dividend from IM Canadian Corporation. We consider this tax efficient because an equivalent amount of interest income Tom earned would garner tax of 43 percent.

When you receive a T3 or T5 slip reporting your dividend income, you'll notice that the slip has boxes that contain both the actual amount of dividends and the taxable amount of dividends paid. Be sure to include only the taxable amount of dividends on your tax return. The T3 or T5 slip will also note the federal dividend tax credit you are entitled to. (Phew!)

In some cases it is possible to pay no personal tax on eligible dividends received because of the basic personal exemption and the dividend tax credit. In most provinces (but not all), you can earn about $49,000 of dividends without having to worry about any type of tax (assuming you don't have any other income sources).

Capital gains are tax efficient

Capital gains are generated when you make a profit on the sale of an asset such as a stock or even a piece of land. See Tip 38 which is dedicated to helping you keep your capital gains tax as low as possible. Capital gains are a very tax-efficient source of investment income because they're taxable only when realized (that is, when your shares are sold or, when you invest in mutual funds, when the securities in the mutual fund are sold). Further, capital gains are just one-half taxable. This makes the tax bill on a realized capital gain exactly one-half of the tax bill on interest income.

Capital gains are calculated by taking the sales proceeds less the tax cost (usually the purchase price) of an investment and less any selling costs. You pay tax on only half of any remaining gain. If you're looking for potential capital gains outside of your registered account, Canadian or foreign equities or mutual funds with stock exposure are your best bet.

 Capital gains are not always taxed more efficiently than dividends — it depends on your tax bracket (Tip #2), province/territory of residence, other sources of income, and the type of dividend. Even at the highest tax brackets the tax bill is very similar for capital gains and dividends, making them both very tax-efficient investment returns. The good news is that Canadian stocks might pay dividends and earn you capital gains, so a Canadian stock investment is generally very tax friendly (Tip #35).

 Assuming you have no other sources of income, you can earn a pretty hefty amount of eligible dividends and pay no tax because of your basic personal amount and the dividend tax credit. Of course the actual amount differs by province. You're looking at close to $50,000 of tax-free eligible dividends in many provinces, which includes the impact of the alternative minimum tax (see Tip #1).

Interest income can be costly

You've probably got the hint by now that interest income is not the most tax-friendly investment return. You'll find interest income is always the least tax-efficient (read: taxed the most!), because it is fully taxed at your marginal tax rate. For example, if your marginal tax rate is 32 percent and you earn $1,000 of interest income, you will pay $320 of tax, meaning your after-tax return is $680. That doesn't mean they shouldn't play a role in your investment portfolio; that depends on your risk tolerance and the purpose of the funds. We simply want to make you aware of the tax exposure.

 Investments that earn interest income include term deposits, guaranteed investment certificates (GICs), Canada Savings Bonds, corporate and government bonds, and money market mutual funds.

#35

Pay Less Tax on Your Stock Investments

*S*o many investment choices are available that you might be confused about where to invest. But when it comes to tax benefits, Canadian stocks rule the roost. When you purchase the stock of a company, you become a *shareholder*, a part owner of that company. As a shareholder you're entitled to dividends declared by the company (although not all companies pay dividends). You also benefit when the company's share price goes up, because you can choose to sell the shares for more than your purchase price. Both Canadian dividends and capital gains are considered tax efficient because the tax rates on these types of returns are about half of what you would pay on interest income.

Understanding the Tax Differences between Public and Private Company Shares

Not all stock investments are created equal. You can make many different types of stock investments, which we cover in this section.

Simply stated, when you invest in a public company share, you're one of many shareholders (thousands, maybe). As the shareholder of a private company, you're likely one of very few shareholders, and may even be the sole shareholder. Public company shares are very easy to purchase. You do so through a stock exchange and would usually use an investment advisor or an online trading account to make your purchases.

A private company share would not be available on a stock exchange. Instead you would set up your own corporation, or purchase shares of an existing corporation by way of a private deal. You might do the negotiations on your own, or use a lawyer or accountant to help with the purchase.

Public company shares

The most common type of stock issued here in Canada is common shares of public companies. This would include shares of the large Canadian banks, insurance companies, and oil and gas companies, among many others. When you're a common shareholder you're entitled to dividends when they are declared by the company. Not all companies pay dividends, so if you're looking for dividends as a source of income do some research. If a company has a strong history of paying dividends in the past, it will generally continue to pay dividends into the future.

Public companies also issue preferred shares. Preferred shares have set dividend rates attached to them and these are paid in preference to the common shareholders.

From a tax standpoint, dividends from Canadian common or preferred public company shares are the same. These dividends are eligible for the dividend tax credit, which greatly decreases the tax burden as opposed to interest income. You can generally expect to pay about half the amount of tax, if you're taxed at the highest marginal rates, with Canadian dividends versus interest income. We talk about the tax advantages of dividends in Tip #34.

Private company shares

Investing in shares of private Canadian companies will produce the same tax benefits as public companies. The dividends you receive are eligible for a dividend tax credit, although it's not always quite as generous as the credit for public company shares. However, if the company is considered a qualified small business corporation (QSBC; see Tips #30 and #31), upon sale you can earn up to $750,000 of capital gains tax free. This capital gains exemption is not available on private company shares.

Foreign shares

Although you may choose to purchase foreign shares to diversify your investment portfolio, keep in mind that any dividends paid on the foreign shares are not eligible for the dividend tax credit. This means that the dividends are essentially taxed like regular income such as interest income or a salary.

Any dividends received should be fully included in your taxable income, after being converted to Canadian dollars. If you paid tax to a foreign jurisdiction on those dividends, you can claim a foreign tax credit for all or a portion of the tax. See Tip #36 for the full details.

Receiving Stock Dividends

A *stock dividend* is a dividend that a corporation pays to its shareholders by issuing new shares instead of cash.

The rules for a stock dividend mirror those for a cash dividend. The only difference, of course, is that you owe tax, but you have not received any cash to pay the tax! The corporation paying the stock dividend will issue you a T5 slip showing the amount of dividend to report on your tax return. The value or amount of the stock dividend in dollars will be determined by the corporation's board of directors. If the corporation is a Canadian resident, the gross-up and dividend tax credit rules we discuss in Tip #34 will apply.

Be aware that a stock dividend and a stock split are not the same thing. A stock split is simply dividing your shares into more shares with no change to the corporation's share capital. You'll owe no tax on stock splits, but you can rack up substantial tax on stock dividends if the board of directors places a high value on the stock issued via the stock dividend.

Transferring Dividend Income from Your Spouse

Say your spouse/common-law partner receives dividends from a Canadian resident corporation but has income, and a resulting tax liability, that is too low to make full use of the dividend tax credit. If this is the case, the dividend tax credit may go partially or fully unused — a tax credit being wasted! (A dividend tax credit in excess of a tax liability does not result in a tax refund.)

To avoid "wasting" part or all of the dividend tax credit, the spouse with the lower income can transfer the dividends to the higher-income spouse to claim on his or her own tax return. When transferred, the dividends will be grossed up and the dividend tax credit can be claimed.

Why in the world would you want to do this? At first glance, you'd think it would result in more tax, because the higher-income spouse is paying tax at a higher rate. But by transferring income out of the lower-income spouse's hands, you may be increasing the spousal credit amount the higher-income spouse can claim. The increase in the credit, together with the fact that the higher-income spouse can use the full dividend tax credit, will more than offset the higher tax rate paid. If it doesn't, then you simply do not make the transfer!

This transfer has a few restrictions:

- ✔ Only dividends received by your spouse or common-law partner can be transferred. Dividends received by other dependants are not eligible.

- ✔ Only dividends received from taxable Canadian corporations (that is, dividends eligible for the 45- or 25-percent gross-up) may be transferred. Foreign dividends do not qualify.

- ✔ All the spouse's eligible dividends must be transferred. Partial transfers are not allowed.

- ✔ This transfer is allowable only if it creates or increases the spousal credit amount you're entitled to.

If you're 65 or older, transferring your spouse's dividends to your return could reduce your age credit if it brings your net income above the current threshold (about $35,000). Moreover, if it increases your income above about $65,000, you'll find you're subject to the Old Age Security (OAS) clawback (Tip #64). The thresholds for the age credit and OAS clawback change annually.

Handling Shares in a Company That's Been Bought Out

Rarely a week goes by without news that a company is being bought out by another company, or a spinoff of a portion of a company is taking place. And when you're a shareholder of that company, it usually means tax implications.

As a general rule, if you're receiving only shares as part of the transaction, and no cash, there are no tax implications. Instead, the adjusted cost base of your original shareholding will carry through to the new shares you will own. In the case of a spinoff you would prorate your adjusted cost base between two shares you now hold. Keep in mind that if you do receive any cash proceeds, that cash is taxable.

If the spinoff relates to a foreign corporation, you might receive a tax slip treating the spinoff as a taxable dividend. If certain conditions are met, you're able to elect to exclude that dividend from your income.

Companies can treat buyouts and spinoffs in many ways. Contact the investor relations department of the company or consult its Web site for details on how to treat the transactions on your tax return. Most companies offer investors very detailed instructions on how to file their taxes.

#36

Know the Rules on Foreign Investments

● ●

*A*s a Canadian resident, your entire worldwide income is taxable. So if you make foreign investments, you must report your investment income on your Canadian tax return. Some special rules apply (of course!), so read on.

Knowing When Foreign Investment Income Is Taxable in Canada

If you earn foreign investment income, it's taxable in Canada. Remember to convert the income to Canadian dollars before reporting it on your tax return.

Some common types of investments and the kinds of returns you might earn are shown in Table 3-2:

Table 3-2   Some Common Investments and Their Returns

Type of Investment	*Potential Returns*	*Currency Conversion Rate*
Foreign stocks	Dividends	Average for the year
	Capital gains/losses	Rate at time stock is sold
Foreign bonds	Interest	Average for the year
	Capital gains/losses	Rate at time bond is sold

(continued)

Table 3-2 *(continued)*

Type of Investment	Potential Returns	Currency Conversion Rate
Foreign rental properties	Rental income (net of expenses)	Average for the year
	Capital gains/losses	Rate at time property is sold
	Recapture/terminal loss	
Foreign mutual funds	Foreign non-business income	Average rate for the year
	Foreign business income	Average rate for the year

The Bank of Canada has some handy currency conversion calculators on its Web site. Check them out at www.bankofcanada.ca/en/rates/exchange.html. The CRA also posts exchange rates on its Web site each year.

When you're calculating the gain or loss from the sale of a foreign investment, convert the purchase price of the investment using the exchange rate in place at the time the purchase was made. The sales price is converted using the rate in place at the time of sale. Any gain from the currency conversion is still taxable; however, the first $200 of exchange gains are not taxable. Likewise, the first $200 of currency losses is not deductible.

Foreign dividends are not treated the same as dividends received from Canadian resident corporations. Here are the details:

- ✓ **Foreign dividends are not subject to the dividend gross-up and dividend tax credit calculations.** This means that foreign dividends are taxed the same as interest income.

- ✓ **Foreign dividends are included in income at their full amount.** Even if the originating country withheld tax on the dividend, the full amount — not the dividend minus the tax withheld — is included in income.

- ✓ **All foreign dividends are included in calculating your taxable income.** Even if the dividend you received is not taxable in the country of origin, it's still taxable here!

What to Do If You Also Paid Tax to Another Country

If you've received income from foreign sources this year, you may already have paid tax to foreign tax authorities. But as we mention at the beginning of this tip, Canadians are taxed on their *worldwide* income, which means that this same income is being taxed in Canada. Does this mean you're being double taxed? Probably not. Luckily for you, Canada lets you claim a tax credit for the foreign taxes you've paid.

Claiming the foreign tax credit can take a bit of work. First, two types of foreign tax credits exist, one for foreign tax paid on non-business income, perhaps better known as "investment income," and one for foreign tax paid on business income. Second, you need to do a separate calculation for each country you paid the foreign tax to.

If you paid a total of $200 or less in foreign non-business taxes, you do not need to do a separate calculation for each country. Generally, the foreign tax credit you can claim for each country is the lowest of either the foreign income tax you actually paid to the foreign country, or the Canadian federal tax due on your income from that country.

For example, say you earned foreign income and paid $5,000 of foreign tax on that income. Then, say that same income would give rise to $3,000 of Canadian tax. In this situation, you'd be allowed to claim only a $3,000 foreign tax credit. Think of it this way: If that income were your only taxable Canadian income in the year, letting you claim a tax credit of $5,000 would actually entitle you to a tax refund in Canada. Why would Canada reimburse you for taxes you paid to another government? The foreign tax credit system is designed to help you avoid paying double tax on the same income, but not to reimburse you for earning income in a higher-taxed jurisdiction.

Use form T2209, "Federal Foreign Tax Credits," to calculate the amount of your foreign tax credit. After you've calculated the amount of foreign tax credits you're entitled to, enter the total in box 14 of schedule 1.

If you paid tax on income from foreign investments (that is, foreign non-business income), your foreign tax credit cannot be more than 15 percent of your income from that investment. However, you may be able to deduct the excess amount on your return at line 232.

You can carry unclaimed foreign business income taxes back three years and forward ten years.

If your federal foreign tax credit on non-business income is less than the tax you paid to a foreign country, you may be able to claim a provincial or territorial foreign tax credit. Complete form T2036, "Provincial Foreign Tax Credit," to determine the amount, if any, of the credit available.

Here's how to claim the federal foreign tax credit. First, ensure you complete the federal foreign tax credit area on schedule 1 and attach form T2209 to your return. Also attach the following:

- ✔ A note showing your calculations. (**Remember:** Show all amounts in Canadian dollars.)

- ✔ Proof, such as an official receipt, showing the foreign taxes you paid. For example, if you paid taxes in the U.S., attach your W-2 information slip, U.S. 1040 tax return, and any other supporting documents. Foreign taxes paid may also be noted on your T3 and T5 slips.

Reviewing the Rules on Foreign Property Holdings

On page 2 of your tax return, you're asked if the total cost of all foreign property you owned in the year was greater than $100,000. If so, you need to answer yes and complete form T1135, "Foreign Income Verification Statement," and file it with your tax return.

The types of property that are considered foreign property include:

- ✔ Funds in foreign bank accounts
- ✔ Shares of foreign companies
- ✔ Land and buildings, such as a rental property, located outside Canada
- ✔ Mutual funds organized in a foreign jurisdiction
- ✔ Non-Canadian government and corporate bonds

Foreign property does not include:

- ✔ Property used exclusively in an active business
- ✔ Vacation properties (must be used primarily as a personal residence, not rental)
- ✔ An interest in a U.S. Individual Retirement Account (IRA)

You'll have to convert the cost of your foreign properties into Canadian dollars to see whether it's more than $100,000. To do this, you need to find out the foreign exchange rate at the time you purchased the asset.

Take a look at some examples. Suppose Karen owns shares of a U.S. corporation with a tax cost of $85,000. She also holds $20,000 in a U.S. bank account. Karen has to file form T1135, because although the cost of each property is less than $100,000, the combined value of all her foreign properties exceeds the $100,000 threshold.

What about Dave? He holds $120,000 of foreign stocks in his RRSP. Does he have to file form T1135? No. You don't have to file this form for assets held in your RRSP.

Note that you can still EFILE your tax return, but form T1135 needs to be mailed off separately to the CRA.

Form T1135 must be filed if the tax cost of a foreign property exceeded $100,000 at any time during the year, not just at the end of the year.

Substantial penalties exist for failing to file form T1135 by April 30. And these penalties increase when the CRA asks you to file a return and you don't comply, or if you're found to have given false information.

Consider Tax-Advantaged Investments

●●

*Y*our goal as an investor is to receive the highest return possible for the amount of risk you can stomach. But you can't just look at the simple returns of each investment to determine how much money you made. To truly distinguish between investment returns, you need to look at the *after-tax returns*. When looking for tax savings, consider some investments available in Canada that offer unique tax benefits.

Don't get us wrong; we're not necessarily recommending these investments. Choosing them is something you should do after research and perhaps working with an investment professional. But understanding these tax benefits is one step toward determining whether these are right for you.

Recognizing the Pros and Cons of Labour-Sponsored Funds

A labour-sponsored venture capital corporation (LSVCC), otherwise known as a labour-sponsored fund, is a venture capital mutual fund established under specific federal or provincial legislation and managed by labour unions or employee groups.

The tax benefit of a LSVCC is in the tax credits. The allowable federal credit is 15 percent of the cost, to a maximum of $750. A $5,000 investment will garner you the full allowable credit. Many provinces also offer credits as well.

If you redeem your fund within eight years, the tax credit you claimed will be clawed back. Make sure this is an investment you're comfortable with for the long term.

You can contribute labour-sponsored funds to your RRSP. If you choose to do so, don't forget to claim an RRSP deduction as well as the federal (and perhaps provincial) tax credit for your investment!

If the first registered holder of the labour-sponsored fund units is a spousal RRSP, either the RRSP contributor or the RRSP annuitant (the spouse) may claim the credit for the investment. (We talk more about spousal RRSPs in Tip #50.)

Attach to your return either a T5006 slip, "Statement of Registered Labour-Sponsored Venture Capital Corporation Class A Shares," or an official provincial/territorial slip documenting your investment. If the labour-sponsored funds went into your RRSP, you must attach an official RRSP receipt to your return as well.

Saving Tax with Flow-Through Shares

When you purchase a flow-through share, you're investing in a Canadian company in the exploration or mining sector. This type of investment is most appropriate for taxpayers taxed at the highest rates because of the sizable deductions and credits available. However, because you normally would want to make a pretty big investment in order to really benefit from the tax savings, make sure you don't overdo it from an investment standpoint. Keep the flow-through investment only a portion of your overall portfolio. The rules of diversification still apply! And remember that the shares may not be liquid — if you need some cash back, you may not be able to get to it easily.

The government allows special tax breaks for investors in the natural resource sector in order to help fund the huge expenditures these companies have to make in the early days of their exploration, before any profits can be made. These companies have a lot of deductions, though, and are allowed to give those deductions to their investors. It's not uncommon for investors to receive a tax deduction for the full value of their investment in the first year or two after the investment was made.

Tax benefits from flow-through shares include:

- Tax deduction for 100% of eligible exploration expenditures
- A 15% non-refundable tax credit for certain investments
- Provincial tax credits in many provinces

The tax cost of flow-through shares is considered nil, so whenever you decide to sell them you'll have a guaranteed capital gain. Flow-through shares, therefore, manage to reduce current taxes and to defer taxes until the future when the shares are sold.

Flow-through shares may benefit you when you have unused capital losses, because you'll have a high chance of generating a capital gain in the future.

Choosing a Tax-Efficient Mutual Fund

Mutual funds are pools of assets managed by professionals. The assets managed range from real estate to mortgages to stocks and bonds. As the mutual fund earns income, or sells some of its underlying assets, income and capital gains may be generated. These income and gains, net of fund expenses, are distributed to the fund's investors.

If you invest in mutual funds, you'll find that most income distributed to you retains its identity in your hands. This means that income earned as capital gains or Canadian dividends by the fund is still regarded as capital gains or Canadian dividends to you. Investors can take advantage of the low rate on Canadian dividends due to the dividend tax credit and pay tax on only 50 percent of capital gains, just like they could if they owned the underlying assets directly.

Highly taxed interest income retains its identity only when you purchase a mutual fund trust and you receive a T3 slip. If you own a mutual fund corporation investment (and if you receive a T5 slip, you do), you'll notice that you never get an interest distribution — it's just not possible (trust us on this one). If you're looking to buy a bond fund, a money market fund, or a balanced fund where a large percentage of the underlying holdings are interest-bearing investments like bonds, consider a "corporate class" mutual fund to minimize tax on your investment returns.

Corporate class mutual funds are also beneficial where you like to make regular changes to your portfolio. Each fund has a variety of underlying pools of investments that you can choose from. If you have a gain from the pool you're currently invested in, and switch to another pool within the same umbrella fund, you won't pay tax on your gains. This means that tax is deferred until you sell out of the fund altogether. With a traditional mutual fund trust, any transfers between funds will give rise to a *disposition* for tax purposes (which means you'll have to pay tax on your gains on your next tax return).

Very often, funds automatically reinvest distributions to the fundholders in new units of the fund. In these situations, although you never see any of the cash, you'll be taxed on the income distributed. This is why you may have received a tax slip this year even though you didn't see any cash coming into your account. Be sure to keep track of the reinvestments, because they will increase your adjusted cost base and can help minimize capital gains when you eventually redeem your mutual fund units.

Buyer Beware: Tax Shelters

Your income is high and you hate paying tax. You want a magical solution to manage your taxes. You've taken advantage of all the deductions and credits you can think of. Now what? Well, some Canadians turn to investment tax shelters, such as limited partnerships (see Tip #29) and flow-through shares (see above).

Although some legitimate and effective tax shelters do exist, not all are created equal. You must weigh the benefit of the tax deduction to the actual merit of the investment itself. Given the large investment most tax shelters require, you may want to have your accountant take a look at the details.

Watch out for these traps with investment tax shelters:

✔ The adjusted cost base on your investment is deemed to be nil, therefore you're deferring tax only until the investment is sold; at that time a capital gain will arise (although that capital gain is taxed at a lower rate than the deduction originally benefited from).

✔ They can be hard to sell in the short term after the tax deductions have been taken. Be sure you don't need liquidity!

✔ You can be hit with alternative minimum tax (see Tip #1) if you take too many deductions.

✔ They may require you to make future instalment payments (see Tip #14), so you must ensure you have ongoing liquidity.

The CRA has not been impressed by many tax shelters and tracks them quite closely. Be assured that if the CRA is offended by any of the activities of the tax shelter (even if it has an identification number), tax benefits will be disallowed. Buyer beware — each year new schemes arise, and CRA is on the lookout. If it seems too good to be true, it usually is. (For more on the CRA's stance on charity tax shelters, see Tip #11.)

Minimize Tax on Capital Gains

A *capital property* is any asset you own — real estate, shares of public and private corporations, bonds, units of mutual funds, cars, boats, jewellery, art, and so on. When you sell a capital property, you can end up with a gain or loss on the sale (well, you could also break even). The gain or loss is referred to as a *capital gain* or a *capital loss*. This chapter deals with tips for capital gains. We discuss capital losses in Tip #39.

What Is a Capital Gain?

To see whether you have a capital gain on the sale of a capital property, you need to know the following three amounts:

- ✔ The *proceeds of disposition* — total funds received and/or to be received from the sale of the capital property

- ✔ The *adjusted cost base* of the capital property — often referred to as simply the "ACB" or "tax cost" of the capital property

- ✔ The costs incurred in selling the capital property, for example legal fees and commissions — referred to as *selling costs* or *outlays and expenses*

You have a gain when the proceeds of disposition are greater than the adjusted cost base of the capital property plus the costs incurred in selling the capital property.

 Depreciable property is a special kind of capital property. The cost of depreciable property can be written off for tax purposes over a number of years by claiming annual capital cost allowance (CCA, or, in other words, "tax depreciation") amounts. Common examples of depreciable property are rental buildings (but not the land, which is not considered to depreciate) and capital assets used to earn income from a business, such as buildings used in a business, machinery, computer equipment, or office furniture and equipment. In addition to incurring a capital gain, you may also be required to add a recapture of prior-year CCA deductions to your income. See Tip #44 for more details.

Calculating Your Taxable Capital Gain

Only 50 percent of the capital gain is taxable. The amount of the capital gain subject to tax is referred to as the taxable capital gain.

Say that Lynne sold 1,000 shares of Public Corporation Limited for $7,500. She received the full proceeds at the time of the sale and paid a selling commission to her investment advisor of $80. The adjusted cost base of the shares is $3,500 (equal to the original purchase price of the shares plus her buying commission). Lynne calculates her capital gain — and taxable capital gain — as follows:

Proceeds of disposition		$7,500
Less: Adjusted cost base		($3,500)
Less: Outlays and expenses	($80)	
Capital gain	$3,920	

Because only 50 percent of the capital gain is taxable, Lynne reports $1,960 ($3,920 × 50 percent) as her taxable capital gain on line 127 of her tax return.

Contrasting Capital Property and Income Property

The judgment on whether a property is capital or income depends on both the nature of the property and the manner in which the owner manages the property. If the owner intends to realize a profit from the property (for example, a speculator in real estate) versus holding the property for the income it produces (for example, a landlord of a rental property), the gain or loss realized on the sale is treated as ordinary income or loss (which is fully taxable/deductible) as opposed to a capital gain or loss (which is only 50 percent taxable/deductible).

In an ideal situation, you would treat your gains as capital and your losses as income. The reason for this is twofold: one, capital gains are only 50 percent taxable, but business income is fully taxable; and two, capital losses can be applied only against capital gains, but a business loss can be applied against any source of income to reduce tax. For the average stock and mutual fund investor, doing this will be difficult. However, if you're planning to sell other types of capital property, it's something to think about.

To understand the difference between capital and income in relation to the taxpayer's intention, think about the scenario of a tree
and its fruit. If you bought the tree with the intention of selling the
fruit, then any subsequent sale of the tree would be on account of
capital. If, however, you purchased the tree intending to sell it and
make a quick buck, then you would treat the proceeds of the sale
as income — and 100 percent of any gain would be taxable.

In deciding whether the gain or loss is on account of income or
capital, tax courts have used the following tests:

- **Period of ownership:** If property has been held for only a
  short period, it may be considered to have been purchased
  to be resold, and, therefore, the profits may be treated as
  income. A property held for a longer period is more likely to
  be treated as capital.

- **Improvement and development:** Where systematic efforts
  are made to make properties more marketable, it may indicate
  a business of selling properties rather than holding properties
  as investments.

- **Relationship of the transaction to the taxpayer's ordinary
  business:** The more similar the transaction is to the taxpayer's ordinary business, the more likely it is that the transaction will be treated as income (for example, the sale of a
  renovated home by a general contractor).

- **Reasons for and nature of sale:** If the sale of a property is the
  result of an active campaign to sell it as opposed to the result
  of something unanticipated at the time of purchase, the profits may be considered on account of income.

- **Frequency of similar transactions:** A history of buying and
  selling similar properties, or of quick turnovers, may indicate
  the taxpayer is carrying on a business.

Even if your transaction does not satisfy one of these tests, that
does not mean the transaction will automatically be considered
capital or income. The courts look at the larger picture, and you
may have the opportunity to argue either way.

Knowing When to Claim
Your Capital Gain

A capital gain is realized and taxable when you sell a capital property. Prior to the time you actually sell the property, the gain is
unrealized, and therefore not taxable. However, there may be

times when you haven't actually sold the asset or received any proceeds, but you have triggered a capital gain because you have a deemed disposition.

Understanding deemed dispositions

What does "deemed" mean? In certain situations, the tax rules consider you to have sold or disposed of something when in the true economic sense you have not. A capital gain can be triggered along with a tax liability on the accrued gain. This can be quite harsh in terms of cash flow — remember, it's only a disposition for tax purposes. It doesn't mean you've received any cash, which you could use to pay your tax bill.

A deemed disposition occurs when you die. At that time you're considered to have sold everything you own for proceeds of disposition equal to the market value at the time of death — so any accrued gains are subject to tax. (An exception to this rule is when assets are bequeathed to a spouse.) Also, when you cease to be a resident of Canada, you're again considered to have disposed of everything you own (with a few exceptions), and tax would be payable on any accrued gains. Both dying and leaving Canada can be expensive in terms of taxes!

Some other situations in which you are deemed to have disposed of a capital property include when:

- ✔ You exchange one property for another.

- ✔ You give or donate property (other than cash).

- ✔ You transfer property to a trust — exceptions to this include transfers to an alter-ego (set up by an individual acting on his or her own) and joint spousal/partner trusts (set up by a couple in partnership). (For more on alter-ego and joint/spousal partner trusts, see Tip #73.)

- ✔ Your property is expropriated, stolen, or destroyed.

- ✔ An option that you hold to buy or sell property expires.

- ✔ You change all or part of a property's use (for example, you change your residence to a rental property, or vice versa).

You may think that just because you haven't received any proceeds from a sale, you have no capital gain (or loss) to report. A common example occurs when you give property to a family member. The problem is that for tax purposes you're deemed to have received proceeds equal to the market value of the property at the time of the gift. It doesn't matter how much cash — if any — actually changed hands.

Many individuals think they can sell a property, such as a cottage, to a friend or family member for $1 so no capital gain is incurred. Well, the selling individual may receive only $1, but for tax purposes he or she is considered to have received proceeds equal to the market value of the property at the time of the sale. It doesn't pay to be nice when it comes to the tax rules!

Understanding how units of a mutual fund can cause capital gains

If you own units of a mutual fund, capital gains can arise for you in two ways:

- ✔ When you sell your shares or units of the mutual fund, a capital gain (or loss) will result from the difference between your proceeds of disposition and the adjusted cost base of the investment.

- ✔ Capital gains realized by the mutual fund from its investment portfolio are usually "flowed out" to you as distributions. Expect to receive information slips from your investment dealer (a T3 or T5 slip) detailing the amounts to be reported.

Timing Sales to Minimize Tax

Because a capital gain is triggered upon a sale or deemed disposition, you generally have some control over the timing of the sale, and therefore your tax bill.

Consider triggering capital gains periodically in your open investment accounts, especially in years when your income is particularly low. Taxpayers with no other sources of income (such as minors, for whom you may have set up "in trust for" investment accounts) can trigger about $20,000 in capital gains (only $10,000, or 50 percent, is taxable) and not attract any tax. This is because each taxpayer has a basic personal tax credit worth about $10,000 to reduce taxes payable (actual amount increases annually). The advantage to this strategy is seen in the future when you actually sell the investment for good.

By triggering gains in years when you have low income, you manage to increase the tax cost of the investment. For example, say you have an investment with a current value of $10,000 and a purchase price, or tax cost, of $4,000. If you choose to trigger the capital gain on the investment this year, you will have a $3,000 taxable gain ($10,000 less $4,000 × 50 percent) to report on your tax return. Assuming you have no other sources of income, you'll face no tax on that gain. However, you've managed to increase the tax cost of the investment to $10,000. If you sell the investment for $12,000 next year, you'll be subject to tax on only 50 percent of that increase in value, or $1,000.

Maximizing Your Adjusted Cost Base

The adjusted cost base (ACB) is a very important figure when calculating your capital gain, because the higher your adjusted cost base the lower your capital gain — and therefore your tax bill. You want to make sure you include everything you can in the adjusted cost base to keep your taxes to a minimum.

The adjusted cost base of a property is usually the purchase price of the property plus any expenses incurred to acquire it, such as real estate commissions and legal fees. However, in many situations figuring out the adjusted cost base is a little more complicated. We give some examples here:

- ✔ If you make improvements to a property, such as a major overhaul of your family cottage, the cost of these improvements will increase the property's adjusted cost base.

- ✔ If you inherit property, or perhaps receive property as a gift, your adjusted cost base of the property will be the market value of that property on the day you took ownership of it (although special rules apply if you inherited the property from your spouse).

- ✔ If you're a newcomer to Canada, your adjusted cost base is the market value (not your purchase price) of your property on the day you became a Canadian resident for tax purposes.

- ✔ If you reinvest distributions — such as dividends in a dividend reinvestment program (DRIP), or mutual funds allocations where you received additional units rather than cash — these reinvestments increase your adjusted cost base. Think of it as receiving the cash and then using the cash to purchase additional shares or mutual fund units. The amount of your investment has increased, so your adjusted cost base should increase as well!

- ✔ If you elected to crystallize — or lock in — a capital gain back in 1994 to use your lifetime capital gains exemption, your adjusted cost base will be higher than the purchase price of the property. We discuss the 1994 capital gains election in the section "Lifetime Capital Gains Exemption" near the end of this tip.

Identical properties

You may have "identical properties" when over time you've purchased shares of the same class of a corporation or units of the
same mutual fund. To determine the adjusted cost base of identical properties sold, you have to calculate the average cost of each
property in the group at the time just prior to a sale taking place.
You determine the average cost by dividing the total cost of identical properties purchased by the total number of identical properties owned (that is, the number of shares or mutual fund units).

Partial dispositions of capital property

When you sell only part of a property, you have to divide the
adjusted cost base of the property between the part you sell and
the part you keep.

Graeme owns 100 hectares of vacant land with an adjusted cost base
of $100,000. He decides to sell 25 hectares of this land. Because 25
is ¼ of 100, Graeme calculates ¼ of the total ACB as follows:

Total ACB	$100,000
The ACB of the part sold ($100,000 × ¼) =	$ 25,000

Graeme's adjusted cost base for the 25 hectares he sold is $25,000.
The adjusted cost base of the remaining hectares is $75,000.

Using Selling Costs to Minimize Your Taxable Gains

You're allowed to deduct the costs incurred in selling a property
(referred to as "outlays and expenses") in calculating a capital
gain. These costs will cause a capital gain to be lower and a capital
loss to be greater.

Common selling costs include fixing-up expenses, finders' fees,
commissions, brokerage fees, surveying fees, legal fees, transfer
costs borne by the seller, and advertising costs.

Investigating the Capital Gains Reserve

When you sell a capital property, you usually receive full payment at that time. However, sometimes you receive the amount over a number of years. For example, you may sell a capital property for $50,000, receiving $10,000 when you sell it and the remaining $40,000 over the next four years. When this happens, you can claim a reserve, which allows you to shift or differ reporting a portion of the capital gain to a later year (or years). In other words, if you have not received the full selling price for your capital property in the year of sale, you don't need to pay all the tax on the capital gain right away! The reserve works as a deduction against the capital gain being reported.

To claim a reserve, you still calculate your capital gain for the year as the proceeds of disposition minus the adjusted cost base and the outlays and expenses involved in selling the property. From this amount, you deduct the amount of your reserve for the year to arrive at the amount of capital gains that will be subject to tax in the current year. What you end up with is the part of the capital gain that you have to report in the year of disposition. This is the part of the capital gain that will be taxed in the year.

The amount of reserve you can take in any particular year is the lesser of the following:

(Proceeds still to be paid/Total proceeds) × Gain

⅕ of the gain × (4 − # of preceding taxation years ending after disposition)

Did you catch all that? Let's take Finlay, for example. Finlay sold capital property this year for $200,000. However, he received only $20,000 upfront. The remaining $180,000 is not due until next year. The adjusted cost base of the property was $150,000. The total gain from the sale of the property is $50,000 ($200,000 proceeds less cost base of $150,000). However, because Finlay did not receive all the proceeds this year, he is eligible to claim a reserve.

This year, the year of sale, his reserve is the lesser of the following:

($180,000/$200,000) × $50,000 = $45,000

(⅕ × $50,000) × (4 − 0) = $40,000

Therefore, this year he can shelter a portion of the $50,000 gain with a $40,000 reserve. He will report only $10,000 of the gain.

Next year, he must include in his income the $40,000 reserve he claimed in the year of sale. Next year's reserve is the lesser of the following:

$0/\$200,000 \times \$50,000 = 0$

$(\frac{1}{5} \times \$50,000) \times (4 - 1) = \$30,000$

Therefore, next year Finlay cannot claim any reserve and must include in his income the remaining $40,000 of the capital gain. This makes sense because he received all the proceeds by the end of the year, so no further reserve should be permitted.

To deduct a reserve in any year, you have to complete form T2017, "Summary of Reserves on Dispositions of Capital Property." The information provided on the back of the form explains the limits on the number of years for which you can claim a reserve, and the amount of the reserve you can deduct. The calculations work such that you report the full capital gain by the end of the fourth year after the year you dispose of the capital property. Therefore, you pay the tax on the capital gain over a maximum period of five years, whether or not money is still owed to you after the five-year period. *Tip:* With respect to the sale of certain farm property, the reserve can be extended to 10 years where the purchaser is your child, grandchild, or great-grandchild.

Checking Out the Lifetime Capital Gains Exemption

Prior to February 23, 1994, everyone had a $100,000 personal capital gains exemption. This meant that every Canadian could generate up to $100,000 of capital gains during their lifetime (up to this date) and not pay tax on those gains. As the saying goes, all good things must come to an end; therefore, in order to get a final benefit from this exemption, in 1994 many people elected to use up their exemption and trigger a capital gain (on form T664, "Capital Gains Election").

If you used this election, you effectively sold capital property to yourself. The sale price chosen was usually a price between the adjusted cost base and the market value of the property — the idea was to trigger a capital gain that could be fully offset by the remaining amount of the $100,000 exemption. You were then considered to have repurchased the capital property at the same price, effectively increasing the adjusted cost base of the capital property so that when the property was actually sold, the capital gain would be that much less.

When selling an asset, be sure to check back to your 1994 tax return to see whether you elected to trigger any gain on the capital property sold. If so, your adjusted cost base will be higher than you think it is — and your capital gain, and tax bill, lower! One of the most common mistakes we see in tax returns is that the "new" adjusted cost bases as a result of making the $100,000 capital gains election is *not* used in calculating the capital gain, because people have forgotten about the election. The original adjusted cost base is used, resulting in the capital gain and tax liability being overstated.

Make the Most of Capital Losses

*W*e all hate to lose money on an investment — and, over time this is a reality many of us will face. However, you can use losses to reduce your current-year taxes and even to get back some of the tax you paid in prior years!

Keep in mind that the losses must be in a non-registered, or open, investment account. Losses in your RRSP or RRIF account are not deductible.

What Is a Capital Loss?

You have a capital loss when you sell, or are deemed to have sold, a capital property such as a stock, bond, mutual fund, or piece of real estate for less than its adjusted cost base and the selling costs.

As we discuss in Tip #38, only 50 percent of capital gains are taxable. In line with this rule, only 50 percent of capital losses are deductible; but there's a catch: capital losses are deductible only against capital gains.

Offsetting Capital Gains with Capital Losses

Capital losses will benefit you for tax purposes only when you have capital gains to offset. Capital gains cannot be used against your other types of income.

In Tip #38 we give the example of Lynne, who incurred a capital gain of $3,920 on her sale of 1,000 shares of Public Corporation Limited. Let's say she also sold 1,000 shares of Private Corporation Limited for $4,000 later in the same tax year. Her adjusted cost base of these shares was $5,000 and she paid selling commissions of $50. In other words, Lynne had both a capital gain and a capital loss this year. Lynne would calculate her total capital gains and taxable capital gains as follows:

Capital gain on sale of 1,000 shares of Public Corporation Limited
$3,920

Capital loss on sale of 1,000 shares of Private Corporation Limited

Proceeds of disposition	$4,000
Less: Adjusted cost base	($5,000)
Less: Outlays and expenses	($ 50)
Capital loss	($1,050)
Net capital gains	$ 2,870

Lynne enters her taxable capital gains — 50 percent of the net of her capital gains and losses in the year — at the bottom of schedule 3 and on line 127 of her tax return.

50 percent of $2,870 $ 1,435

What if a taxpayer has only capital losses?

So, what happens when the only share sale Lynne had in the year was the sale of the 1,000 shares of Private Corporation Limited? She would report the $1,050 capital loss on schedule 3, and at the bottom of schedule 3 she would report a net capital loss of $525 (50 percent of $1,050).

Can Lynne carry the loss to line 127 of her return so the loss is effectively deducted against her other sources of income (employment income, interest income, and so on) in calculating her taxable income? Would it not be logical that if 50 percent of capital gains are subject to tax, then 50 percent of capital losses should be deductible in computing taxable income? (We wish it would!)

Sadly, it doesn't work that way. Lynne cannot carry the net capital loss of $525 to line 127 because line 127 is for taxable capital gains only. However, Lynne has other options. She can't get any tax relief this year from the loss because she has no gains to offset the loss against. However, if she has reported taxable capital gains on her tax return in any or all of the prior three years, the net capital loss can be "carried back" to those years to be applied against the taxable capital gains she reported previously. Doing this will result in a tax refund for the year or years to which Lynne has carried back the net capital loss.

Say Lynne reported taxable capital gains of $300 three years ago, $2,500 two years ago, and none last year. In filing her current return, Lynne would include form T1A, "Request for Loss Carryback," indicating she wanted $300 of her current net capital loss of $525 to be carried back or applied against the gains from three years ago, and the remaining $225 to be applied against the taxable capital gains from two years ago. The CRA will reassess Lynne's prior-year returns and issue her a refund cheque for these years, as the loss application reduces the taxable capital gains that were subject to tax in those years.

You must use form T1A to request net capital loss carrybacks. Don't file amended tax returns for the years in which the taxable capital gains were reported!

Losses can be carried back to a previous year only to the extent they cannot be used to reduce gains realized in the current year.

In most circumstances, request that net capital losses be carried back to the third previous year if you reported taxable capital gains in that year. This will be your last chance to recoup taxes paid on capital gains from that year, because losses can be carried back for only three years.

What if a taxpayer has not reported taxable capital gains in the last three years?

Can Lynne get any tax relief from her current-year net capital loss if she has not reported any taxable capital gains in the last three years? Yes! Any net capital loss that cannot be carried back to a prior year can be carried forward to a subsequent year and be applied against taxable capital gains reported in those years. No time limit is placed on using the losses.

If Lynne doesn't incur a taxable capital gain until a future year, she can apply the current net capital loss against the taxable capital gain reported in that year. It would be reported on line 253, "Net capital losses of other years," on Lynne's future return. The loss carryforward would not impact the schedule 3 filed with Lynne's future or the amount she would report on that year's line 127.

Watching Out for the Superficial Loss Rules

Sell your losing investments only if you no longer like them and do not wish to repurchase that same investment for at least 30 days after the sale. If you repurchase the same investment within 30 days, your loss will be denied. For the techies out there, these are known as the "superficial loss rules." If you want to purchase the investment back, wait for 31 days between settlement dates.

Consider selling your loss investment and then contributing the proceeds to your RRSP up to your contribution room limit. This will trigger the loss for tax purposes while also providing you with cash to put into your RRSP — for even more tax relief! Do not directly transfer the investment into your RRSP: a capital loss in this case is considered to be nil by the *Income Tax Act.* You also cannot repurchase that same investment you sold for a loss within your RRSP for at least 30 days. This is also a superficial loss, which means your loss will be . . . well . . . lost. Instead, choose a different investment altogether inside your registered account, or wait until your 30-day period is up.

Exploring the Special Rules in the Year of Death

Normally capital losses can be carried forward indefinitely to offset capital gains generated into the future. However, upon death no more tax returns will be filed for the deceased, meaning the capital losses may be permanently lost.

A special tax rule is in place to assist in this situation. If a taxpayer dies with unused net capital losses of earlier years, these losses can be deducted against any type of income, such as employment income, interest income, or pension income reported in the year of death as well as in the year preceding death. The amount deductible will be restricted if the taxpayer had ever claimed the capital gains exemption.

Use Insurance Products as Investments

• •

*L*ife insurance is commonly used to cover tax liabilities on death and to help provide a source of income for heirs. However, some products available through life insurance companies can help you manage your current tax bill as well.

Investing inside a Life Insurance Policy

If you purchase a "permanent" life insurance policy, such as a universal life policy, you can combine your insurance coverage with a side investment fund. From a tax standpoint, this side fund works very much like an RRSP in that the investments inside grow tax free and you won't face a tax bill until the funds are withdrawn or the policy is surrendered (you don't get a tax deduction for amounts put into the fund, though). Most universal life policies have a decent selection of investments to choose from, which means that the investment component of the policy has the potential to grow at a respectable rate of return.

 Unlimited, tax-sheltered growth sounds too good to be true — and it is. Our tax law places a ceiling on the amount that can be in the investment account, and you'll be charged penalties if you build up too much investment in your side fund. Your insurance company will work with you to ensure you stay onside.

This type of strategy isn't for everyone. Because you'll have to pay premiums for insurance, you must weigh these costs against the benefits of tax-free growth. However, if you already need insurance, the investments are a nice add-on feature. Of course, this strategy is based on the presumption that you're insurable.

Life insurance proceeds (including any investments held within the policy) received on the death of the insured are received tax free.

Create Tax-Efficient Income with Annuities

If you're retired, or are approaching retirement, you may be concerned about generating stable income from your non-registered investments. Many decide they want to play it safe and choose fixed-income products like GICs. One problem with a full fixed-income portfolio is that the interest income is highly taxed at your marginal rate, which could be up to 50 percent of the income earned!

Enter annuities. *Annuities* are investment contracts you establish with a life insurance company. In return for an initial deposit, the contract will provide you with level and guaranteed payments for a certain time period, or for life. Part of the payment to you is taxable, but not all of it, which is why an annuity enhances your after-tax cash flow.

It's possible to purchase an annuity with registered funds. In that case, the entire annuity payment to you is taxable, just like any other payment out of the RRSP or RRIF.

The taxation of the annuity depends on the type of annuity you hold. In a non-registered account, you can have a prescribed or non-prescribed annuity. In either case, part of the payment to you is taxable as interest income, and part is considered a tax-free payment of your initial capital. With a *prescribed annuity* you'll have a level taxable portion each year, which is great for planning for your tax bill. It can also allow for some deferral of taxes because the taxable portion in the earlier years is less than it would be under a non-prescribed annuity. With a *non-prescribed annuity,* you'll have more taxable interest income in the early years, and very little in later years. Your insurance company will help determine the right taxable versus non-taxable portion.

Report the interest income earned from an annuity at line 121, unless you're 65 years of age or older and receiving retirement income, in which case you report the interest at line 115, "Other pensions or superannuation."

Let's look at an example. Lou has $250,000 to invest. He's looking at a fixed-income investment that will pay him 4.5 percent, but he is taxed at a 40 percent marginal tax rate. With that investment, he would earn $940 per month, but would net only $565 after tax. If Lou instead purchased a life annuity with his $250,000, his monthly

Income would increase to $1,740 and his net after-tax income would increase to $1,620!

An annuity purchase is not reversible. You're giving up your capital in return for the guaranteed income payments. Ensure you're fully aware of the features of the annuity before you sign on the dotted line.

If you want to preserve your capital for your estate, you can purchase an insured annuity that will add permanent life insurance coverage onto your contract. Let's say Lou added this feature to his annuity. If $250,000 of insurance coverage was purchased with a cost of $551 per month, his net after-tax income would still be $1,070, almost double what it was with his original fixed-income investment, and his chosen beneficiaries would receive a $250,000 payment on his death.

Your particular numbers will differ from those shown here depending on your age, insurability, and other factors.

Knowing When Segregated Funds Make Sense

Segregated funds are similar in many respects to mutual funds, where your investment dollars are pooled with those of other investors and managed by a fund manager. Segregated funds are offered by insurance companies, and therefore have added insurance benefits not offered by traditional mutual funds.

The actual benefits you receive depend on the terms of your insurance contract. At a minimum, the contract will offer you a guarantee of at least 75 percent of your initial investment deposit at fund maturity or the death of the policy holder. Some guarantee up to 100 percent. In addition, some segregated funds allow you to lock in investment increases and base the future guarantee on this reset value.

Segregated funds offer some non-tax benefits including creditor-proofing in certain situations. This is often important for business owners or professionals who are afraid of being sued, and want to protect their savings in the case of a lawsuit. Another benefit is the ability to pass the assets outside of probate, which can save on probate fees on death in provinces where these fees are high. (For more on probate, see Tip #74.)

From a tax standpoint segregated funds allocate income to investors each year, so you can expect to pay tax on dividends, capital gains, and interest. Segregated funds can also allocate out capital losses (mutual funds cannot), so investors will benefit from any losses realized by the seg fund if the investor has capital gains to offset. The income is allocated on a time-weighted basis, so if you held the seg fund for only a portion of the year your income allocations will be prorated. Again, this is not available with a mutual fund.

Any top ups offered by the contract in the form of resets or guarantees are not taxable at the time they are given to the investor. Instead, they may be taxable only when the fund is sold, or on death. Consider Sue, who invested $10,000 in a seg fund that guaranteed 75 percent of the value upon maturity in 15 years. In 15 years, the fund was worth only $5,000. The seg fund would top up her fund to $7,500 (75% of the initial investment of $10,000). If she continued to hold the fund, this top up would not be taxable at this time. It would be taxable when the fund is sold or on Sue's death.

Upon sale or upon death, the difference between the proceeds of disposition and adjusted cost base of a seg fund is taxable as a capital gain.

If you dispose of your seg fund for proceeds equal to or less than the adjusted cost base plus selling costs, you'll have no net tax bill, even if a maturity or death benefit was paid. This is because you did not receive proceeds of more than you invested.

Invest in a Tax-Free Savings Account

*T*here's a new type of investment account in town, and the name says it all. The Tax-Free Savings Account (TFSA) introduced in 2009 allows Canadians aged 18 plus to save funds in a tax-friendly way. Its uses are many, and in our opinion all Canadians should have one where possible.

Discovering Why TFSAs Are So Tax Friendly

What's so neat about the TFSA? Well, the tax-free part! After you set up a TFSA, you can make investments inside the account. You don't get a tax deduction for the actual contribution into the TFSA (like you would for an RRSP), but the investments you purchase with the contribution can grow tax-free and any income earned on the investments, such as dividends and interest, is also tax free.

You're able to contribute to a TFSA for your spouse without having to worry about attribution rules (which would normally tax investment earnings back to you). Because a TFSA is not taxable to start with, no attributable earnings exist. So, if you can, maximize contributions to both your and your spouse's TFSA annually.You can also fund a TFSA for an adult child without any tax worries.

Withdrawals from your TFSA are not subject to tax. This is much different from an RRSP, where the full withdrawal is taxed at your marginal tax rate. Therefore, TFSAs are very useful for those trying to manage a tax bill, such as high income earners, and seniors who are trying to avoid the OAS (Tip # 64) or age credit (Tip # 67) clawbacks.

Considering the Uses for a TFSA

Due to its flexibility, the TFSA has a variety of applications including:

- ✔ **Short-term or emergency-type savings:** Normally you would put these funds into a cash-like equivalent such as a money market fund or a high-interest savings account. A TFSA will shelter the highly taxed interest income from tax but will allow you easy access to the funds when needed.

- ✔ **Retirement savings:** RRSPs are highly taxed upon withdrawal, and non-registered investment account withdrawals may also give rise to tax if accrued gains exist in the account. It's helpful to supplement the savings with a TFSA so that you have access to some tax-free income in retirement. Plus, because earnings can grow tax free, you don't have to worry about tax draining your investment returns.

- ✔ **Education savings:** RESPs are a tax-efficient way to save for a child's education (Tip #57); however, limits exist to what you can contribute, and if the child does not go to school penalties may apply. If you're looking to supplement your child's education, you can save in a TFSA and withdraw the funds when your child goes to school.

- ✔ **Estate planning:** Wealthy individuals may have more investment savings than they will use during their lifetimes. On death, they may plan to leave their assets to family members or friends. Instead of paying tax on the investment income each year (some of which you might not even need), and potential tax and probate fees on death, you might wish to start giving away assets during your lifetime.

- ✔ **The TFSA can be used twofold in this process:**

  - You can establish a TFSA for yourself, and depending on your province you can possibly name a beneficiary on the account, which makes this an efficient way to transfer those assets later on.

  - You might choose to set up TFSAs for your heirs now, and fully fund them each year. Perhaps tell them that you will continue to fund the TFSAs as long as they don't make withdrawals out of the accounts! You've managed to pass assets on now, in a tax-efficient way.

 A TFSA is a good location for any interest-bearing investments you would like to hold, particularly if you're a highly taxed individual, because the tax rate on interest income is so much higher than the rate on dividends or capital gains.

Adding Up the Contribution Limits

All Canadian residents age 18 or older are entitled to $5,000 of contribution room in a TFSA each year. The contribution room is not income tested. If you don't have the funds to make a contribution in a particular year, your room will carry forward. So, for example, if you didn't use your $5,000 of room in 2009, you'll have $10,000 of room to use in 2010. The room carries forward indefinitely. No age limit is placed on a TFSA.

The contribution room is set to increase annually to the rate of inflation and will increase in $500 increments.

In some provinces (currently Newfoundland and Labrador, New Brunswick, Nova Scotia, British Columbia, and the territories), the age of majority is 19. In those areas you cannot open a TFSA until you're the age of majority. However, the contribution room accumulates from age 18, so your overall ability to contribute to the TFSA doesn't change, just your timing.

Withdrawals from a TFSA are not taxable, either. What's more, if you make a withdrawal from your TFSA more room opens up. Say you contribute $5,000 to your TFSA in 2009 and in 2010 you want to remove some funds to go on a vacation. The account at that time contains $5,300; $5,000 of your initial contribution and $300 of growth. You can withdraw the whole $5,300 tax-free and open up another $5,300 of contribution room for future years!

Shopping Around for TFSAs

TFSAs can be set up at pretty much any bank, credit union, or financial services provider in Canada such as an investment dealer or life insurance company. Make sure the financial institution can offer you the types of investments you wish to hold in the TFSA. For example, a bank will be able to offer you investments such as mutual funds, GICs, money market funds, and the like; an investment dealer may be able to add in publicly traded stocks and bonds.

You can make the same types of investments in your TFSA as are allowed in your RRSP. However, you do have to make sure the financial institution you work with is licensed to sell the types of investments you want.

It's possible to establish more than one TFSA, but keep in mind that if you go over your contribution limit the CRA can charge penalties.

Here are some questions to ask before determining where you want to set up your TFSA:

✔ What types of investments do you offer?

✔ What fees do you charge, such as account opening costs, transaction fees, monthly or annual maintenance fees, or any special product-related fees?

✔ Will I get investment advice, or do I make my own investment choices?

✔ What other services come with my TFSA, including financial planning help?

Invest in an RRSP

• •

*N*ext to the ability to sell your house tax free due to the principal residence exemption, the RRSP is Canada's best tax shelter. Many people believe a tax shelter is some very creative tax-planning idea available only to the wealthy. Not true! Almost every taxpayer who has a job or is self-employed can take advantage of RRSPs. In this tip, we tell you how.

What Is an RRSP?

To easily understand what a registered retirement savings plan (RRSP) is, think of it as your own personal pension plan that has been CRA approved ("registered").

An RRSP is an arrangement that allows you to save for your retirement on a tax-friendly basis when you've earned certain types of income but haven't necessarily been able to contribute to an employer's pension plan. You control when contributions are made to your plan, the investments made in the plan, and when withdrawals are made (at least up until age 71).

Tax Savings Provided by RRSPs

The government wants you to save for your retirement. To encourage this, an RRSP offers two main tax advantages:

- ✔ A tax deduction for contributions made to an RRSP
- ✔ Tax-free growth while the funds remain in the RRSP

With an RRSP, no tax is payable until you make a withdrawal from your plan. You hope that the tax payable on RRSP withdrawals will be less than the tax saved when you took the deduction for making an RRSP contribution. This will occur if you're in a lower tax bracket during your retirement years than the tax bracket you were in when you made your RRSP contributions.

A better idea is to have the withdrawal taxed in your spouse's hands if he or she is in a lower tax bracket than you are at the time of the withdrawal. This is especially advantageous when you already have significant retirement income (say, pension income from an RPP) and your spouse has little. We know this sounds too good to be true, but you can do it by making spousal RRSP contributions. We discuss spousal RRSP contributions in this tip.

 In addition to spousal RRSPs, seniors can take advantage of pension-splitting legislation to pay less tax on certain RRSP withdrawals. You must be at least age 65 to use pension income splitting. Check out Tip #68 for the lowdown.

Setting Up an RRSP

You can set up an RRSP in many places: a bank, a trust company, through your investment planner, or online through a direct investing account. It's as simple as filling out a form and handing over the money. After you contribute to the RRSP, you'll be provided with an official RRSP receipt. This is what you'll use to support the RRSP deduction you claim on your tax return.

 Are you reading this after December 31? Don't worry — it may not be too late to set up an RRSP and get a tax deduction for last year's tax return! Contributions made to an RRSP within 60 days of the new year qualify for a tax deduction on your last year's tax return. (Neat, eh?)

Determining How Much You Can Contribute

By now you might be convinced that an RRSP would be a great way to save for your retirement and to gain some tax benefits. So, why not sell the farm, so to speak, and put all your net worth into the RRSP? Well, slow down, Nelly. Not just anyone can set up an RRSP, and limits apply to how much you can contribute.

Generally, any person who has "earned income" in Canada can contribute to an RRSP. The amount that you're allowed to contribute is based on a formula involving three numbers:

- 18 percent of your prior year's "earned income," to a dollar limit maximum set by the Department of Finance (the maximum for 2009 was $21,000)

- Less your pension adjustment, PA, if you're a member of a registered pension plan

- Plus the pension adjustment reversal, PAR, which might occur if you're a member of a registered pension plan

Understanding earned income and how it is calculated

The main consideration in determining your RRSP deduction limit is 18 percent of your prior year's "earned income." For purposes of determining your RRSP deduction limit, earned income consists of the following:

✔ Your salary, including taxable benefits (box 14 of your T4)

✔ Self-employed business income

✔ Rental income and royalty income

✔ Taxable spouse and child-support payments received

✔ Amounts from supplementary unemployment benefit plans

✔ Research grants

✔ CPP and QPP disability pension

To compute earned income, deduct the following:

✔ Union or professional dues deducted on your tax return (line 212)

✔ Employment expenses deducted on your tax return (line 229)

✔ Losses from self-employment

✔ Losses from rental operations

✔ Support payments deducted on your tax return (line 220)

Knowing the limit set by the Department of Finance

As we mention earlier, the maximum amount you can contribute to an RRSP in a given year is limited by earned income and amounts set by the government.

The maximum amount you may contribute to your RRSP will increase in future years (although you're still limited to 18 percent of your earned income). The 2009 limit is $21,000. The limits are scheduled to rise as follows:

2010	$22,000
2011	Indexed to inflation

If you did not make your full RRSP contribution for any year from 1991 on, this unused entitlement carries forward.

You can make RRSP contributions up to the end of the year you turn 71. Prior to 2007, you could make contributions only until the end of the year you turned 69.

Finding out your RRSP contribution limit

You can find out your RRSP contribution limit in four ways:

- **Look at your Notice of Assessment.** You receive this assessment from the CRA after filing your return. Your current year's RRSP contribution limit is highlighted on the assessment.

- **Call the TIPS (Tax Information Phone Service) toll-free number** (1-800-267-6999) and ask what your limit is.

- **Calculate it yourself.**

- **Go to My Account on the CRA Web site** (www.cra-arc.gc.ca).

Exploring Your Investment Choices for an RRSP

An RRSP is not an investment in itself; the money you put into it must be used to purchase investments. The contribution you make to your RRSP is usually in cash. You can leave the RRSP in cash if you want, but you'll get little to no future return on your money. Instead, it's a good idea to invest the funds according to your risk tolerance, so you can maximize the eventual amount you'll have to withdraw in retirement. Discuss your needs with the person you meet with to set up your RRSP.

For the most choice and flexibility in your RRSP investing, consider a "self-directed RRSP." Don't worry — "self-directed" doesn't mean you're on your own. You can work with your investment advisor to decide which investments are appropriate for your RRSP given your investment goals and risk-tolerance levels. For example, you may choose to hold a variety of mutual funds, stocks, bonds, other specialty investments, or even cash in your RRSP.

An annual cost to maintain a self-directed RRSP applies; to justify this cost, wait until your RRSP assets reach $20,000 before setting up this type of plan.

The following is a list of investments you may hold inside your RRSP:

- ✔ Cash, guaranteed investment certificates, term deposits, and Treasury bills

- ✔ Canada Savings Bonds, Canada RRSP bonds, and government bonds

- ✔ Publicly traded shares and bonds, warrants, options, and Canadian limited partnerships. You can hold Canadian or foreign investments without limit.

- ✔ Certain private-corporation shares, as long as you and your family own less than 10 percent

- ✔ Mutual funds, segregated funds, and labour-sponsored funds

- ✔ Certain mortgages, including a mortgage on your own home (although special rules apply)

- ✔ Investment-grade gold and silver bullion coins and bars (great news for all you pirates out there!)

If your RRSP holds an ineligible investment, it will be subject to a tax of 1 percent per month on the value of the ineligible investment.

RRSP Contributions in Kind

Wanna set up an RRSP or contribute to an existing RRSP, but find yourself short on funds? Well, provided you already own an investment that's eligible for an RRSP (we provide a list above), why not contribute the investment itself to your RRSP? This is called a *contribution in kind*. But be careful. If you contribute an investment that has gone up in value from the time you acquired it, a capital gain will be triggered that will be taxed on your return. If the investment has gone down in value, you would think you would be entitled to a capital loss. No such luck. Why not? Because the taxman says so.

If you're thinking about contributing investments that have declined in value, then sell the investment, claim the loss, and donate the cash. This way, you won't lose out on claiming the capital loss. Don't repurchase that same investment back in the RRSP, though — this will mean you still won't be allowed to claim your capital loss. Instead, use the cash to repurchase something similar (but not the identical investment) — or, if you'd prefer, something totally different — inside your RRSP.

Overcontributing to an RRSP

Generally, the amount you contribute to your RRSP will be equal to the RRSP deduction you take on line 208 of your return. However, the total amount you have contributed to your RRSP may exceed the amount you claim as a deduction when you do one of the following:

- ✔ **You accidentally overcontribute to your RRSP:** You're permitted to overcontribute to your RRSP. However, the overcontribution is not tax deductible in the year it's made. And if your overcontribution exceeds $2,000, you'll find yourself in a penalty situation if you don't withdraw the excess contribution. The penalty is 1 percent per month of the overcontribution in excess of $2,000 — that amounts to 12 percent per year!

- ✔ Many people will overcontribute by exactly $2,000, because there is no penalty and the funds can earn income inside the RRSP tax free. Moreover, the $2,000 can be deducted on a subsequent year's tax return where you may not have contributed up to your maximum.

- ✔ A major undertaking by the tax authorities to review RRSP overcontributions is underway. So, even if your overcontribution has gone unnoticed in the past, this may not continue to be the case. We recommend you fix the problem now either by forgoing some future contributions (allowing you to deduct your overcontribution amounts) or by withdrawing the excess. You need to fill out special forms to ensure the withdrawal is not taxable, though.

- ✔ **You don't deduct some or all of the RRSP contribution you have made.** Why would you not take a tax deduction when it's available? Well, you may plan on being in a higher tax bracket in the future. Even though you make an RRSP contribution during the year, you don't need to take the deduction that same year. You can save the deduction for a tax year when the deduction is more valuable. You don't have to worry about those pesky penalties in this situation.

Making Special One-Time RRSP Contributions

Some special situations exist where you're permitted to make additional RRSP contributions, or where you may choose to overcontribute for future tax savings.

Receiving a retiring allowance

If you're going to receive a severance or retiring allowance from an employer you worked for since before 1996, you may be able to put all or a portion of the payment directly into your RRSP. (Sorry, it can't go into a spousal RRSP.) This is referred to as a "transfer," and it's attractive for two reasons:

- ✔ No income tax needs to be withheld on the portion of the payment being transferred directly into your RRSP. A direct transfer means the cheque goes from your employer to your RRSP — you don't even get to touch the money!

- ✔ The portion transferred to your RRSP is in addition to your regular RRSP contribution limit. You can still contribute up to your RRSP contribution limit, in addition to the portion of the severance transferred to your RRSP.

 It's not critical that you roll your retiring allowance directly into your RRSP — this transfer can be made later. But be sure to make the contribution within 60 days following the end of the year in which you received your payment. If you don't contribute before this time, the special contribution room is lost forever!

 If any portion of your retiring allowance or severance cannot be transferred directly to your RRSP, consider using it to make a regular RRSP contribution (or a spousal contribution). In fact, you can ask your employer to directly transfer your ineligible retiring allowance into your RRSP and no tax has to be taken off the payment.

Seniors overcontribution

The tax rules require you to wind up your RRSP by December 31 in the year you turn 71. However, you might still work and have earned income and therefore RRSP contribution room that you won't be able to utilize. Instead of wasting contribution room that's accumulated in years after the age of 71, an additional contribution can be made in the year you turn 71. The contribution should be made as late in the year as possible; December is best.

Provided you've already maximized your RRSP contributions to date, an additional contribution will result in an overcontribution. The CRA charges a penalty of 1 percent per month on the overcontribution in excess of $2,000. This means that an overcontribution of $21,000 made in December would attract a penalty of $190. (Calculated as $21,000 less the allowable contribution of $2,000 times 1 percent.) Come January 1 of the year after you turn 71, you'll be entitled to RRSP contribution room based on your earned income of the previous year. Therefore, your excess contribution will be used up, and the penalty stops accruing.

How will this benefit you? Well, assuming your marginal tax rate is 45%, a contribution of $21,000 will save you $9,450 of tax, a saving well worth the $190 penalty. In addition, you'll reap the benefits of tax-free compounding.

Using a Spousal RRSP for More Tax Savings

When you make your RRSP contribution, you have the option of putting the contribution in your own RRSP or in a spousal RRSP, or a combination thereof. A spousal RRSP is an RRSP to which you contribute the funds, although your spouse is the one who receives the funds when withdrawn. This means your spouse — not you — makes withdrawals from the plan and pays tax on those withdrawals.

Ideally, both you and your spouse should have equal incomes in retirement. Make a spousal contribution if your spouse will be in a lower tax bracket than you when the money is eventually withdrawn. This way, you get the reduction at a high tax rate, and your spouse pays the tax at a lower one.

But beware: If your spouse makes a withdrawal from a spousal plan in the same year or within two calendar years of when you last made a spousal RRSP contribution, you — not your spouse — will be subject to the tax on the amount of the withdrawal that relates to contributions you made during this three-year period.

You're not entitled to additional RRSP contribution room in order to make a spousal contribution. The total contributions to your own plan, plus your spouse's, cannot be greater than your total RRSP contribution limit. (Your spouse's contribution limit does not affect how much you can contribute to a spousal RRSP.)

Now that pension income splitting is allowed on RRSP withdrawals for those over age 65, you might wonder whether spousal RRSPs are obsolete. We say no! Where your spouse has little or no income, you can benefit from using both spousal RRSPs and pension income splitting. With a spousal RRSP, all the income from that plan can be taxed in your spouse's hands. With pension splitting, a maximum of 50 percent of the withdrawals can be taxed to your spouse. Having a spousal RRSP therefore provides you with more income-splitting options for the long term.

#43

Manage Your RRSP and RRIF Withdrawals

. . . .

*A*s we discuss in Tip #42, registered retirement savings plans (RRSPs) are government-sanctioned plans that Canadians can use to save for their retirement. RRSPs are tax friendly because you get a tax deduction for contributions you make to the plan (within limits), and earnings within the plan grow free of tax — that is, until you make withdrawals. You can choose when you want to make withdrawals unless the plan is considered locked in. You might have guessed that at the point you make withdrawals you have income to report on your tax return.

A registered retirement income fund (RRIF) is created when you convert your RRSP — which must be done by the end of the year in which you turn 71 (although you could do it earlier). When your RRSP is converted to an RRIF, you're *required* to make annual taxable withdrawals (withdrawals from an RRSP are optional). RRIF withdrawals, like RRSP withdrawals, are taxable.

Investigating How Your RRSP and RRIF Withdrawals Are Taxed

After you've placed funds in an RRSP, you're generally able to withdraw those funds whenever you want. However, we don't normally recommend you make withdrawals prior to retirement. Because your RRSP assets are supposed to help fund your retirement, you'll be taxed on the withdrawals. You may choose to withdraw funds on a tax-preferred basis, though, using the Home Buyers' Plan or the Lifelong Learning Plan. We talk about these plans in this tip.

Withdrawals prior to RRSP maturity

Unless you've locked in funds, you're allowed to withdraw funds from your RRSP whenever you want. However, the amount of the withdrawal is included in your income and is fully taxable, just like a salary or interest. This means the tax hit could be quite severe.

In addition, these withdrawals will be subject to withholding tax at source. See Table 3-3 for the required withholdings. This means the financial institution where you hold your RRSP is obligated to take some tax off the payment being made to you, and then remit that tax to the CRA on your behalf. You'll receive a T4RSP at tax time outlining the amount of taxable payment made to you, as well as the amount of tax withheld. Report the full RRSP withdrawal amount on line 129 of your tax return, and the withheld tax on line 437.

Table 3-3	Withholding Tax Amounts at Source	
Withdrawal Amount	**Province other than Quebec**	**Quebec**
$0–$5,000	10%	21%
$5,001–$15,000	20%	26%
$15,000 and over	30%	31%

In many cases the amount of withholding tax will not be enough to cover your actual tax liability when you file your tax return, so you'll want to make sure you keep enough money on hand to pay your tax bill in April. For example, say you live in British Columbia and you expect your total income for the year to be $40,000. You want to take $5,000 out of your RRSP this year to go on a vacation to Mexico (not that we recommend a withdrawal for this purpose!). You can expect to pay about 30 percent tax on this withdrawal, or about $1,500. If only 10 percent of tax ($500) was withheld for taxes when the withdrawal was made (which is the required amount in all provinces but Quebec), you'll have to come up with just over $1,000 when you file your tax return next year. Something to ponder over your margarita.

Withdrawals from spousal RRSPs

A spousal RRSP is an RRSP that you've contributed to but that names your spouse as the "annuitant." This means that all retirement funds out of this RRSP will belong to your spouse and not to you, the contributor (although you do get the upfront tax deduction). A spousal RRSP is usually used by individuals who have much higher incomes than their spouses and wish to "split" their retirement income rather than have the entire amount included in their income.

A withdrawal from a spousal RRSP has very special rules that seek to dissuade individuals from placing money in a spousal RRSP and then withdrawing it soon after, to take advantage of the spouse's lower marginal tax rate. If these rules are violated, the income will be attributed back to the contributing spouse, which means it will be added to his or her income and taxed at that person's marginal tax rate instead. This would be the same outcome had that person contributed to his or her own RRSP and then withdrawn the funds.

If your spouse withdraws money from a spousal RRSP that you've contributed to in the year or in the previous two years, the withdrawal will be taxed in your hands and must be included on line 129 of your return. It does not matter if your spouse's name is on the T-slip! For example, if your spouse withdraws money from a spousal RRSP in 2010 that you contributed to in 2010, 2009, or 2008, the withdrawal will be included in your income, not your spouse's.

If the contributor is separated from his or her spouse, or was deceased at the time funds were withdrawn, the government will not attribute the income back to the contributor.

Contribute to a spousal RRSP at the end of the year (instead of on January 1) to reduce the waiting time on withdrawals from three years to just over two.

Withdrawals of unused contributions or overcontributions to an RRSP

Sometimes taxpayers are a little overzealous when it comes to contributing to their RRSPs. However (as you can imagine), we're not allowed to put unlimited amounts into our retirement savings plans. When you put more than you're allowed into your RRSP, you are said to have overcontributed.

Other taxpayers contribute within the allowable limits, but decide for one reason or another not to deduct the contribution on their tax return. This is referred to as having an undeducted contribution.

It may make sense to create an undeducted contribution when you find yourself in an unusually low tax bracket. If you save the RRSP deduction for a year when your marginal tax bracket is higher, your tax deduction will be worth more. To do this, you still include the contribution on the RRSP deduction workchart (line C), but then simply choose to not claim the deduction this year (line D). This will result in the calculation of an undeducted contribution on line G of the workchart. By including the contribution on this year's tax return, you ensure the CRA knows the contribution was made, and avoid problems in future years when you actually want to claim the deduction.

Generally, any withdrawals of contributions to your RRSP, even those that exceed your contribution limit, are reported on line 129 and taxed as income. This is the case even when you withdraw any undeducted contributions to the RRSP! Luckily, relieving provisions exist that allow you an offsetting deduction against these income inclusions. (After all, you didn't get a deduction for the contribution, so why should you pay tax on the withdrawal?)

Time limits exist, however. Specifically, you must withdraw the overcontribution in the year the contribution was made or in the following year, or in the year an assessment is issued for the year the contribution was made or for the following year. For example, if you made the overcontribution in 2010, you have to take it out of your RRSP in 2010 or 2011 to be entitled to the offsetting deduction. If your 2010 tax return is assessed in 2011 (as it probably will be), you then have the added option of removing the overcontribution by the end of 2012 to take advantage of the tax relief. These tight timeframes make it very important to remove the overcontribution from your RRSP as soon as you find out about it. If you wait too long, you'll be taxed on the withdrawal or will face penalties for the overcontribution. Neither is a very positive outcome.

If you're going to withdraw your RRSP overcontribution, use form T3012A, "Tax Reduction Waiver on the Refund of Your Undeducted RRSP Contribution." When you submit this form to the CRA, it will direct your financial institution not to withhold tax on the withdrawal of funds. If you withdraw funds without form T3012A, the issuer of the plan will withhold tax. In this case, use form T746, "Calculating Your Deduction for Refund of Undeducted RRSP Contributions," to calculate the amount of your tax deduction given that you have already paid withholding tax.

Withdrawals after age 71

An RRSP matures on December 31 of the year you reach 71 years of age. At this time, the government requires you to convert your RRSP to a *registered retirement income fund* (RRIF) or an annuity. You can also choose to convert early if you wish to earn a retirement income.

Withdrawing from your RRIF

The transfer of the assets in your RRSP to your RRIF can take place without triggering any current tax. You simply need to contact the financial institution where your RRSP is held, or your financial advisor, to request your RRSP be converted to an RRIF. They will take care of the required paperwork.

Like the RRSP, the RRIF earns income, tax free, inside the plan. An RRIF is different from an RRSP, however, in that you can no longer contribute to the plan, and you must make a minimum income withdrawal from the plan each year following the year in which the RRIF was established. The minimum withdrawals can be paid monthly, quarterly, semi-annually, or annually. All RRIF withdrawals are considered taxable income.

You're allowed to withdraw as much as you want from your RRIF each year (unless it's locked in), but you must take at least a minimum payment. The minimum payments are legislated and are based on your age and the RRIF value at the end of the previous year. For example, the year after you turn 71 you must take at least 7.38 percent of the value. The year after you turn 90 you have to take at least 13.62 percent of the value.

Conversion from an RRSP to an RRIF (or annuity) must take place when you reach age 71 — however, you might choose to do this conversion early. Some reasons to do so include:

✔ You need the income.

✔ You are at least 65 and want to take advantage of the pension credit on the first $2,000 of pension income or pension income splitting (Tip #68).

✔ You are currently in a low tax bracket and expect to pay very little tax on your withdrawals.

Of course, if you can afford to, it generally makes sense to keep the funds in your RRSP/RRIF for as long as possible in order to defer the tax hit on withdrawal.

Minimum required withdrawals from an RRIF are not subject to withholding tax, except in Quebec. However, if you withdraw more than the minimum amount, these withdrawals will be subject to withholding tax.

You don't have to make any withdrawals from your RRIF in the year you set up the plan. In fact, you can (and should, if you're financially able) defer making a withdrawal until December of the year after your RRIF is set up in order to defer tax for as long as possible.

Using an annuity

Instead of converting to an RRIF, you can also use your RRSP funds to purchase a life annuity to convert your savings to a source of income. A *life annuity* is a contract with an insurance company. The insurance company will promise you a set income for life, in exchange for a lump sum payment.

The amount of payment you will receive from your annuity depends on factors such as your age, sex, health, current interest rates, and special features you choose to attach to your contract such as inflation protection, guarantee periods, and joint and survivor payments.

An annuity is beneficial when you prefer to know exactly what your income will be each year and have a need for income for life. The drawback is that if the markets do well, you won't benefit like you might with an RRIF because the payments are not based on the market value of the plan assets each year. In addition, an annuity purchase is irrevocable. After you purchase the contract you no longer own the assets; rather, you own a right to the income. You're not able to access any payments other than your contracted income amount. If you die early on in the contract, your survivors could be left with nothing, although that can be rectified by purchasing an annuity with a guarantee period so that at least some amount of payment can be made to a beneficiary if you die prematurely.

Ask lots of questions and give lots of information when you're purchasing an annuity. If you have a spouse you want to ensure the spouse will continue to get annuity payments after you're gone. This is known as a joint and survivor annuity. You can also choose to purchase an annuity that's indexed to inflation.

Income paid to you out of an annuity contract that originally came from registered funds is fully taxable to you just like payments out of an RRSP or RRIF. They are not subject to withholding tax. Annuities can also be purchased using cash or non-registered funds. These annuities are subject to different tax rules. See Tip #40 for more on annuities.

Minimizing Tax on Your Withdrawals

Withdraw money from an RRSP only when you really need the income, so you can defer the resulting tax for as long as possible. And if you do have to make a withdrawal, try to use some of these strategies to keep the tax bill to a minimum.

Withdraw in low-income years

Try to withdraw amounts during a year in which you anticipate having a lower income. This will reduce the tax bite when the amounts are eventually included in income.

Further, if you're married, remove money from the RRSP of the lower-income earner first. This will reduce the tax paid by the family, because the lower-income earner probably has a lower marginal tax rate and will pay less tax on the withdrawal.

Use the pension credit

If you're 65 years of age or older, report your minimum required RRIF withdrawal at line 115. Why? As we discuss in Tip #67, income reported at line 115 is eligible for the $2,000 pension credit at line 314.

If you've taken advantage of pension splitting (Tip #68), you and your spouse could each benefit from the $2,000 pension credit. Each spouse wanting to claim the credit must be age 65.

If you're age 65 or over but do not have sufficient pension income to qualify for the full credit (that is, your pension income is less than $2,000), you can create pension income by converting all or part of your RRSP to an RRIF or life annuity.

Take advantage of pension income splitting

As you accumulate more funds in your RRSP, you might find your tax rate in retirement increasing because the payments you'll be required to withdraw from the account will push you into a higher tax bracket.

If you have a spouse who is taxed at a lower tax rate than you, take advantage of the pension income splitting rules in order to shift some income, and tax, to your spouse's tax return. The result will be less tax for the family as a whole. In fact, if you have few other sources of income, it may be to your advantage to convert your RSP to an RRIF or life annuity at age 65 so that you can tax advantage of pension income splitting (and the pension credit!). See Tip #68 for the full details on pension splitting.

Base withdrawals on the age of the younger spouse

If your spouse is younger than you, consider basing your minimum withdrawals on your spouse's age to defer the tax hit from your RRIF for as long as possible.

Why does this work? As we discussed earlier, after you have an RRIF you're required to withdraw at least a minimum amount of income each year. The actual percentage withdrawal increases with your age. If your spouse is younger, the percentage of withdrawal will be less. This will reduce the amount you're required to withdraw each year, allowing you to defer tax and leave more assets in your RRIF for future growth.

Split withdrawals over two tax years

By taking funds out at the end of December one year and in January the next year, you'll be splitting the withdrawal over two tax years, thus reducing the tax hit in any one year. In addition, tax will not be payable on the January withdrawal until April 30 of the following year — so, if you withdraw money from an RRSP in January 2010, additional tax will not be payable on this amount until April 30, 2011.

In the past, it was recommended to take registered fund withdrawals in increments of $5,000 or less to keep the tax withholdings to a minimum. The CRA has spoken out on this practice and now requires financial institutions to take higher future withholdings when you take out several smaller lump sum amounts that in total put you into a higher withholding bracket.

Use your RRSP for a home purchase

Although the general rule is that withdrawals from your RRSP are taxable, in some special circumstances the government allows you to withdraw funds with no tax. The first situation occurs when you withdraw money from your RRSP to purchase a home under the Home Buyers' Plan. If you qualify, you're allowed to withdraw up to $25,000 from your RRSP under this plan and not pay tax on the withdrawal.

Of course, your tax obligations aren't over yet. You're required to repay the amount you withdrew for your Home Buyers' Plan to your RRSP. And if you don't? You guessed it — the shortfall will be added to your income at line 129. See Tip #55 for further details.

Use your RRSP to go to school

As is the case with the Home Buyers' Plan, you can withdraw funds from your RRSP on a tax-free basis to help you go back to school. This program is called the Lifelong Learning Plan.

If you don't pay back funds withdrawn under the Lifelong Learning Plan according to the required schedule, they are included in your income at line 129 every year that the payment is missed. Also, if you withdraw the money but do not use it for education, and if you do not return the funds to the RRSP by the end of the calendar year following your withdrawal from the educational institution, the entire amount will be included in income. For more on the Lifelong Learning Plan, see Tip #56.

Special Rules for Locked-in Retirement Accounts

Different withdrawal rules exist where you have a locked-in RRSP. A *locked-in RRSP* or *locked-in retirement account* (LIRA) is created when you transfer funds from a registered pension plan to an RRSP.

When you have a regular RRSP, you can withdraw funds whenever you want if you're willing to pay tax on the withdrawal (although it's not always recommended). However, you're not always allowed to make withdrawals at will if the funds are locked in. Withdrawals from locked-in plans are legislated in each province and may be limited. Even when you convert the locked-in RRSP to a source of retirement income you might find you have both a minimum and maximum withdrawal to consider.

Registered pension plans are legislated federally or provincially. After you transfer pension funds to your own retirement account, you're governed by that same federal or provincial legislation — which will affect your withdrawal options.

You must convert your locked-in RRSP or LIRA to a source of income by the end of the year you turn 71. When you convert the plan to a source of income, you generally have the following options:

- ✔ Purchase a life annuity like you could with a regular RRSP.
- ✔ Transfer the funds to a life income fund. A LIF is almost identical to an RRIF except that annual maximum withdrawals and age limits apply in some provinces.

Some provinces offer additional options as well. Your financial advisor or financial institution will be able to help you with your options.

Manage the Tax on Property Investments

When you purchase property investments, such as a rental property, you might earn various types of returns that give rise to tax. You might earn income from renting out the space, or gains on the sale of the property. In any case, the good news is that lots of deductions are available. In this tip we let you in on rules that can help you minimize your tax bill.

Real Estate Rentals — What's Deductible, What's Not

Rental income is earned from renting out properties such as a building, a house, a room in a house, an apartment, office space, machinery, equipment, vehicles, and so on. Most types of rental income are considered to be "income from property" and therefore are reported on line 126, although if you rent out properties as a business, you report it as self-employment income.

On the line for rental income on your tax return you'll see a line for *gross income* (line 160) and a line for *net income* (line 126). Gross income is the full amount of rental income you received in the year, before taking into account expenses you incurred to earn that income. Net income is the amount left over after expenses.

 Rental income is always reported on a calendar-year basis — that is, January to December. If you co-own a rental property, your share of the rental income or loss will be based on your percentage of ownership. Arbitrary allocations are not acceptable.

If you're renting out real estate, you likely incur a variety of costs in order to earn that income. You can deduct many of these costs for tax purposes. You will need to keep track of your deductible expenditures during the year and then list them on form T776 when you file your tax return. Take a good look at this form, because it will also help you remember all the types of expenses you might be able to claim. ***Note:*** You don't have to send in your receipts for rental expenses when you file your tax return, but keep them on file in case the CRA asks to see them.

The most common expenses incurred that may be deducted against rental income include the following:

- ✔ Mortgage interest
- ✔ Property tax
- ✔ Insurance
- ✔ Maintenance and repairs
- ✔ Heat, hydro, water
- ✔ Accounting fees
- ✔ Condo fees
- ✔ Landscaping
- ✔ Office supplies
- ✔ Fees paid to find tenants
- ✔ Advertising
- ✔ Management and administration fees
- ✔ Salaries or wages paid to take care of property
- ✔ Legal fees to collect rent or prepare rental documents
- ✔ Lease cancellation fees (amortized over the remaining term of lease to a maximum of 40 years)
- ✔ Mortgage application, appraisal, processing, and insurance fees (deducted over five years)
- ✔ Mortgage guarantee fees (deducted over five years)
- ✔ Mortgage broker and finder fees (deducted over five years)
- ✔ Legal fees related to mortgage financing (deducted over five years)

Real estate rentals can create losses for tax purposes. These losses can be used to offset other types of income you report on your tax return, thereby reducing your overall tax payable in the year — see Tip #39 for more on dealing with capital losses.

Costs you cannot deduct include mortgage principal, any penalties or interest assessed by the CRA, the value of your own labour, and other personal expenses relating to the property.

If you own one rental property in addition to your principal residence, you can deduct motor vehicle or travel expenses to conduct repairs and maintenance or to transport tools and materials to the rental property provided the property is located in your general area of residence. If you own only one rental property (and no other residence), you cannot deduct travel expenses to collect rent; this is considered a personal expense. Also, you cannot deduct travel expenses for a property outside your area of residence.

If you own two or more rental properties, you can deduct all the above expenses plus travel to collect rents, supervise repairs, and generally manage the properties. Your rental properties have to be located in at least two different sites away from your principal residence.

Real estate commissions or legal fees paid in connection with the purchase or sale of the property are not deductible as incurred. Instead, they must be added to the cost base of the property.

Sussing Out the Special Rules for Undeveloped Land

The tax treatment of undeveloped land is a tricky issue. If you rent out this undeveloped land (or even if you don't!), you need to ensure you do not run afoul of the rules.

Deductibility of interest and property taxes

If you rent out vacant land, you'll be allowed to deduct any interest and property tax only to the extent of the net rental income earned on the land (that is, income after other expenses are deducted). In other words, you cannot use the interest and property tax to create a loss on vacant land not used to produce income.

If, on the other hand, the land is used or held to carry on a business, or if the land is held primarily for the purpose of gaining or producing income, the interest and property tax can be deducted in excess of earned income. This distinction allows land under buildings and land used in a business (for example, a parking lot) to avoid the interest and property tax restrictions.

Capital assets

If the vacant land is considered a capital asset (it normally would be if you purchased it to hold as a long-term investment), the non-deductible interest and property tax will be added to the cost of the land. This will reduce the capital gain (or increase the capital loss) on sale when the land is eventually disposed of.

Renting Out Your Personal Space

When renting out a residence that you also use personally, you have to determine which expenses relate solely to the rental activity and which ones are shared with the whole house:

- ✔ **Expenses of rental activity:** Expenses such as advertising, cleaning, and cutting keys are incremental costs of owning and renting the property. These expenses are 100-percent deductible against rental income.

- ✔ **Expenses shared with the rest of the house:** Expenses such as taxes, insurance, water, hydro, heat, maintenance, and mortgage interest would have been incurred even if a portion of the house were not rented out. These expenses are allocated between the rental and the rest of the house. This is because your personal portions of expenses are not deductible.

The CRA accepts two ways of allocating expenses:

- ✔ **Based on the number of rooms in the house:** If the house has ten rooms and two are rented, allocate $\frac{2}{10}$ of the household expenses to the rental units.

- ✔ **Based on the square footage:** If the house is 2,000 square feet and the rental is 400 square feet, allocate $\frac{400}{2,000}$ of the house expenses to the rental portion.

As tempting as it might be, do not claim capital cost allowance (CCA) when renting out part of your home. The reason? When you claim CCA against your rental income, the part of your home that is rented stops being your principal residence. This means that when you sell your home, part of your proceeds will be taxable because they're no longer exempt under the principal residence exemption. (We touch on CCA more at the end of this tip and in Tip #32.)

It has been proven in the Canadian courts that as long as no personal or hobby element to an activity (such as a rental activity) exists, losses cannot be denied if there have never been profits or there may not be profits in the future. However, say you own a cottage that you and your family regularly use, but you also rent it out to others a few weeks a year. In this case, you're supposed to report the rental income you receive on your tax return, and you're also entitled to deduct some of your cottage expenses. Sounds inviting, huh? However, a personal element exists here, and because you're essentially deducting some costs as rental expenses that you would have incurred even if you hadn't rented out part of your premises (think of property taxes, insurance, maybe even mortgage interest), if you claim losses on that rental activity a "reasonable expectation of profit" test can be used to deny your losses. The lesson here? Don't get greedy when looking for tax deductions.

Keeping Track of Property Improvements

Unless you're a slumlord, you're likely going to incur some expenditures on your rental property. The question is whether you can deduct these expenses against your income.

Expenses of a property can be divided into two main categories: current expenditures and capital expenditures. Current expenditures are the operating or recurring expenses that provide short-term benefits. These expenditures tend to maintain or keep the property in the same shape. Think of your garden. You might pay someone to weed the flower bed, but alas, the weeds will grow back. The gardener is a current expense. Other examples include repairs and maintenance, window cleaning, heat, hydro, property tax, and interest expense on the mortgage. Capital expenditures, on the other hand, are the expenses of purchasing the property or substantially improving it. Capital expenditures are expenses that give lasting benefits that improve the property beyond its original condition. Back to the garden. If you planted new trees and a perennial garden, these would be expected to last for many years. They would be a capital expenditure. Other examples of capital expenditures include major repairs to the property such as a new roof, additions to the property, new windows, new plumbing or electrical wiring, and a new furnace or coalscuttle. (We just mentioned coalscuttle because we like the word.)

The key concept in determining whether a repair is a capital or current expenditure is the concept of betterment. If a repair improves what was initially there, it will be classified as a capital expenditure. If the repair only restores what was there initially, it is a current expense.

Capital expenditures are not expensed in the year of occurrence; rather, they are amortized or deducted over time using the capital cost allowance system, which we discuss in the next section.

Capital expenditures to assist the disabled are fully deductible in the year of occurrence. These expenses are given current-expense treatment in an attempt to encourage landlords to install them, and may include the following: installing hand-activated power door openers; installing ramps; modifying bathrooms, elevators, or doorways to accommodate wheelchairs; modifying elevators to assist the blind; and installing telephone devices for the hearing impaired and computer equipment or software to assist people who have disabilities.

Capital Cost Allowance

Capital cost allowance is a method of writing off the cost of a capital item over time, because the cost of capital assets cannot be deducted all at once in the year of acquisition (see Tip #32). The length of time that the tax laws permit you to "write off" the asset is supposed to represent the time it takes for the asset to wear out or become obsolete. The amount you're allowed to deduct each year is called the capital cost allowance (or CCA).

How do I determine how much CCA I can claim?

The yearly amount of CCA you're permitted to claim depends on the type of asset you own and when the asset was purchased. The Income Tax Act puts each type of asset into a specific asset group, or "class." Each class has a predetermined amortization rate. For example, office furniture and equipment are class 8 assets, and therefore the cost of any new purchase of office furniture or equipment gets added to this class. Think of it as a running total of the value of like-assets you own.

How do you know what class to put your capital asset in? The CRA's Rental Income guide has a good discussion of CCA classes. See the CRA Web site at www.cra-arc.gc.ca.

Various CCA classes also have different rules regarding the treatment of assets in the first year that their costs are added to the class. Most classes require you to use the "half-year rule" for new additions. This rule allows you to claim only half the normal CCA in the first year an asset is added to a class. This rule was designed to prevent individuals from buying assets on the last day of the year and claiming a full year of amortization (too bad!).

You don't have to claim the maximum CCA every year. This is a discretionary deduction, meaning you can choose to claim any amount from zero to the maximum allowed. If you don't owe tax in a particular year, for example, you may not wish to claim CCA that year and instead preserve your deduction for other tax years when you might need it. Remember, though, a maximum amount you can claim each year applies even if you forgo deductions in previous years. No double-dipping!

Combining rental income to calculate CCA

You can't use CCA to create a loss on rental income. The government requires you to combine all rental income and losses from all properties before calculating CCA. In this way, you're prevented from using CCA to create or increase net rental losses.

Let's say Jack owns two buildings. Both buildings are in class 1. The income and loss on the rental buildings are as follows:

	Building 1	Building 2
Net income (loss) before CCA	$10,000	($15,000)

Because Jack has to combine the income of both buildings, he has a net rental loss of $5,000. Because Jack is in a net rental loss position, he cannot claim CCA on either building without increasing the rental loss. If this rule did not exist, he could claim CCA on Building 1 to bring income to zero and claim no CCA on Building 2. The result would be a net rental loss of $15,000.

Foreign Rental Income

For tax purposes, you must include in your Canadian income any rental income that you receive on property located anywhere in the world, converted to Canadian dollars. The same rules and restrictions apply to foreign-source rental income as apply to Canadian-source rental income, including the CCA rules.

If you also had to pay tax to another country on your foreign rental income, you may be eligible for a foreign tax credit when you calculate your rental income for Canadian tax purposes. This system helps to ensure you're not paying double the tax on the same income. See Tip #36 for more on investing in foreign property.

Calculating the Capital Gain or Loss from the Sale of Property

Rental buildings (but not the land, which is not considered to depreciate) and capital assets used to earn rental (and business) income — such as buildings used in a business, machinery, computer equipment, or office furniture and equipment — are considered depreciable property. We talk about the CCA rules earlier in this tip. You can write off the cost of the property by claiming capital cost allowance over a number of years — meaning that at the time the asset is sold, undepreciated capital cost will likely be less than the original purchase price.

When you dispose of depreciable property, you may have a capital gain but not a capital loss — capital losses on depreciable property are simply considered to be nil. That may seem unfair at first, but the tax implications don't end there.

In addition to incurring a capital gain, you may also have recapture or a terminal loss. Recapture and terminal loss are adjustments you must make when you dispose of assets and find (based on your selling price) that the assets either were not depreciated enough over time, or were depreciated too much. To recapture means to reverse CCA taken in excess of the actual depreciation in value of the asset. To claim a terminal loss means to claim additional CCA when an asset has depreciated in value more than the allowed capital cost deductions. Neither recapture nor terminal losses can be claimed while assets are still in a CCA class (that is, if you had more than one asset of the same type being depreciated). When all assets in a class have been disposed of, you will be able to determine whether you over- or underdepreciated assets.

Let's say Lisa sells her class 1 building for $1,000,000. She originally bought the building for $500,000. Over the years, she has claimed $300,000 of CCA. Because this building is the last asset in the class, we can calculate recapture or terminal loss. At the time of sale, Lisa's undepreciated capital cost balance was $200,000 ($500,000 − $300,000 = $200,000).

Because the building increased in value and did not depreciate, Lisa had been entitled to CCA tax deductions in prior years that did not reflect the actual wear and tear of the building. Although the CCA deductions were valid at the time she took them (because the tax laws state how much you are entitled to deduct as CCA), now that Lisa is disposing of the asset she will be required to include $300,000 of recapture in her income for the year of disposition.

#45

Know the Implications of Purchasing U.S. Property

*I*t's an annual tradition for many Canadians: A trek down to the United States for a reprieve from our Canadian winters. Instead of renting, you might be thinking about buying your own property down south. But anytime you purchase a property in another country you'll have tax implications, and that's very true of property purchases in the U.S. In this tip we tell you what to watch out for.

Be Aware of the Implications of Receiving Rental Income

We've said it before and we'll say it again. As a Canadian resident, you're liable for Canadian tax on your worldwide income. If you're earning rental income from your U.S. property, that income is taxable in Canada. (We talk about the Canadian taxation of that income in Tip #44.)

Your U.S. rental income is also taxable in the U.S., and you have some choices regarding how you fulfill your U.S. tax requirements.

Option 1: 30 percent withholding tax on gross rental income

Under this option, the gross rents you earn are subject to a 30 percent withholding tax. Did you get the gross part? Under this method you're not allowed a deduction for any expenses. This means a pretty hefty tax bill unless you have absolutely no deductions at all. This is an easy option, though, as you don't have to file a U.S. tax return. You can claim a foreign tax credit for the withholding tax paid to the U.S.; however, be warned that you'll not likely get a full foreign tax credit in Canada because you can't receive more Canadian tax via a foreign tax credit than the amount of tax payable to Canada on that income. So, in summary, this is the easy but expensive choice of the two.

Option 2: Net rental basis

Under this option, you're required to file a U.S. non-resident tax return, called form 1040NR. On this form you'll report your gross rental income as well as allowable deductions. These deductions may include mortgage interest, property taxes, insurance, utilities, management fees, and advertising. A mandatory deduction for depreciation also applies. The gross income less deductions is equal to your net rental income, and it's on this amount that you will pay U.S. tax. The tax you pay can be used as a foreign tax credit in Canada. Due to the allowable deductions, you'll likely pay much less tax using this method.

Selling a U.S. Property

When you sell your U.S. property, you're required to report the sale on your Canadian tax return. If you sell the property for more than its tax cost, you'll have to report a capital gain in Canada. In addition, because the property is physically located in the U.S., the U.S. has the right to tax the sale. You're required to file a U.S. tax return to report the capital gain or loss and pay tax on any profit. Like the taxes on the rental income, any tax paid on the capital gain in the U.S. can be claimed as a foreign tax credit in Canada.

It may be possible to avoid taxes in Canada if the U.S. property is considered your principal residence.

Be very careful about gifting U.S. property. A U.S. gift tax may apply. In addition, if you keep the property for life, it's possible that U.S. estate tax will be charged on a portion of your estate value. You'll want to visit a cross-border tax pro to assess the damage and suggest solutions.

#46

Pay Less on the Sale of Personal-Use Assets

*E*ven if you don't have the extra cash to buy investments or start your own business, you may have personal items with nominal or even considerable value that you plan to sell. Further, you may have other assets such as a family home or cottage that you use personally. Because Canadians are taxed on all income earned worldwide in a year, as a general statement, any gains you bring in from selling those assets are taxable. Some special rules, however, can work in your favour to reduce the tax hit.

Taxing Personal-Use Property

A personal-use property is an asset you hold and use for your own personal enjoyment. Common examples of personal-use property include your home, family vacation properties (such as your cottage or ski chalet), cars, boats, art, jewellery, and the like. The asset itself doesn't make it qualify as a personal-use property; an asset is determined to be personal-use property through your use of the asset.

In most cases — with perhaps the exception of their homes and vacation properties — people are not affected by the capital gains rules when they own assets for their personal use. When you sell such property, usually you do not end up with a capital gain. This is because these types of property generally don't increase in value over the years. In fact, because many personal-use assets depreciate in value, you may actually end up with a loss.

Although you have to report a capital gain on the sale of personal-use property on your tax return, you're not ordinarily allowed to claim a capital loss. (We agree that this seems unfair, but them's the rules!) However, you can claim a loss under the following circumstances:

- ✔ If you disposed of personal-use property such as art or jewellery that is considered "listed personal property" (see the next section).

✔ If a bad debt is owed to you from the sale of a personal-use property to a person with whom you deal at arm's length (in other words, a non-related third party). In this case you can claim the bad debt owed to you as a capital loss.

Capital gains and, where allowed, capital losses incurred on personal-use property — that is not listed personal property — are reported in section 7 of schedule 3 ("Personal use property").

To calculate any capital gain or loss realized when you dispose of personal-use property, follow these rules:

✔ If the adjusted cost base of the property is less than $1,000, its adjusted cost base is considered to be $1,000.

✔ If the proceeds of disposition are less than $1,000, the proceeds of disposition are considered to be $1,000.

If both the adjusted cost base and the proceeds of disposition are $1,000 or less, you don't have a capital gain or a capital loss. Do not report the sale on schedule 3 when you file your return.

If you sell your home — your principal residence — for more than it cost you, you usually do not have to report the sale on your return or pay tax on any capital gain due to the principal residence exemption.

Taxing Listed Personal Property

Listed personal property (LPP) is a type of personal-use property that usually increases in value over time. Listed personal property includes the following capital properties:

✔ Rare manuscripts or rare books

✔ Prints, etchings, drawings, paintings, sculptures, or other similar works of art

✔ Jewellery

✔ Stamps and coins

Report capital gains or losses from selling such items in part 8 of schedule 3.

To determine the value of many of these items, you can have them appraised by book, art, jewellery, stamp, or coin dealers. Because listed personal property is personal-use property, the $1,000 minimum proceeds of disposition and adjusted cost base rules apply.

One very important difference, for tax purposes, exists between personal-use property that *is not* listed personal property and personal-use property that *is* listed personal property: If you have a loss when you dispose of listed personal property, these losses are not, well, lost. In fact, the losses can be used to offset gains generated on listed personal property this year, in the previous three years, or in any of the seven subsequent tax years.

 Keep a record of your listed personal property losses that have not expired, so you can apply these losses against listed personal property gains in other years. A listed personal property loss expires if you do not use it by the end of the seventh year after it was incurred.

Minimizing Tax on Your Residence and Vacation Properties

When you sell your home, you may realize a capital gain — that is, you may make money on it. Congratulations! If the property was your only principal residence for every year you owned it, you don't have to report the sale or the capital gain on your tax return. However, if at any time during the period that you owned the property it was not your principal residence, or you owned more than one property, you may have to report all or a portion of the capital gain and pay tax on it. In this section we explain the meaning of a principal residence, how you designate a property as such, and what happens when you sell it so hopefully you can save a few bucks of tax.

 If after reading this section you need more information, read the CRA's Interpretation Bulletin IT-120R6, "Principal Residence," available on the CRA Web site at www.cra-arc.gc.ca.

Determining your principal residence

Your principal residence can be a house, cottage, condominium, apartment, trailer, mobile home, or houseboat. A property qualifies as your principal residence for any year if it meets the following conditions:

✔ You own the property alone or jointly with another person.

✔ You, your spouse, your former spouse, or any of your children 18 years of age or younger lived in it at some time during the year. In the case of a vacation property, staying there only occasionally during the year is okay; it can still be designated as your principal residence.

✔ You designate the property as your principal residence for the year. (You don't need to make this designation until you sell, or are deemed to have sold for tax purposes, a property that can qualify for the principal residence exemption.)

The land on which your home is located can also be part of your principal residence. Usually, the amount of land you can consider part of your principal residence is limited to one-half hectare (about one acre). However, if you can show that you need more land to use and enjoy your home, you may consider more than this amount as part of your principal residence — for example, this may happen if the minimum lot size imposed by a municipality at the time you bought the property was larger than one-half hectare.

Figuring out whether you can have more than one principal residence

For 1982 and later years, you can designate only one home as your family's principal residence for each year. If you're married or are 18 or older, your family includes you, your spouse (unless you were separated for the entire year), and your children (other than a child who was married during the year or who was 18 or older). If you're not married or are not 18 or older, your family also includes your mother and your father, and your brothers and sisters (who were not married or 18 or older during the year).

For years before 1982, more than one housing unit per family could be designated as a principal residence. Therefore, for these years a husband and wife could designate different principal residences (for example, a house and a cottage) to help minimize capital gains (and taxes) on a sale. After 1982, only one residence per family can be named the principal residence. Therefore, it's important to calculate the potential capital gains on each property you own so you can take maximum advantage of the principal residence exemption.

Disposition of your principal residence

When you sell your home, usually you don't have to report the sale on your return and you don't have to pay tax on any gain from the sale. This is the case if the home was your principal residence for every year you owned it. For many Canadians, this is a no-brainer because they have only one home.

However, for those fortunate enough to have a family cottage, or even more than one home, the principal residence exemption is not quite as straightforward. Things are complicated further if you didn't actually live in the home, cottage, or whatever during a particular year. If your home was not your principal residence for every year you owned it, you have to report the part of the capital gain on the property that relates to the years when you did not designate the property as your principal residence.

If you have a loss when you sell, you're not allowed to claim the loss because your home is considered personal-use property.

If only part of your home qualifies as your principal residence and you used the other part to earn income, you may have to split the selling price between the part you used for your principal residence and the part you used for other purposes (for example, rental or business purposes). You can do this by using square metres or the number of rooms, as long as the split is reasonable. Report only the gain on the part you used to produce income. Don't worry, however, if the income-earning activity was ancillary to the main use of the residence (i.e., say you rented out a small portion of the house) and you have not claimed capital cost allowance on the income-producing portion of the home in the past. In these cases, the whole residence can still be considered your principal residence and no portion of any capital gain on sale will be taxable to you.

If you're renting out a portion of your home, avoid claiming capital cost allowance (CCA) on that portion of the home. If you do, you won't be able to shelter the entire gain using the principal residence exemption when you eventually sell the home.

If the principal residence exemption does not completely shelter the capital gain on the sale of a property, form T2091, "Designation of a Principal Residence," will help you calculate the number of years for which you can designate your home as your principal residence, as well as the part of the capital gain, if any, that you have to report and pay tax on.

Include form T2091 with your return only if you have to report a capital gain. In other words, if your gain is fully sheltered by the principal-residence exemption, you don't have to report anything on your tax return.

Doing the math when selling a principal residence

If you sell a residence on which all the capital gain is not fully shel-tered from tax by the principal residence exemption, the following formula calculates what portion of the gain is tax exempt:

1 + The number of years the home was designated as principal residence

Exempt gain equals (total number of years you owned the home after 1971) × gain

Because an individual can designate only one home as a principal residence for any given year, the 1 + in the formula allows you to protect the principal residence exemption when you sell and pur-chase a home in the same year.

#47

Know When to Deduct Investment-Related Expenses

*I*f you're an investor with a non-registered investment account, you likely incur expenses to manage the investments and account for the investment income you earn. It's important to keep track of those expenses — many of them are tax deductible.

Understanding What Expenses Are Deductible

Certain expenses you incur to earn investment income are tax deductible. These include:

- ✔ Investment counsel and management fees (only the portion of these fees related to services for your non-RRSP investments are deductible)

- ✔ Safekeeping, custodial, and safety-deposit box fees

- ✔ Tax-return preparation fees, if you have income from a business or from your investments (sometimes called income from property). This includes interest, dividends, rents, and royalties.

- ✔ Interest on money borrowed to earn investment income, such as interest and dividends — but not capital gains

Brokerage commissions are not tax deductible as a carrying charge because they form part of the tax cost on the purchase of an investment or reduce the proceeds on the sale. In other words, these commissions will reduce your ultimate capital gain, or increase your capital loss on sale, but are not deductible on an annual basis against other sources of income.

Detail eligible carrying costs and interest in Part IV of schedule 4 of your tax return, "Summary, Carrying Charges and Interest Expenses." Then enter the total on line 221.

At the time of writing, a set of draft rules (yes, they are still draft — the suspense is killing us!) in the *Income Tax Act* threatens to deny interest deductions and other investment expenses when no reasonable expectation of cumulative profits exists (excluding capital gains) from the investment in question. Plainly stated, your deductions may be denied if you're not expecting to earn enough interest and dividends from your investment over the expected holding period to cover your interest costs over that same period.

If you live in Quebec, you have additional rules to worry about. Specifically, for Quebec tax purposes, you can deduct interest (and other investment expenses) only to the extent you've reported investment income in the year. Investment income for these purposes includes taxable capital gains. Any interest that is not deductible can be carried forward to offset investment income you have in future years.

Special Deductions for Exploration and Development Investments

Did you invest in an oil and gas or mining venture? The type of investment may have been called a "limited partnership," a "flow-through share" investment, or simply a "tax shelter." Whatever the term, if you did invest, you're probably entitled to some special tax deductions. One of the attractive features promoted in the selling of oil, gas, and mining investments is the tax write-offs (slang for "deductions") available.

If you're contemplating an investment in an oil, gas, or mining venture, be sure you completely understand the risks associated with the investment. A general rule is that the greater the tax saving, the riskier the investment. Be sure that such an investment falls within your risk-tolerance comfort zone. Invest based on the quality of the investment — not the tax saving provided by the investment.

Why are these tax deductions made available? The government thinks it's a good idea to encourage oil, gas, and metal exploration in Canada, so the Act contains provisions to encourage these activities. The Act provides oil, gas, and mining companies with significant write-offs for the following:

- ✔ Canadian exploration expenses (CEE) — 100 percent deduction
- ✔ Canadian development expenses (CDE) — 30 percent deduction
- ✔ Canadian oil and gas property expenses (COGPE) — 10 percent deduction

In addition, a temporary 15 percent mineral exploration tax credit is set to expire March 10, 2010. This credit was put in place by the government to help companies raise capital for mining exploration.

Because many exploration companies do not have sufficient money to go out and explore for oil, gas, and metals, the Act permits these companies to turn to you for the funds. You're the one actually funding the exploration and development, so you get the attractive tax deductions. This is referred to as the expenses being "renounced" to you. Because exploration is the government's main initiative, and the exploration phase has the greatest chance of failure, the write-offs are greatest when funds are expended on exploration.

The promoter of the oil, gas, or mining venture will provide you with all the information you need. Depending on the structure of the investment, you'll receive a T101, T102, or T5013 slip. Instructions are provided on the back of these forms to assist in calculating your deduction.

You don't have to take the maximum deduction. Any amount not claimed will carry over to the following year for a potential deduction using the same percentage figures. Why would you not want to take a deduction? Perhaps you expect to be in a higher tax bracket next year, so the deduction will be worth more in tax savings if you wait.

Make and Keep Interest Deductible

Given the large amounts of debt carried by Canadians, you want to ensure you get a tax break for the interest paid whenever you can. And lots of situations arise where the interest is deductible when the debts are properly structured.

 Leveraged investing — that is, taking out a loan and using the proceeds to invest — is popular because you use other people's money (usually the bank's) to make money for yourself! The idea is that over the long term you can achieve higher effective rates of return on your investments and may even reach your financial goals faster than if you simply used your free cash flow to invest. And, of course, the interest on the loan is tax deductible. It does come with risks, though, so ensure you talk to your banker and financial advisor to see if it makes sense for you.

Determine When Interest Is Deductible on Your Tax Return

The government makes it very clear when interest on debts is deductible for tax purposes. And if you're planning to take out a loan and deduct the interest, you'll want to ensure you are onside with those rules.

For your interest to be deductible, the following four criteria must be met:

- There must be an obligation to pay the interest costs.
- The interest costs must be paid or payable during the year.
- The interest costs must be reasonable.
- The borrowed money must be used to earn business income or income from property.

When funds are borrowed from a bank or other lending institution, a legal obligation exists to pay the interest annually. And because the investor and the bank are not related to one another, it's safe to say that the interest costs are reasonable. Therefore, provided the interest is paid during the year or the lender could legally enforce payment, it is clear that the first three criteria are met.

The fourth criteria states that the borrowed money must be used to earn business income or income from property. The term business income is simple. It means you earn income from operating your own business or investing in someone else's business. It gets a bit trickier when we consider income from property, which includes interest, dividends, rentals, and royalties — but not capital gains. The tax law is clear — when funds are used to generate primarily capital gains, the interest is not deductible.

The most common types of items purchased with debt where you will be able to deduct your interest include bonds, mutual funds, public company shares, and rental properties. Interest on debts incurred to purchase personal assets like a house is not deductible, although you're able to use the equity in your home to secure a loan that is used for investment purposes. In that case the direct use of the borrowed funds is investing; therefore, the interest is deductible.

If you borrow to invest in an RRSP, your interest is not tax deductible. Consider using your tax refund to pay off at least part of your loan in order to keep your non-tax-deductible debt to a minimum.

Leveraged investing is not for everyone, because it's considered risky. Ask yourself whether you have a long-term investment horizon, sufficient personal cash flow to make loan payments (particularly in years where the investment cannot generate the cash flow to support its loan), and a high risk tolerance.

Even if your interest cost exceeds your investment income, you're still entitled to deduct the excess against other sources of income if you're expecting income in the future. (Well, this last statement is not completely true. The excess of interest expense over investment income can be deducted for federal tax purposes, in all provinces/territories except Quebec.)

Make Interest Tax Deductible

Many of us pay interest on personal borrowing, such as mortgage interest, car loans, lines of credit, and credit cards, but few of us can deduct that interest on our tax returns. A way exists, however, for some of us to convert that non-deductible interest into a tax deduction. This strategy is commonly known as *debt-swapping*.

Debt-swapping is possible if you have both non-deductible interest and non-RRSP investments such as shares, bonds, or mutual funds. Here's how you do it:

1. Sell your investments, ideally choosing those that have not greatly appreciated in value since you purchased them (because you are responsible for paying tax on any capital gains you trigger on the sale).

2. Use the proceeds from the sale to pay down your non-deductible debt.

3. Take out a new loan with the bank and use it to repurchase the investments you sold.

At the end of the day, you have the same amount of debt and the same amount in investments as before the sale (assuming you didn't have tax to pay on any capital gains), but because a direct trace occurs between the borrowing and the investments, the interest you pay each year can be deducted on your tax return!

Keep the Interest Deductible

Just because the initial purpose of your borrowing is to invest, this does not mean you're guaranteed a tax deduction for the interest paid in the future. To ensure your interest remains tax deductible, avoid withdrawing any capital from your investment account (which includes both the growth and any reinvested distributions) for personal purposes. Doing so will result in losing a portion of your interest deduction, unless you're withdrawing the funds to put into another investment.

If you've borrowed to invest but later sell your investment at a loss, and use all the proceeds you have to pay down the loan, the interest on the remaining loan is still tax deductible.

Part IV
Tips for Families

The 5th Wave

By Rich Tennant

"I got excellent advice on my tax return from a very knowledgeable guy. All the while he cleaned my windshield and checked the air pressure in my tires."

In this part . . .

Family life is sure to be full of events with financial — and tax — implications. From marriage to divorce, to the birth of children to them leaving to go away from school, and everything in between, you and your family have tax rules aplenty to deal with. The good news is that many of the rules mean more money in your pocket. But you have to know about them to claim them, and thankfully Part IV fills you in on all the deductions, credits, and special programs available to help you run your household in a tax-efficient manner.

#49

Know What Tax Credits Are Available for You and Your Family

*L*ots of non-refundable tax credits are available for you and your family — you just have to know which ones you can claim. Non-refundable tax *credits* directly reduce the amount of income tax you owe. In this way they differ from tax deductions, which are subtracted in computi   ng your taxable income. These credits are referred to as "non-refundable" because if they exceed your tax you don't get a refund of the excess.

For all but one of the non-refundable tax credits (the donation credit) the federal tax savings is 15 percent of the non-refundable tax credit amount to which you're entitled. The federal non-refundable tax credits are indexed each year. This means you're entitled to larger credit amounts — tax savings — as the years go on.

 Report federal non-refundable tax credit amounts on schedule 1 of your tax return. Each province/territory also calculates its own non-refundable tax credits to help offset provincial/territorial taxes. These credits are reported on your provincial/territorial tax calculation forms.

Looking at the Basic Personal Credits for You, Your Spouse, and Your Children

Every Canadian can claim personal tax credits on the annual tax filing forms, and if you have a spouse and/or children or other dependants you might be able to claim credits for them as well. These credits mean you're able to earn a basic amount of income each year and not pay tax on it.

Basic personal credit amount

Each and every Canadian filing a tax return is able to claim this credit. The amount changes every year, but it is in excess of $10,000. In other words, the first $10,000 or so of income you earn is not subject to tax!

Here's how this actually works. Assume your taxable income is $10,000. The tax rate at this income level is 15 percent, so your tax equals $1,500. On schedule 1 you calculate the non-refundable tax credits available to you. If the basic personal amount is $10,000 (and it's likely more), the 15 percent tax credit equals $1,500. See a pattern? The tax credit completely offsets the tax, so your final tax liability is nil.

Spouse/common-law partner credit amount

The spouse/common-law credit amount is another credit worth at least $10,000. Again, the amount changes every year. Assuming the credit is $10,000 and you're able to claim the full amount, the federal tax savings will be $1,500 ($10,000 × 15 percent).

How do you qualify? Well, first you have to have a spouse. For income tax purposes, "spouse" includes the person you're legally married to or a person who is your common-law partner. (Of course, if you happen to have both, you can make a claim for only one these "spouses"!) Common-law partners are defined as two persons, regardless of sex, who cohabit in a conjugal relationship that has been continuous for at least 12 months or, if fewer than 12 months, have a child, natural or adopted, together.

As you might have guessed, more qualifications exist. If your spouse had any net income for the year, the credit amount is reduced dollar for dollar. If your spouse's income is greater than the credit amount, the amount available to you is reduced to zero. Your spouse's net income is the amount reported on line 236 of his or her tax return.

If you separated during the year and were not back together by December 31, reduce the credit amount by your spouse's net income before the separation only.

If you cannot claim the spousal amount (say, because the credit amount calculation works out to zero), or you have to reduce the credit claimed because of your spouse's net income, you still may be able to claim the credit, or an increased credit amount, if your spouse's income for the year includes dividend income from

Canadian corporations. You do this by claiming your spouse's dividend income on your return so that his or her income is lowered to permit the credit amount you claim — or, perhaps, a greater credit amount than originally calculated.

Child tax credit amount

If you have a child, then this credit is for you! The child tax credit amount is at least $2,000 for each child under the age of 18 at the end of the year. No receipts required! The credit amount changes each year, but assuming a credit of $2,000 the actual federal tax saving is $300 per child ($2,000 × 15 percent)!

If you don't need all the child tax credit to reduce your federal tax to zero, you can transfer any of the unused portion to your spouse or common-law partner.

If you'll be eligible to claim the child tax credit in the future, you might want to let your employer know so that your taxes at source can be reduced throughout the year. Otherwise, you have to wait until you file your tax return to benefit from the credit. You can inform your employer via a letter or by filling out form TD1 (you can download it from the CRA Website). Your payroll department should also have copies on hand.

Credit amount for an eligible dependant

This credit amount (often referred to by its previous moniker, the "equivalent-to-spouse" credit amount) of at least $10,000 is available to you if you have a dependant and you were single, divorced, separated, or widowed at any time during the year. In other words, you did not have a spouse/common-law partner, or if you did you were not living together. Not just any dependant will qualify for this credit — unfortunately, you can't claim a credit for your 28-year-old son who still lives in your basement, even if he does eat all your food. Your dependant must be the following:

- Your parent or grandparent
- Your child, grandchild, brother, or sister who was under 18 or, if not under 18, was physically or mentally infirm
- Living with you in a home you maintain

This claim is usually made by a single parent for a child, although claims by children for a parent and by one sibling for another are fairly common as well. Give details of the claim for an eligible dependant (name, age, income) on schedule 5 of your tax return.

Like the spousal/common-law partner amount, the amount for an eligible dependant is reduced by the dependant's income on a dollar-for-dollar basis. If the credit this year is $10,000 and the dependant's net income is $10,000 or greater, the credit amount for an eligible dependant will be zero. The actual credit amount will vary each year and is increased annually by the inflation rate.

You cannot claim this amount if someone else in your household is claiming it for the same dependant.

You can claim this credit for a dependant who lives away from home while attending school, if that dependant ordinarily lives with you when not in school.

Credit amounts transferred from your spouse/common-law partner

Your spouse/common-law partner can transfer to you any part of certain tax credit amounts that he or she qualifies for but does not need to reduce his or her federal income tax to zero.

The credit amounts that may be transferred from one spouse/common-law partner to another are the age amount (Tip #67), the disability amount (Tip #61), the pension amount (Tip #67), and the tuition, education, and textbook amounts (Tip #56). For additional details and to calculate the amounts that can be transferred, refer to schedule 2 of your tax return. In the identification area on page 1 of your return, be sure to report your marital status and your spouse/common-law partner's name and social insurance number so your claim is not rejected.

Examining Additional Credits for Your Kids and Other Dependants

In recognition that the costs of supporting dependants can be high, and in order to support parents and caregivers, other tax credits are available to help lessen the load. In addition to the credits below, if you have a disabled family member, other credits may be available to you. See Tip #62 for more details.

Credit amount for adoption expenses

A non-refundable tax credit is available to help with adoption expenses. Eligible adoption expenses include fees paid to an adoption agency; travel costs for the parents and child; and court, legal, and administration fees. The adoption can be within Canada, or international, to qualify. The expenses must be claimed in the year the adoption is finalized, and they can be shared by the parents. The total amounts claimed cannot exceed the lesser of the actual adoption expenses or a maximum per child. The actual maximum changes each year, but it is at least $10,600 per child. At a maximum of $10,600, the federal tax savings would be $1,590 ($10,600 × 15%)!

Keep your receipts for this one.

Children's fitness tax credit amount

A credit of up to $500 is available to parents who pay to register a child in certain physical activity programs. The child must be under age 16 at the end of the year to qualify.

To be eligible for this credit, the program must be ongoing (at least once a week for eight weeks, or five consecutive days in the case of camps), supervised, and suitable for children.

The program also must include a significant amount of physical activity that provides cardiorespiratory endurance plus one or more of muscular strength, endurance, flexibility, or balance. Common Canadian activities that generally qualify include hockey, lacrosse, soccer, dance, and gymnastics, along with many others.

The maximum you can claim is the lesser of the actual cost paid or $500 per child. So, if karate camp costs $350, the maximum you could claim would be that $350. If that same child also took skating lessons that cost $125, your total claim for that child would be $475. On the other hand, even if you spend thousands on the activity, the most you can claim as a credit amount is $500 per child.

Keep your receipts for any activities you put your children in during the year. Although the receipts don't have to be filed with your tax return, the CRA might ask to see them later.

#50

Income Split for Family Tax Savings

*O*ne of the most effective ways for a family to save tax is to split income. *Income splitting* involves shifting income from the hands of one individual who pays tax at a high tax rate to another who pays tax at a lower tax rate. The result is that less tax is paid by the family! Of course, it's not as easy as simply putting some of your income on your spouse or kids' tax returns — some limitations do exist. But where it's possible, income splitting can potentially save you a load of tax!

Why Income Splitting Can Save Tax

In Canada we pay tax at graduated rates. Basically, your taxable income is split into bands (or brackets), and income within each band is taxed at increasingly higher tax rates. If you have family members who are taxed in the lower bands, and you're in a higher band, you can save on taxes if you can manage to get some income taxed to those family members.

Let's look at some numbers. Say you're an employee and earn a salary of $150,000. At this income level you're taxed at the highest marginal tax rate. If you also earn investment income, all that income will be taxed at high tax rates because your salary has already pushed you into the highest tax bracket. If the highest marginal tax rate in your province is 45 percent and you earn $10,000 of interest income, you will pay $4,500 of tax on that interest income alone! However, if you can manage to get that interest taxed in the hands of your spouse or children, and if they have no other sources of income, they will pay no tax on $10,000 of interest. You've now saved $4,500 of tax as a family!

Watching Out for the Attribution Rules

To make income splitting difficult, the *Income Tax Act* includes a bunch of rules, called the "attribution rules," which state that if you try to split or shift investment income (i.e., interest, dividends, and rents) to your spouse/common-law partner or to a minor child, grandchild, niece, or nephew, you — not they — will be taxed on the income earned on the invested funds. In addition, if you wish to split or shift capital gains with a spouse/common-law partner, you may find the attribution rules also work against you! Oddly, perhaps, the attribution rules will not negatively impact your plans to shift capital gains to your minor child. Hey, here's a tax-planning opportunity! We talk more about this under "Loaning money to family members."

The good news is that we can tell you some ways around the attribution rules (legal ways, of course!) so you can make income splitting work for you and your family.

Investigating Ways to Split Income

Income splitting isn't necessarily easy. You can't shift a salary to lower taxed family members. But when proper steps are taken, income splitting is possible with certain types of income — including investment income, pension income, and business income.

Loaning money to family members

If you give your spouse or minor child funds to invest, the interest and dividends (in other words, the investment income) earned on the invested funds will be subject to tax in your hands — not in the hands of your spouse or minor child. The investment income earned will be "attributed" to you and your tax return, where it will be subject to tax at your tax rate. In other words, you're in the same position as had you invested directly yourself — you have not successfully income split!

If you loan, instead of gifting, money to a spouse or minor child to be used for investment purposes, you can avoid the investment income earned on the loaned funds being taxed in your hands. However, as with everything, there's a catch. Interest-free loans or even low-interest loans won't cut it! To avoid the attribution rules, you must charge interest on the loan at an interest rate at least equal to the CRA's prescribed interest rate at the time of the loan. Your spouse or minor child must pay the interest owing to you by no later than January 30 (not 31!) of the year following the year in which the interest was incurred — and it must be included in your income. Your spouse or minor child can deduct this interest from the income earned on the investment.

The CRA announces its prescribed interest rates every quarter. The rates can be found on the CRA's Web site at www.cra-arc. gc.ca/interestrates. (At the time of writing, the CRA's prescribed interest rate was a historically low 1 percent!)

You'll manage to split income, and save tax, only if the investments earn a rate of return higher than the CRA's prescribed interest rate at the time the loan is made.

You can lock in the prescribed interest rate that was in effect at the time the loan was made for the entire term of the loan, so you're not at risk should the CRA's prescribed interest rates go up in the future. If the rates drop, consider repaying your loan and taking out a new loan to lock in at the lower rate.

If you give money to a minor child to invest, the investment income (interest and dividends) will be taxed in your hands. However, if the funds were invested and capital gains were incurred (due to a sale of an investment where proceeds are greater than the cost of the investment, or a capital gain allocated from a mutual fund), the capital gain will not be taxed in your hands — it will be taxed in the hands of the child. Individuals can have a taxable income of up to about $10,000 because of your basic personal amount (which changes annually) and pay no tax — a minor child can actually report capital gains of double that and pay no tax, because only 50 percent of capital gains are subject to tax.

If you're giving a minor child funds to invest, make sure the investments focus on generating capital gains (stocks and equity-based mutual funds) as opposed to interest and dividends. If you're looking for a more balanced investment mix, corporate-class mutual funds will avoid generating interest income, even though the underlying investment exposure could be traditional interest-bearing investments.

Using second-generation income

If you give or lend money to a spouse or minor child to invest (with no interest or at an interest rate below the CRA prescribed interest rate at the time of the loan), any income earned on the investments will be attributed back to you and taxed in your hands. The good news? *Second-generation income* — that is, "income on income" — is not attributed back.

Second-generation income works like this: Lend or give money to your spouse or minor child, then transfer any income earned each year to a separate investment account in the spouse's or minor child's name. Future earnings in that second account are not subject to the attribution rules. Income splitting has been achieved!

Using trusts to income split

You might want to income split but are uncomfortable with giving your money directly to a family member, especially one with a love for fast cars or expensive handbags. You get the drift. In these cases, you could gift or loan funds into a family trust instead. With a trust, your family member benefits from the funds in the trust, but does not necessarily get direct access to the funds. They are, however, taxed on the investment income each year; although you still need to give heed to the attribution rules. A common reason for setting up a family trust occurs when you have a fairly significant wealth level, pay for your child's expenses out of your after-tax income (think private school), and want to income split. You can put money in the trust and have the trust pay the child's expenses instead. If you're the right league for a trust, speak to a tax professional; specific paperwork must be drawn up.

Splitting retirement income

If you're retired or nearing retirement, consider these easy and effective ways to use income splitting to pay less tax on your retirement income.

First, for those already retired, up to 50 percent of certain pension income can be split, shifted, or allocated from a high-tax-bracket spouse to a lower-tax-bracket spouse. This results in the couple paying less tax! Many types of income can be split, including income from an employer pension plan and RRIF income if you're over the age of 65. See Tip #68 for all the details.

Pension splitting may serve to permit another pension credit amount of up to $2,000 for a spouse age 65-plus who otherwise would not be eligible.

Be wary of the impact of the increase in income of the lower-income spouse as a result of pension splitting. The extra income can cause a reduction in the age credit amount (Tip #67), as well as causing or increasing the Old Age Security (OAS) clawback (Tip #64).

Next, married or common-law partners who are at least 60 and live together can elect to share CPP payments on the portion of CPP earned during their time together. A portion of CPP payments of a high-tax-bracket individual can be shifted — or shared — with a lower-tax-bracket individual. This will result in tax savings for the couple!

If only one individual was a CPP contributor, the two individuals can share one pension. Remember, you must apply to share your CPP pension!

Finally, for those still saving for retirement, your optimum goal is for each spouse/common-law partner to have equal incomes during retirement. This will accomplish perfect income splitting and keep the total family tax bill to a minimum. You can achieve this by using spousal RRSPs. Spousal RRSP contributions work like this: You contribute to an RRSP under which your spouse is the annuitant. You claim the tax deduction for the amounts put into the plan, and when money is withdrawn for retirement, your spouse is taxed on the withdrawal. Talk about shifting retirement income from one spouse to the other! (See Tip #42 for more on spousal RRSPs.)

Even with the new pension-splitting rules, contributing to a spousal RRSP remains a sound tax-planning idea for a number of reasons. Spousal RRSPs are still a way to income split for those who are not yet a "senior" — say, to fund a maternity or education leave or for early retirement. The types of pension income eligible for pension splitting are quite restrictive for those under 65.

Paying wages to family members

If you have your own business, consider paying a salary or wage to members of your family. Of course, they must actually work in the business (and no, you won't get away with paying your 4-year-old son to colour pictures you use for advertising or your 2-year-old daughter to lick stamps). In addition, the salary you pay them must be reasonable for the work they do.

The advantage to paying wages to family members is that you can claim the amount paid as a deduction on your business statement, so your taxable income and your taxes are reduced. On the flip side, the family member includes this amount in his or her income. You can pay a child who has no other source of income up to their basic personal amount (over $10,000 per year, and the amount increases annually) without generating a tax bill for that child. Assuming your marginal tax rate is 45 percent, that's a savings of about $4,500 in tax!

Transferring money for business purposes

If you give or lend money to family members to use in a business as opposed to for investing, you can avoid the dreaded attribution rules. Even if it's a loan, there's no need to charge interest. Because the funds will earn business income and not investment income or capital gains, you don't have to worry about having the business income or gains taxed in your hands.

Investing more for lower-income family members

If your ultimate goal is to invest your funds for the future, you would like the investments to be made by a family member who will pay the least amount of tax on those investments. You can accomplish this for a spouse and for children in various ways.

One way to get more funds into the hands of the lower-income spouse is to have the higher-income spouse pay all the daily living expenses. This includes groceries, mortgage or rent payments, credit card bills, gas for the car, and so on. This frees up more cash in the hands of the lower-income spouse to earn investment income that is taxed at a lower tax rate.

 Another idea is for the higher-income spouse to pay the income tax liability and instalments of the lower-income spouse. Because the amount is not invested by the spouse, the attribution rules won't apply. Any funds the lower-income spouse would have used to pay the tax liabilities are now free to be used for investment purposes.

You can also invest for children in a tax-effective manner. One way is to use the government benefits paid on behalf of the child for investment purposes. This includes the non-taxable Canada Child Tax Benefit (CCTB) that is paid monthly to qualifying families until their children reach 18 years of age. The amount paid varies based on the family's income. It also includes the taxable Universal Child Care Benefit (UCCB), which is paid to all families with a child under 6. The payment is $100 per month.

 Both these benefit payments can be invested in your child's name and earn any type of income without the attribution rules kicking in. Make sure these funds are deposited directly into an investment account for your child.

You can also invest for a child tax-efficiently using *registered education savings plans* (RESPs). These plans are used to help build an education fund for your child or grandchild. But RESPs are also a great way to income split. Although contributions made to an RESP are not tax deductible, they do grow tax free. When the funds are taken out for educational purposes, you won't be the one to foot the tax bill. The income earned in the plan is taxed in the child's hands, not yours. (See Tip #51.)

Registered disability savings plans (RDSPs) also allow parents to save funds, in a tax-efficient manner, to provide for a disabled child. The purpose of these plans is to provide for the long-term financial security of an individual who has a prolonged and severe physical or mental impairment. Just like an RESP, contributions made to an RDSP are not tax deductible, but they do grow tax free. When the funds are taken out, they are taxable in the hands of the disabled person, which again achieves income splitting. (See Tip #63.)

Income splitting after death using trusts

If you expect to leave or receive an inheritance that will end up being invested, consider a special kind of trust called a testamentary trust to provide income splitting after death. A testamentary trust is provided for in your will and requires your heirs to hold their inheritance in a trust instead of in their personal names. Many benefits to this structure exist, but from our standpoint the advantage is tax savings!

A testamentary trust is taxed like an individual with graduated tax rates. So, if an heir already earns income and is taxed at a fairly high tax rate, any investment income earned from the investment of the inheritance would lose quite a chunk to tax annually. By instead having the trust pay the tax on the investment income, your heir can essentially income split with the trust after you're gone.

A testamentary trust must be provided for in your will, so if this would be to your benefit, speak to a lawyer. And if you would benefit from having a trust for an inheritance you might receive in the future, speak to the person who will be leaving money to you to see if they would provide for such a trust in his or her will. Tip #73 discusses using trusts in your tax and estate planning.

Fund Your Child's Education Tax-Effectively

• •

*T*he cost of postsecondary education in Canada is rising, and with students graduating with ever larger debts many parents are thinking about a head start on saving for education. In this tip we suggest some tax-effective ways to save for a child's education, the most popular being the RESP.

Using RESPs for Tax Benefits

Registered education savings plans, or RESPs, are one of the most popular and effective ways for Canadians to save for a child's education. In a nutshell, here's how they work: A "subscriber" (usually a parent or grandparent, but it could be someone else) places funds in the plan for a child's benefit. Although no tax deduction for RESP contributions applies (like exists for RRSP contributions), funds within the plan can grow tax-sheltered. Plus, the government provides an extra bonus, the Canada Education Savings Grant, to help pump up the savings!

Contributing to an RESP

Contributions to an RESP can be made at a bank, through your investment advisor, or through companies that specialize in these types of plans. You need to have a social insurance number for the child, and the child has to be a resident of Canada.

No annual limits to what you can contribute to an RESP apply, although the lifetime limit is $50,000 per child.

The federal government currently kicks in an additional 20 percent of the amount contributed to an RESP, to a maximum of $500 per year per child. The extra 20 percent is called the Canada Education Savings Grant, or CESG. You will get the maximum grant each year if you contribute $2,500 per child, but if you happen to miss a year don't worry — the grant room carries forward. The most grant the government will pay in a year if you missed out on prior-year grants is $1,000, which would be received with a $5,000 contribution. For years you missed prior to 2007, the maximum grant is $400. Don't miss out on free money for your child's education!

The CESG increases to 40 percent for the first $500 contributed by families with income up to about $40,000. Where family income is between about $40,000 and $80,000, the CESG will be 30 percent of the first $500 contributed. Note that these income levels change annually and are only approximate. If you're looking for the exact thresholds for the increased CESGs, visit the CanLearn Web site at www.can-learn.ca/eng/saving/. Whatever the income level, the maximum CESG a child is eligible for is $500 per year and $7,200 per lifetime.

Contributions can be made into an RESP for 31 years, which will be helpful if your children decide to go on with their schooling at a later age or if you have a family plan. You also can make contributions for a beneficiary who is up to age 31. If the beneficiary qualifies for the disability tax credit, contributions can be made up to age 35. However, in most cases to receive the CESG the beneficiary must be no more than 15 years old during the calendar year. You might qualify for a CESG at the age of 16 and 17 if at least $2,000 had been contributed into RESPs for that child prior to age 16 and at least $100 per year was contributed in any four years before the year the child turns 16. Confused? If your child is 16 and never had an RESP before, no CESG will be paid.

Even if you don't have the funds to contribute to your child's RESP, you might be eligible for a Canada Learning Bond to help you get a kick-start on education savings. If your child was born after December 31, 2003, and you receive the National Child Benefit Supplement, the government will start off the RESP with $500, plus deposit $100 a year for up to 15 years as long as you receive the National Child Benefit Supplement.

For free brochures on RESPs, the CESG, and the Canada Learning Bond, call 1-800-O-CANADA.

Earning investment income in an RESP

After you set up the RESP and contribute funds into it, the next step is to choose investments — because it's the growth of the investments that will help pump up the RESP value and provide more funds for the child's education.

The investment income earned by an RESP is not taxable each year, so the earnings can grow on a tax-deferred basis. This helps the RESP grow at a faster rate than if tax had to be paid each year.

Understanding What Happens When Your Child Goes to Postsecondary School

When your child goes to school, and is age 16 or older, it's time to start making withdrawals from the RESP. The payments are known as Education Assistance Payments (EAP).

Taxing RESP withdrawals while in school

The EAP has two portions. The first is the accumulated investment income earned in the plan and the second is the CESG that has accumulated.

The EAP from the RESP is considered to be tax deferred because it does eventually become taxable. It becomes taxable income of the student when he or she removes the money for educational purposes. However, the advantage of having the tax paid by the student is that the student probably has little or no other income and can claim the tuition, education, and textbook credits to reduce any tax he or she may owe (see Tip #56). It's quite possible there will be no tax at all to pay on the withdrawals in the future.

It's not until funds are withdrawn from the plan that tax is payable, and only the growth (including growth derived from the CESG) in the plan is taxable.

You might be wondering about your initial contributions. Because no deduction is available for contributions, it doesn't make sense that the withdrawal of your contributions would be taxable. So, you or the student is able to withdraw the original contributions out of the plan without any tax implications.

Full-time students can withdraw only up to $5,000 of EAP in the first 13 weeks of enrollment. Part-time students are limited to $2,500 in that time frame. After that, the withdrawals must be reasonable to fund the education needs, although no specific restriction exists on what the funds are used for.

Investigating what types of educational programs qualify

RESP withdrawals to be taxed to the student can be made only if the child is attending a qualifying education program on a full- or part-time basis. For full-time students the program must be at the postsecondary level and last at least three consecutive weeks. It must require the student to spend no fewer than ten hours per week on courses and work in the program. For part-time students the student must spend at least 12 hours per month on the courses. The course must last at least three consecutive weeks at the postsecondary level.

Proof of enrollment is necessary to receive an EAP. Contact the school for the necessary paperwork.

Examining the Options If Your Child Doesn't Go On to School

If the beneficiary of the RESP does not attend an institution of higher education, the contributions and the income earned from these contributions (accumulated income payments) can be returned to the contributor. The initial contributions can be withdrawn tax free, but the accumulated income can be withdrawn only when one of the following circumstances applies:

- ✔ The plan must have existed for at least ten years, and the beneficiary must be at least 21 years of age and not be attending an institution of higher learning.

- ✔ The beneficiary of the RESP has died.

- ✔ The plan has been in existence for 35 years. An RESP has to be closed by December 31 of the 35th anniversary year of the plan (it's 40 years if the beneficiary is entitled to the disability tax credit). Prior to 2008, a 25-year limit existed. This caused some issues when there was a large age gap between the children who were beneficiaries of the plan, and one or more of the children had not yet begun postsecondary education. The extra ten years will help to alleviate this problem.

If these requirements are met, the contributions and the accumulated income can be withdrawn, although the CESGs and any Canada Learning Bond payments received by the RESP must be paid back to the federal government. Any growth in the RESP due to the CESGs being invested can be withdrawn. CESG repayments are not taxable.

Any income returned to the contributor is taxable, and a special penalty surtax of 20 percent applies on top of the regular tax payable on this income. The surtax can be completely or partially avoided when the accumulated income is transferred directly to the contributor's RRSP. The maximum amount that can be transferred is subject to a lifetime limit of $50,000. Sufficient RRSP contribution room must be available to transfer funds to an RRSP. If the contributor passes away, the contributor's spouse can make use of the RRSP transfer option instead.

Exploring Other Options for Education Savings

RESPs clearly have some tax benefits but also some drawbacks, particularly if the child does not go on to school. In addition, if you plan to fully fund your child's postsecondary education, you might find that the limits imposed by the RESP will not allow you to save enough over the long run. In these cases you may need to use other savings plans to top up the savings.

One way to save for the child is to set up an in-trust account. With an in-trust account you contribute money into an investment account that is held for the child's benefit. If the account is set up so that the funds are essentially a gift to the child, the child (not the parent) will pay tax on any capital gains earned each year at assumedly a lower tax rate than the parent would pay. Interest and dividends would be attributed back to the contributing parent or grandparent and taxed in that contributor's hands. Sound too good to be true? The big drawback to an in-trust account is that when the child reaches the age of majority the funds can be withdrawn and used for any purpose the child so chooses.

If you don't like the idea of the child accessing the funds, you might simply want to save in your own account, and earmark the funds for education savings. That way you still pay tax on any investment earnings each year, but you can keep the funds in the future if the child doesn't go to school.

If you save funds in your TFSA and earmark them for education savings, you won't pay tax on the investment earnings each year, and the child won't have access to the funds at age of majority. See Tip #41 for more details.

If you don't save enough for postsecondary education, or if you simply don't intend to fund all the costs, don't forget there are many sources of funds out there for your children to explore including government loans, bank loans, scholarships, bursaries, and good old summer jobs.

#52

Know What Benefits Are Available for Your Children

*R*aising children is an expensive endeavour; those costs are even higher when you have a disabled child. In this tip we offer some additional benefits available if you have young children or a disabled child.

Even if you're not in a taxable situation, you should still file a tax return if you have children. Refer to Tip #3 for ideas on how to get free money from the government via the tax system.

Getting the Universal Child Care Benefit

Starting in July 2006, the government began paying families $100 per month for each child under the age of 6 in a household. This Universal Child Care Benefit is meant to provide financial support for childcare for preschool children, although it's not required that the child actually attends preschool for this benefit to be paid.

The Universal Child Care Benefit is taxable to the lower-income spouse (or the recipient, where two parents are not living together). You must include the payments you received on your income tax return on line 117 (but don't worry — you'll receive statement RC62 showing the amount you received during the year). These payments will not affect your entitlement to Old Age Security, Employment Insurance, or the childcare expense deduction, where applicable.

You must apply to receive the Universal Child Care Benefit. An application can be found at www.cra-arc.gc.ca/E/pbg/tf/rc66/. With payments of up to $1,200 per year, per child, it's worth your while even if it is taxable!

Claiming Disability Amounts

If you have a disabled child, the child might be eligible for a disability tax credit and disability supplement to help reduce taxes payable. However, the child may not have any income, so these credits go wasted. If you have a disabled dependant, be sure to read Tip #62 where we cover all the bases.

#53

Understand the Tax Implications of a Marriage Breakdown

*M*oney and finances are usually a big stressor when it comes to divorce. The lawyers will usually help hash out the financial settlements, but the tax implications to those settlements can play a big role in how much you actually have to shell out or how much you will receive in the settlement. Taxes should never be ignored in a marriage breakdown.

Support Payments

Support is a word synonymous with "alimony" and "maintenance" payments. Support refers both to payments made for spousal support and to payments made for child support. It's important to differentiate between spousal and child support because each has its own criteria regarding permissible tax deductions.

 You'll see that the deduction/income inclusion criteria for support payments mirror each other. Where one taxpayer has a deduction, one will have an income inclusion. If no deduction is available, no income inclusion applies.

 Though it can be emotionally draining to go through the process of finalizing the agreement, our experience in dealing with many separated and divorced individuals is that the agreement is vital in maintaining some sanity and in ensuring your financial protection. Contact a lawyer specializing in family law as soon as possible to protect your rights to support, your assets, and your children.

Spousal support

Payments to an ex-spouse — including an "estranged" (separated) spouse — are in most cases tax deductible, and on the flip side, taxable to the recipient. To support the deduction, you must have a written agreement or court order signed by both you and your ex-spouse that specifically stipulates the amounts to be paid. If no agreement or court order exists, the amounts paid are not tax deductible. However, an agreement can provide for at least some of the pre-agreement spousal support payments to be tax deductible, as we explain later in this section.

The support payments must be periodic; that is, monthly. Lump-sum payments do not qualify for a tax deduction.

Any payments you made prior to the date of a court order or a written agreement can be considered to have been paid under an order or agreement, and therefore are tax deductible. However, the order or agreement must stipulate that any prior payments made are considered to have been paid (and therefore are potentially deductible) pursuant to the agreement. Only payments made in the year that the order or agreement is finalized, and the preceding year, qualify for the retroactive treatment. Get the separation agreement drawn up promptly!

Child support

Child support rules took a dramatic shift over ten years ago. Three sets of rules are now in place, and you need to determine which ones apply to you. Your child support payments may or may not be tax deductible/taxable. The three sets of rules are detailed below.

Child support order or agreement made before May 1, 1997

If you're making payments under an order or agreement made before May 1, 1997, your payments are tax deductible. The ex-spouse receiving the payments will include the amounts in his or her income.

Child support order or agreement made on May 1, 1997, or later

Payments made under a May 1, 1997, or later agreement or order are not tax deductible and are not taxable in the hands of the recipient.

Modification of a pre–May 1, 1997, child support order or agreement

If you're making tax-deductible payments under a pre–May 1, 1997, order or agreement, you may find your payments suddenly cease to be tax deductible (and the payments received no longer taxable) under one of the following circumstances:

- ✔ The order or agreement is amended to increase or decrease child support payments (and, therefore, considered a new agreement and subject to the new rules).

- ✔ You and your ex-spouse elect to have the newer rules apply to your old agreement.

Recognizing When to Deduct Legal Expenses

In the past, very few legal expenses incurred on a marriage breakdown were deductible. However the rules have been expanded and now cover off many more types of legal costs, including costs to

✔ Obtain an order for child support

✔ Collect late support payments

✔ Establish the amount of support payments

✔ Seek to obtain an increase in your support payments

✔ Seek to make child support non-taxable

However, you cannot claim the costs to get a separation or divorce, or to establish custody or visitation arrangements for your children.

You're not permitted to claim legal costs you incur to establish, negotiate, or contest the amount of support payments you pay.

Ensure your lawyer details the bill such that fees for tax-deductible services are highlighted!

Distinguishing Which Parent Can Claim Dependant Credits

If you're a single parent, you're able to claim a credit amount for an eligible dependant. This used to be known as the "equivalent-to-spouse" credit. Basically it's like getting another basic personal credit in order to give you some tax help for supporting a household with a dependant on your own.

This credit is available if you have a dependant and you were single, divorced, separated, or widowed at any time during the year (so it's not solely available on marriage breakdown). You can find a full discussion on who qualifies in Tip #49.

A claim isn't allowed if you were required to make support payments for the dependant child during the year.

Other credits you might qualify for after your marriage is dissolved include:

> ✔ **GST credit for you and your children.** If you share custody,
> the government will put you on a shared eligibility schedule
> for the GST credit.
>
> ✔ **Canada Child Tax Benefit.** Again, a shared eligibility schedule
> may apply.
>
> ✔ **Amount for children aged 18 or younger.** You and your ex
> must negotiate who will claim this credit. It cannot be shared
> and cannot be claimed by more than one person. If you can't
> agree, no one is allowed to make a claim.

Taxing Assets Transferred on a Marriage Breakdown

In the course of your negotiations, you'll have to discuss who is
going to get what. The "what" might include assets such as registered assets, non-registered investment accounts, the family home,
vacation properties, and pension assets.

From a tax standpoint, assets can pass between spouses on a marriage breakdown without current tax implications. For example,
registered assets such as an RRSP can simply be rolled from one
spouse's RRSP to the other. And assets that might have appreciated in value such as stocks or mutual funds held in non-registered
accounts, or a vacation property, can transfer at their tax costs
instead of at their current values, which might give rise to capital
gains.

This is not to say tax never applies on these assets. The recipient spouse will have to pay tax on registered assets any time a
withdrawal is made, and that withdrawal is taxed at that person's
marginal tax rate. And although the capital gain on other assets is
deferred, it does become taxable upon sale. At the time of disposition the capital gain is calculated as the difference between the
final sales price and the original tax cost of the asset, not the value
at the time of marriage breakdown.

Ensure the embedded tax liabilities are taken into account during
your negotiations. If one person gets the family house, where no
tax would ever be payable because of the principal residence
exemption, and the other person gets RRSP assets, the RRSP assets
would be worth much less after tax.

You must complete special tax forms to avoid paying tax on the
transfer of the assets. For RRSP assets, fill out form T2220 and
ensure the assets are transferred directly from one registered
account to another.

#54

Claim Childcare Expenses

*O*ur government recognizes that many of us incur childcare expenses in order to be able to work, go to school, or train for a job. If you pay childcare expenses, make sure you get the most bang for your buck, tax-wise!

Finding Out What Types of Expenses Are Deductible

To claim a deduction for a child, the child must be your child, your spouse's child, or a child dependant on you or your spouse; and the child must have a net income less than the basic personal amount (about $10,000 but the amount changes each year).

Eligible childcare expenses include payments to the following:

- ✔ Individuals providing childcare services. This could be a nanny, a home daycare, or payments to a babysitter while you're at work. Payments to the child's mother, father, or a related person under 18 are not eligible. Individuals providing childcare must provide a receipt with their social insurance number noted. Other childcare providers simply need to provide you with a receipt.
- ✔ Daycares, childcare centres, and day nursery schools
- ✔ Schools where part of the fee is for childcare (such as before- and after-school care)
- ✔ "Day" camps and "overnight" camps

Sports lessons, such as your child's weekly swimming lesson or dance class, are not considered a childcare expense. However, they may qualify for the children's fitness tax credit.

Discovering the Maximum Claim Amount

Childcare can be expensive. However, limits are placed on the maximum amount you can claim as a tax deduction. Here are the maximum childcare expenses that can be claimed per eligible child:

Disabled child — regardless of age	$10,000
Child under age 7 on December 31 of the year	$7,000
Child aged 7 to 16 on December 31 of the year	$4,000

For example, if you hired a nanny and paid her $12,000 in the year to watch your 4-year-old child, you can claim only $7,000 as a tax deduction.

The maximum deductible is also restricted to two-thirds of your "earned income." Don't get the definition of earned income for purposes of the childcare deduction mixed up with the definition of earned income for your RRSP deduction. For purposes of the childcare expense deduction, earned income consists of:

- ✔ Employment income, including tips and gratuities
- ✔ Self-employment income
- ✔ Research grants
- ✔ CPP/QPP disability benefits
- ✔ Government payments under a plan to encourage employment

So, say you earn $10,000 in the year from a part-time job. Your spouse earns $60,000 per year. You have your 3-year-old child in preschool and pay $8,000 per year for that. Your childcare deduction is the lower of $7,000 (the maximum childcare deduction for a child under the age of 7) and $6,667 (two-thirds of your income). Therefore, you can claim only $6,667 as a childcare deduction.

Where payments are made to facilities providing overnight lodging and boarding, such as overnight sports schools, boarding schools, or camps, the eligible deductible amount is restricted to:

- ✔ $175 per week per disabled child of any age
- ✔ $175 per week per child under age 7 on December 31 of the year
- ✔ $100 per week per child aged 7 to 16 on December 31 of the year

Complete form T778, "Child Care Expenses Deduction," when you file your tax return to provide the CRA with all the details it requires to assess your childcare claim.

Determining Who Claims Childcare Expenses

If a child lives with both parents, the parent with the lower income claims the childcare expense deduction. However, as with everything, exceptions apply to this general rule.

Are you the only supporting person? If so, you make the claim for the childcare expenses deduction.

Creating income to avoid wasting the deduction

Where one of two supporting persons has no net income, the deduction for childcare expenses will be "wasted." We often see this when someone is self-employed but has so many business expenses in the year that no net income exists. Therefore, where possible, try to ensure the supporting person with the lower income has "earned income." For example, if you're self-employed, you might want to forgo some of your discretionary tax deductions such as CCA to create more income from which to deduct your childcare expenses. As noted earlier, the deduction for childcare expenses cannot exceed two-thirds of earned income. So, for a maximum claim, the earned income of the lower-net-income supporting person needs to be three-halves (or 150 percent) of the eligible childcare costs incurred.

Deducting childcare on the higher-income parent's tax return

Can the supporting person with the higher net income ever deduct childcare expenses? Yes, if the supporting person with the lower net income was in one of these situations:

- In school (the school can be a secondary school, college, university, or an "educational institution" certified by Human Resources and Skills Development Canada [HRSDC] for courses that develop or improve occupational skills).

- Not able to take care of children because of a mental or physical disability

- In jail for at least two weeks in the year

What to do when supporting persons live apart

Where supporting persons were living apart for all of the year by virtue of a marriage breakdown (whether a legal or common-law relationship), each is entitled to a deduction for childcare expenses. The aggregate claimed by the supporting persons cannot exceed the overall limits noted above.

If you separated from your spouse in the year and you're the higher-net-income supporting person, you can make a claim if you and your spouse were living apart on December 31 of the year. A claim will be allowed to you if you and your spouse were separated for at least 90 days beginning sometime in the year and the child-care expenses claimed by you were actually paid by you. The claim period is restricted to the period of separation. See Tip #53 for more on the special circumstances of a marriage breakdown.

#55

Make the Most of Your Family Home

● ●

*F*or most Canadians, the family home is their most valuable asset. So, tax tips relating to the home are relevant to almost everyone! In this tip we explore how to purchase, renovate, sell, and rent out your home on a tax-friendly basis. You're sure to find a tip or two that can help your family!

Purchasing a Home Using the Home Buyers' Plan

Normally, withdrawals from your RRSP are fully taxable to you in the year of withdrawal. However, when you withdraw money from your RRSP to purchase a home under the Home Buyers' Plan, the withdrawal is exempt from tax. This can provide a much needed down payment for your home and help you to cover closing costs, making your RRSP a tax-friendly source of funds for a home purchase.

Of course, your tax obligations aren't over. You're required to repay the amount you withdrew for your Home Buyers' Plan to your RRSP. If you don't? You guessed it — the shortfall will be added to your income (at line 129 of your tax return).

As with anything tax-related, rules to the game apply. First, you can withdraw up to $25,000 from your RRSP tax-free to buy a home, as long as you or your spouse hasn't owned a home that you occupied as your principal place of residence in the past four years. Your spouse can make use of the HBP too, leaving a potential for $50,000 to go toward the home purchase, provided your spouse also hasn't owned a home in the past four years and you are purchasing the home jointly.

The withdrawal is treated as a loan from your RRSP, to be repaid over a period of no more than 15 years. The first repayment, a minimum of one-fifteenth of your HBP withdrawal, must be paid back in the second calendar year following the year in which you made the withdrawal. If you took out a $40,000 HBP loan in November

2009, for example, you must repay at least $1,333 (one-fifteenth of $20,000) before the end of 2011. If you don't make the repayment, the $1,333 is included in your income. Yikes!

It's easy to make an HBP repayment — you simply make a contribution to your RRSP. On schedule 7 of your tax return, you note the total of your RRSP contributions and then allocate a portion of the contributions to the annual HBP repayment. (That amount doesn't qualify for an RRSP deduction because it's simply a repayment of an amount borrowed from your RRSP.)

If you contribute to your RRSP and then withdraw the funds within 90 days for the HBP, you won't be able to claim a deduction for that contribution. Always allow your contributions to sit for 91 days or more before making a withdrawal under the HBP.

No restriction on speeding up your HBP repayment exists. It makes good financial sense to repay the withdrawals as soon as you can, because the sooner the funds go back into your RRSP, the greater the tax-free growth in value!

Limited time offer: Home renovation tax credit

For 2009, the Canadian government offered a tax credit worth up to $1,350 for eligible home renovations. The credit applies to eligible expenses of more than $1,000 and you receive the maximum credit with reno costs of $10,000. To qualify, the reno costs must be incurred after January 27, 2009 and before February 1, 2010.

The home renovation tax credit (HRTC) applies to a wide range of projects in your home. The key is that the work done must be "of an enduring nature and integral to the dwelling." The cost of supplies and materials, labour, and professional services can all be included. Financing costs cannot, nor can general home maintenance costs such as snow removal or house cleaning.

Some examples of eligible improvements include:

✔ Renovating a kitchen, bathroom, basement, or other room in your home

✔ Landscaping

✔ Installing new flooring

✔ Painting

✔ Replacing your roof

✔ Replacing windows or doors

Getting into the ecoENERGY Grant

If you're planning to renovate your home and the reno will improve your home's energy efficiency, be aware that a grant of up to $5,000 could be available to you from the federal government. Some provincial governments top up the grant. This is free money to help with costs you were going to incur anyway, so it's definitely worth a look!

The first step is to hire an energy advisor certified by Natural Resources Canada who will evaluate your home's current energy effectiveness. You can find an advisor at the following Web site: `http://oee.nrcan.gc.ca/residential/personal/new-home-improvement/contact-advisors.cfm?attr=4`. You'll receive a report outlining the grant you will receive by making specific improvements to your home. Some examples might include replacing your home's furnace, air conditioning or water heating system, or installing energy-efficient windows.

This grant is not claimed on your tax return; however, it's possible you could claim the 2009 home renovation tax credit and the ecoENERGY grant on the same expenditures. This program is set to end on March 31, 2011.

Selling Your Family Home Tax-Free

One of the last great tax shelters in Canada is the ability to sell your principal residence, a fancy name for your family home, without having to pay tax on the gains. If you own only one family residence, you have nothing to worry about. You can safely sell your home and not have to claim the gain on your tax return. Easy peasy.

If you own more than one property that could be considered your principal residence, you'll eventually have to pay tax on the gains on one property. This is most often seen where you have a home and a vacation property like a cottage or ski chalet. In that case you can usually choose which property to designate as your principal residence so that you can avoid the capital gains tax on one of the properties. See Tip #46 for all the details.

Tips When Renting Out Your Own Residence

Do you rent out space in your home? If so, the income you earn is taxable and must be reported on form T776 when you file your tax return. Thankfully it doesn't end there. You're allowed to claim a portion of your expenses to help offset that income and lower your tax bill. We talk about real estate rentals in Tip #44. The only difference between renting out a space that you live in, versus a space that you don't, is that not all of your expenses are deductible.

 You have to split your expenses so that you're not deducting any personal expenses on your tax return. If you have expenses that relate only to the rented space, such as advertising costs to get a new tenant or repairs and maintenance of the space, those expenses are fully deductible. Any expenses that related to the property on a whole such as mortgage interest, property taxes, or utilities must be divided between the personal part and the rented part.

The method you use to split the expenses must be *reasonable*. Generally, the CRA will allow you to split the expenses if you use the square footage of the rented space divided by the square footage of the entire space, or the number of rented rooms divided by the total number of rooms in the house. Some rooms may be used by you and the tenant. In that case you need to use a reasonable method to allocate the expenses, such as estimating the percentage of time the tenant uses those shared rooms.

 We don't recommend you claim capital cost allowance on your home. If you do, you'll lose a portion of the principal residence exemption when you eventually sell your home. And because real estate usually goes up in value, that exemption may be worth more than a small deduction each year.

 Avoid claiming a loss on the rental of your home, or other personally used property. If you do, a "reasonable expectation of profit" rule could be applied that will prevent you from claiming expenses against your rental income.

#56

Claim Credit for Tuition and Textbooks

*1*n this tip we tell you how claim the 15 percent non-refundable federal tax credit — for eligible tuition, education, and textbook costs and any unused amounts you weren't able to use that are carried forward from previous years. If you can't use it you may be able to share the credit with a family member.

Amounts carried forward are shown on your Notice of Assessment. Enter the details of your tuition and education amounts on schedule 11 of your return.

Qualifying courses include the majority of those at the post-secondary level or those that develop or improve skills in an occupation. You must also have paid more than $100 during the year to each educational institution whose fees you claim. You can't claim other expenses related to pursuing your education, such as board and lodging. These costs are the reason why an education amount is available to students.

You can claim the tuition you paid for courses you took in the current year. If you missed claiming tuition you paid for in previous years you will need to file a T1 Adjustment (to correct that year's tax return) in order to claim the credit.

Making the Claim

You can claim the education tax credit for each whole or part month in the year in which you were enrolled in a qualifying educational program. Your educational institution has to complete and give you form T2202, "Education and Textbook Amounts Certificate," or form T2202A, "Tuition, Education and Textbook Amounts Certificate," to confirm the period in which you were enrolled in a qualifying program.

To claim tuition fees paid to an educational institution outside Canada, you must receive from your institution a completed form TL11A, "Tuition, Education and Textbook Amounts Certificate — University Outside Canada."

Currently, you can claim $400 for each month in which you were enrolled as a full-time student, or $120 for each month in which you were enrolled in a qualifying part-time program. You cannot claim more than one education amount for a particular month.

A *full-time program* is a program at the post-secondary level that lasts at least three weeks and requires at least ten hours per week on courses or work in the program. A *part-time program* must also last at least three weeks, but it does not have a ten-hour-per-week course or workload requirement.

You can claim $400 a month if you attended your educational institution only part time because of a mental or physical impairment. In this case, you have to complete part 2 of form T2202, "Education and Textbook Amounts Certificate," to make your claim.

Offsetting the Cost of Textbooks

In addition to receiving some tax relief through the tuition and education credit amounts, students can also claim a non-refundable credit amount to offset the cost of their textbooks. The credit amount is calculated as follows: $65 for each month for which you qualify for the full-time education tax credit amount; or $20 for each month for which you qualify for the part-time education tax credit amount.

Transferring or Carrying Forward Credit Amounts

In many cases, students simply do not have the cash flow to pay for their own education. However, for tax purposes, the student — not the person who paid the fees — gets first crack at the tuition, education, and textbook tax credit amounts. It's only when you don't need the full tax credit from these amounts to reduce your tax bill to zero that you can transfer the tuition, education, and textbook tax credit amounts to another person.

If you don't need all the tuition, education, and textbook tax credit amounts to reduce your taxes to zero, you can transfer some or all of your unused credits to another person. If you don't transfer your unused amount to your spouse, you can transfer it to your or your spouse's parent or grandparent, who would claim it on line 324 of his or her return. Complete the back of form T2202 or form T2202A, as well as schedule 11 on your tax return, to calculate and designate this transfer. The maximum amount you may transfer to a spouse, parent, or grandparent is $5,000 (for federal tax purposes).

If you're transferring a tuition, education, or textbook tax credit amount to another person, don't transfer more than the person needs to reduce his or her federal income tax to zero. That way, you maximize the benefit of the credit and can carry forward the unused amount to a future year to offset your future tax bill.

You can carry forward the part of your tuition, education, and textbook tax credit amounts that you did not need to use and did not transfer for the year in which they were incurred. However, if you carry forward an amount, you won't be able to transfer it to anyone else in the future.

You must claim your carryforward amount in the earliest year possible — when you have a federal tax liability that needs to be sheltered with a federal tax credit. You can't pick and choose the tax years in which to claim the credits. The federal carryforward amount and the amount, if any, used in the year to reduce a tax bill are to be detailed on schedule 11 of your tax return.

Receiving a Transfer of Credits

A student who does not need tuition, education, and textbook tax credit amounts to reduce federal income tax to zero may be able to transfer the unused portion to you if you are a parent or grandparent of the student or of the student's spouse. The maximum amount that each student can transfer is $5,000 (for federal tax purposes) minus the amount the student needs, even if an unused amount greater than this still exists.

To calculate the transfer amount and to highlight to whom the amount is being transferred, the student has to complete the reverse side of form T2202, "Education and Textbook Amounts Certificate," or form T2202A, "Tuition, Education and Textbook Amounts Certificate."

If a student's spouse claims amounts on line 303 (spousal or common-law partner amount) or 326 (amounts transferred for spouse) for the student, a parent or grandparent cannot claim the tuition and education amounts transfer.

Know What Education Income Is Tax-Free

*P*ost-secondary education is increasingly expensive, and you've got to pay for it somehow. Sadly, any income you receive at that summer job slinging fries is taxable, but the CRA doesn't tax every cent you put toward your education. In this tip, we look at some education income that isn't taxable, and consider income that you might not expect to be taxable.

Scholarships, Bursaries, and Fellowships: Tax-free

All scholarship, bursary, and fellowship income you receive is not taxable when that income is received in connection with a program for which you will get an education tax credit. (See "Claiming Credit for Tuition") for details on who is eligible for an education tax credit.

If you're not eligible to claim the education amount, then only the first $500 of the award is tax free. Sadly, you need to report amounts you receive in excess of $500 on line 130 of your tax return.

Elementary and secondary school scholarships and bursaries are not taxable and are not subject to the requirement that they be eligible for the education amount.

Research Grants and Education Assistance Payments: Taxable

Unfortunately, not all income you receive for education is non-taxable. In this section, we cover two taxable sources of income that might surprise you.

Research grants

Research grants are taxable, but you can deduct any expenses you incurred to conduct research against them. Eligible expenses include the following:

- ✔ Travelling expenses, including all amounts for meals and lodging while away from home in the course of your research work;

- ✔ Fees paid to assistants; and

- ✔ The cost of equipment, and laboratory fees and charges.

You can't deduct personal and living expenses (including your pet goldfish's food, even though you would never have survived those long nights in the lab without her) or amounts for which you have been reimbursed.

Report only the net amount of your grant income on line 104 of your return. To calculate your net income, subtract your expenses from the grant you received. Your expenses cannot be more than your grant.

 You're allowed to deduct only research expenses you paid for in the same year that you receive the research grant. You may incur research expenses before or after the year in which the grant is received in certain circumstances. CRA will consider those expenses to be deductible in the year the grant is received as long as you've been notified the grant is payable and they are paid within one year before or after the grant is received.

Education assistance payments

Also taxable are income amounts earned in a *registered education savings plan* (RESP), called *educational assistance payments* (EAPs). If you're the beneficiary of an RESP you need to include the EAPs in your income for the year you receive them. Don't include the original contributions you made to an RESP in your income when they are returned to you — you've already paid tax on this money. Taxable payments from an RESP are shown in box 40 or box 42 of your T4A slip. See Tip #51 for more details on RESPs.

Study the Other Deductions and Credits Available to Students

· ·

*W*e know that being a student may not be the most glamorous or lucrative time of your life (let's hear it for mac and cheese, folks!), and fortunately, the CRA does, too. That's why, in addition to the tuition and textbook credits we cover in Tip #56, the CRA offers additional deductions and credits just for students, which we cover here.

Deduct Your Student Moving Expenses

If you relocated during the course of the year, either to work a summer job or to take up full-time attendance at your college or university, it's possible you can deduct your moving expenses.

Your moving expenses are deductible if your residence is at least 40 kilometres closer to your new workplace or school than your old residence was. However, they can be deducted only against either employment income at your new location or, when you're moving to go to school, against taxable award income such as research grants.

Moving-expense deductions are less common for students than they used to be. This is because the expenses are deductible only against "taxable" income from scholarships, fellowships, research grants, and similar awards that are reported on your Canadian tax return. Since 2006, most of these types of income are no longer taxable. However, when the student is also working (such as moving home to work for the summer), the moving expenses would qualify under the general moving expense rules.

If moving expenses can't be deducted in the year, they can be carried forward to the next year and claimed against employment or self-employment earnings in that year.

Student moving expenses would include transportation costs such as your train or plane ticket. If you used your car, you can claim gas expenses and the cost of any meals and lodging en route. Also deductible is the cost of up to 15 days of temporary accommodation near your new or old residence. Receipts need not be filed with your return, but should be kept in case the CRA asks to see them later.

You'll need to complete Form T1-M and send it along with your tax return in order to make the claim. See Tip #26 for more details on claiming moving expenses.

Get More Credit for Your Student Loan Interest

You're eligible for a non-refundable tax credit for your student loan interest if your loan was obtained under the *Canada Student Loans Act, Canada Student Financial Assistance Act,* or a similar provincial or territorial government law for post-secondary education.

The credit can be claimed only by you, the student, even if the interest was paid by another person.

You can carry forward your unused interest credits for up to 5 years. Consider saving your loan interest credit (if you're in a low tax bracket now) to claim against your employment income when you finally get that job and you'll have more money to pay down your loan.

You cannot claim interest paid on any other kind of loan, or on a student loan that has been combined with another kind of loan. So even if you will be eligible for a lower interest rate if you renegotiate your student loan with a bank or include it in an arrangement to consolidate your loans, the interest on the new loan does **not** qualify for this tax credit. Take this into account when you're running the numbers!

File a tax return even when you have no income to tax

Even if you have no tax to pay this year, filing a tax return is a great idea. It's the only way to receive the following benefits that may be owing to you:

✔ **GST credit:** If you're 19 or over, you're eligible for the annual GST/HST credit. To obtain this money, which is paid quarterly, you have to apply for it by filing a tax return and completing the GST/HST application section of your return.

✔ **Provincial tax credits:** Some provinces provide tax credits for low-income taxpayers, which are paid in the form of a tax refund. As a student you probably qualify, so check out what's offered in your province. You may be able to get a tax refund even if you never paid any tax!

✔ **CPP repayment:** If you worked last summer and tax was deducted from your pay, you can probably recover most of the tax, and some of the CPP premiums, when you file your return. If your net income is low enough, you may even be able to save your parents or your partner some tax by transferring your unused credits to them.

To maximize savings, take advantage of as many deductions and credits as you can, and don't waste any that are available. Tuition fees, the education amount, and the textbook tax credit that you don't need this year can be transferred or carried forward so that you can use them in a future year when your income is higher.

Use Your RRSPs for Higher Learning: The Lifelong Learning Plan

If you or your spouse is considering the possibility of continuing your education, or if you're currently enrolled in an education program, you now have an alternate way to finance your studies. Great news in times like these!

You can take advantage of the Lifelong Learning Plan as long as you or your spouse is enrolled as a full-time student in a qualifying education program. You can also participate in the Lifelong Learning Plan if you're disabled and attend school on a part-time basis.

Give me the money

The Lifelong Learning Plan allows you to withdraw up to $20,000 (the annual limit is $10,000) tax-free from your RRSPs to assist you or your spouse with education expenses. Subject to certain restrictions, amounts may be withdrawn as often as needed over a period of up to 4 years, and repaid over a period of no more than 10 years.

The Lifelong Learning Plan is similar to the Home Buyers' Plan in that you must make sure not to withdraw any of the RRSP contributions you made in the immediately preceding 90 days, otherwise you won't be allowed to deduct them on your return. You can avoid this by not making your withdrawal from the same RRSP to which you contributed in the immediately preceding 90 days, or, alternatively, by making sure the balance in the RRSP immediately after the withdrawal is greater than the total contributions made during the preceding 90 days.

Payback time

Generally, you need to repay 1/10th of your original Lifelong Learning Plan balance until you repay the full amount you withdrew.

The timing of when you need to start making those repayments depends on your status as a student. If you're entitled to the education amount as a full-time student for at least three months in a year, you don't need to start making repayments. If you don't meet this education amount condition two years in a row, your ten-year repayment period begins in the second of the two years.

 Attention perpetual students! If you continue to meet the three-month condition every year, your repayment period will start in the fifth year after your first LLP withdrawal. Sorry guys — you can't put off repayment forever!

Sometime when a program is a short one and you begin it near the end of a year you may not be entitled to the education amount for three months in any year. When this happens, your first repayment year is the second year after the year of your LLP withdrawal.

Part V
Tips for Special Tax Planning Circumstances

In this part . . .

"**D**eductions and credits" — always good words to a taxpayer! Many taxpayers in special circumstances (say, those incurring significant medical expenses, being disabled or supporting someone who is or, simply, being a senior and receiving pension income) could use a few more dollars to assist with living expenses. The tax rules acknowledge special needs and circumstances and work to offer taxpayers a number of tax breaks that we discuss in the this part. Take these breaks when they're available — the CRA won't remind you to claim them!

Sadly, it's not all deductions and credits in this part. If you're a U.S. citizen or Canadian and own U.S. property, the Internal Revenue Services (IRS) of the U.S. has an interest in you for both U.S. income taxes while you are alive and U.S. estate taxes on your death. (And you thought Canadian taxes were hard enough!)

Finally, as the saying goes, "death" and "taxes" go together. Unless you have found the fountain of youth or are somehow immortal you cannot cheat death. However, you can take advantage of some tax tips on to minimize the income tax arising on death. (Unfortunately, we can't say "cheat tax" because that would get us into trouble.) The lower the tax the greater the funds available to your heirs! They will thank you for undertaking some of the income, estate and probate planning tips we recommend in this part.

Make the Most of Your Medical Expenses

• •

*B*eing ill can be quite unsettling (to say the least), and it can be costly to keep up with health care and prescriptions. The good news is that our tax rules provide some small saving grace in that eligible medical expenses can provide a tax break for you.

Restrictions apply on the amount of medical expenses that can be claimed, but you have some flexibility in choosing the period in which you claim them. (*Hint:* It doesn't need to be a calendar year.) You also have some options on who actually claims your medical expenses.

Claim a Tax Credit for Medical Expenses

First, the restrictions. You can claim only the total of eligible medical expenses you have incurred that exceeds the lesser of 3 percent of your net income (line 236 of your tax return), and $2,011.

So, if your medical expenses do not exceed the greater of 3 percent of your net income and $2,011, then you're not entitled to claim your medical expenses and your tax credit is, therefore, zero. (It may also mean you're pretty healthy, or you have really good medical insurance coverage!) As we discuss later in this tip, you may be able to claim the medical expenses on the following year's tax return or perhaps it's best, in terms of family tax minimization, if your spouse/common-law partner claims *your* medical expenses.

If you do the math you will see that the $2,011 threshold is reached when a taxpayer has a net income of $67,033 or greater.

Choose the Best Period to Claim Medical Expenses

You'd think the tax rules would state that if you incurred a medical expense in, say, 2008, it could be claimed only on a 2008 tax return. However, that's not the case. In an example below we show how a 2008 medical expense can be claimed on a 2009 tax return — and the result is "taxpayer friendly!"

The income tax rules let you pick the best "medical expense year" or 12-month period so you can maximize the tax savings from medical expenses. In going "non-calendar," you're able to pick the period when you incurred the highest medical expenses and therefore minimize the impact of the "3 percent of net income/$2,011" restriction noted above that serves to reduce the tax saving.

12-month period

In reporting your medical expenses on your 2009 return you can gather your expenses for any 12-month period that ends in 2009.

Say you incurred $1,500 of eligible medical expenses in December 2008 and this was the total of your 2008 medical expenses. You did not claim the $1,500 of medical expenses on your 2008 return — you knew the tax savings would be zero because the amount was below the 2008 threshold.

The $1,500 of medical expenses in 2008 would have been "wasted" (in terms of tax savings) were there not the possibly of choosing a "non-calendar" period when completing your 2009 tax return.

Continuing the example, let's say you incurred $2,000 in medical expenses in November 2009. Also assume that for 2009 your net income was $67,033 (or above), so your medical expenses had to exceed $2,011 for you to receive any tax savings. If in 2009 you chose the calendar year to report your $2,000 in medical expenses, your tax savings would, as in 2008, be zero.

Now for the better way! In preparing your 2009 return, choose the 12-month period of December 1, 2008 to November 30, 2009 to report your medical expenses. Then, the total reported is $3,500 — which is reduced by your threshold of $2,011 to leave $1,489 available for a tax credit. At 15 percent, your federal tax savings is $223 — plus you're also entitled to provincial/territorial tax savings. Not a bad result for simply "going non-calendar" with your medical expenses.

24-month period

In the year of death an individual can claim any previously unclaimed medical expenses for a 24-month period that includes the date of death. This permits medical expenses that may have been paid after the date of death to be claimed on the individual's final personal tax return.

Choose the Best Person to Claim Medical Expenses

In preparing your tax return you're allowed to claim medical expenses you paid for yourself and for your spouse/common-law partner. You can also claim medical expenses paid for by your spouse/common-law partner or vice versa.. Essentially, all medical expenses can be claimed on your tax return or on the tax return of your spouse/common-law partner regardless of which one of you paid or who the expense was for. This flexibility brings good news! (Tip #60 explains how you can claim medical expenses incurred for other family members as well.)

Because the total of medical expenses available for tax credit is reduced by the lesser of "3 percent of net income or $2,011," it's usually best that the spouse/common-law partner with the lowest net income claims the medical expenses to maximize the tax savings available to the family. Where both you and your spouse/common-law partner have a net income of $67,033 or above, the tax savings from the medical expenses will be the same — you both will be subject to the restriction that only medical expenses in excess of $2,011 are eligible for a tax credit.

Understand What Medical Expenses Are Eligible

Eligible medical expense include

> ✔ **Fees for professional medical services:** These include the services of doctors, dentists, surgeons, chiropractors, acupuncturists, nurses, physiotherapists, speech language pathologists or audiologists, naturopaths, or professional tutors that a medical practitioner certifies as necessary because of a person's learning disability or mental impairment.

✔ **Payments for apparatus and materials, and repairs thereto:** Eligible apparatus and materials include artificial limbs, wheelchairs, crutches, hearing aids, prescription eyeglasses or contact lenses, dentures, pacemakers, orthopedic shoes, reasonable expenses relating to renovations or alterations to a dwelling of an impaired person, reasonable moving expenses if incurred by an impaired person moving to a more accessible dwelling, and so on.

✔ **Medicines:** These include costs of prescription drugs, vaccines, insulin, oxygen, and so on.

✔ **Fees for medical treatments:** These treatments include blood transfusions, injections, pre- and postnatal treatments, psychotherapy, speech pathology or audiology, and so on.

✔ **Fees for laboratory examinations and tests:** These include blood tests, cardiographs, X-ray examinations, urine and stool analyses, and so on.

✔ **Fees for hospital services:** These include hospital bills, use of the operating room, anaesthetist, X-ray technician, and so on.

✔ **Amounts paid for attendant care and care in a retirement or nursing home:** Seniors eligible to claim the disability amount tax credit (Tip #61 and Tip #62) can claim the cost of care in a retirement or nursing home. When in a retirement home the claim is limited to $10,000 per year or $20,000 in the year of death. If more than these amounts are claimed the disability amount tax credit cannot be claimed. If the senior is in a nursing home the cost of the care can be claimed as a medical expense but the individual cannot claim the disability amount tax credit.

✔ **Ambulance charges**

✔ **Expenses for guide and hearing-ear animals**

✔ **Premiums paid to private health services plans** including travel medical insurance.

✔ **Travel expenses,** if medical treatment is not available locally.

✔ **Services** such as real-time captioning for individuals with a speech or hearing impairment, note-taking services for individuals with mental or physical impairments, and reading services for the blind.

✔ **Marijuana,** under restricted circumstances.

Understand What You Cannot Claim as Medical Expenses

Things you cannot claim as medical expenses include

- Toothpaste;
- Maternity clothes;
- Athletic club memberships;
- Funeral, cremation, or burial expenses;
- Illegal operations, treatments, procured drugs, and so on.

Similarly, you're not allowed to claim any vitamins, herbs, bottled water, or organic or natural foods, even when prescribed by a licensed medical practitioner, if those items are not "recorded by a pharmacist." In other words, only prescription drugs that you must buy from a pharmacist qualify.

Take Advantage of the Refundable Medical Expense Supplement

The refundable medical expense supplement provides monetary assistance of $1,067 (in 2009) to lower-income taxpayers who incur significant medical- or disability-related expenses (see Tip #61). To receive the supplement the taxpayer's employment and/or self-employment income must be at least $3,116. The supplement is calculated as the lower of $1,067 and 25 percent of the aggregate of the medical expenses and the disability supports deduction claimed. The available supplement is reduced where family income (both spouses'/common-law partners' incomes together) exceeds $23,363. The reduction is 5 percent on every dollar of family income over $23,363. At a family income of $44,703 or above, the supplement works out to zero.

#60

Claim All the Medical Expenses of Your Family

● ●

*B*eing sick is no fun. Having sick family members is no fun. However, if a bright side exists, it's that in addition to medical expenses you pay for yourself you can also include the medical expenses paid for your family members in calculating your tax savings.

Determine Total Medical Expenses for You and Your Family

The medical expenses eligible for you (or your spouse/common-law partner) to claim in preparing your tax return include medical expenses paid by you or your spouse/common-law partner in regard to:

- ✔ You and your spouse/common-law partner

- ✔ Your children and grandchildren and the children and grandchildren of your spouse/common-law partner

- ✔ Other individuals' children who were under 18 at the end of the year who depended on you or your spouse/common-law partner for support, and

- ✔ Your parents, grandparents, brothers, sisters, uncles, aunts, nieces, and nephews who depended on you for support.

Medical Expenses of Children

The amount of medical expenses eligible to claim on a parent's, grandparent's, or supporting person's tax return depends on the child's age at the end of the year.

Children under 18

No income restriction applies on the amounts claimed for medical expenses of each child under 18 at the end of the year. In other words, the income of the child dependant does not factor into the amount of the child's medical expenses that can be claimed.

The parent, grandparent, or supporting person claiming the medical expenses is still restricted to the overall limits highlighted in Tip #59. The total amount of medical expenses you (or your spouse/common-law partner) may claim needs to exceed the greater of 3 percent of your "line 236" net income (or spouse/common-law partner's net income if he or she is claiming the medical expenses) and $2,011.

Claiming medical expenses of your children or grandchildren 18 or older

Where you (or perhaps your spouse/common-law partner) are claiming medical expenses regarding your own child or grandchild who is 18 or older at the end of the year the amount of medical expenses eligible to be claimed is reduced by the lesser of

- 3 percent of the child's or grandchild's net income (line 236 on his or her 2009 tax return), and
- $2,011.

A separate calculation needs to be done for each child or grandchild for whom medical expenses are being claimed.

Even when after the above reduction the medical expenses eligible to claim are greater than $10,000, the maximum that can be included in your (or your spouse's/common-law partner's) tax return is $10,000 of medical expenses per child or grandchild 18 or older.

After the 18-year-old-or-older child or grandchild's medical expenses are reduced by the "3 percent of net income/$2,011" restrictions noted above, the restrictions are NOT again applied in calculating the overall amount the parent or grandparent may claim regarding themselves and other dependants.

Restrictions in claiming medical expenses of other dependants 18 and over

In claiming medical expenses of other dependants (that is, not your spouse/common-law partner, children, or grandchildren), three restrictions apply. The first two restrictions are identical to the restrictions noted above related to medical expenses being claimed regarding children or grandchildren who are 18 years of age or older at the end of the year.

The first restriction is that the amount of medical expenses for each dependant relative to be claimed are reduced by the lesser of

✔ 3 percent of the dependant's net income, and

✔ $2,011.

The second restriction is that the maximum medical expenses of the dependant you can claim on your (or your spouse/common-law partner's) tax return is $10,000.

Finally, the third restriction is that for you (or your spouse/common-law partner) to claim the dependant's medical expenses, the dependant must have lived in Canada at some time in the year.

Support your medical expense claim

Attach your receipts and other documents to your tax return if you're paper-filing. If you file electronically, keep your receipts, as the CRA often asks to see them *before* they assess your return. If you have a significant amount of medical expenses we recommend paper-filing your return to avoid delays in the assessing of your tax return.

Receipts for attendant care or therapy paid to an individual need to note the individual's name and social insurance number.

Claim the Disability Tax Credit Amount and Disability Supports Deduction

*T*he income tax rules offer disabled individuals some tax savings to leave a few extra dollars around to assist with the additional medical-, school-, and work-related costs incurred as a result of the disability.

The most well known tax saving provisions available to a disabled individual are the disability tax credit and, when the disabled individual is under 18, the additional disability supplement. We look at these in this tip and also cover the less well known "disability supports deduction."

In Tip #62 we comment on how an individual can claim a disability tax credit regarding a spouse/common-law partner, child, or other dependant's disability. In Tip #63 we discuss the new saving and tax planning idea of *registered disability savings plans,* or RDSPs.

Claim the Disability Tax Credit Amount

You may be able to claim the disability credit amount of $7,196 (for 2009) on schedule 1 of your tax return, resulting in a federal income tax savings of $1,079 (15 percent). Provincial/territorial income tax savings are also available.

Examining eligibility criteria

To claim the disability tax credit amount, you must have a *qualified practitioner* (such as a medical doctor, optometrist, psychologist, occupational therapist, audiologist, speech-language pathologist, or physiotherapist) certify the following:

- ✔ You had a severe impairment in mental or physical functions which caused you to be blind or markedly restricted all or almost all the time in a basic activity of daily living or subject to life-sustaining therapy.

  You may be *markedly restricted in a basic activity of daily living* if you're blind or are unable to feed or dress yourself, control bowel and bladder functions, walk, speak, hear, or lack the mental functions for everyday life (perceive, think, or remember). You may also be markedly restricted if it takes you an extremely long time to perform any of these basic activities of daily living, even with therapy and the use of appropriate aides and medication.

  Examples of life-sustaining therapy include

  - Chest physiotherapy to facilitate breathing (used in the treatment of cystic fibrosis)

  - Kidney dialysis to filter blood

  - Insulin therapy to treat Type 1 diabetes in a child who cannot adjust the insulin dosage

- ✔ Your impairment was prolonged — meaning it lasted, or is expected to last, for a continuous period of at least 12 months.

Getting certification

Certification of your disability by a qualified practitioner needs to be documented on CRA form T2201, "Disability Tax Credit Certificate." If you're claiming the disability credit amount for the first time, you have to submit the form T2201 with your tax return. The CRA will review your claim to determine whether you qualify before it assesses your return. Once approved, you'll be able to claim this amount for future years as long as your circumstances do not change.

If you've filed the form in a previous year you needn't file it again. The CRA may contact you every few years to request an updated certified form T2201.

Claiming the disability tax credit versus claiming the cost of attendant care as a medical expense

A riddle? No, not really — perhaps just a number-crunching exercise!

If you require attendant care, restrictions apply in claiming this cost as a medical expense and also claiming the disability tax credit. Should you claim greater than $10,000 as a medical expense for the cost of your care, your disability tax credit will not be permitted.

 Depending on the cost of your full-time attendant care it may be beneficial, in terms of tax savings, to forgo claiming your disability tax credit and claim the cost of your full-time care as a medical expense. Because the disability tax credit amount for 2009 is $7,196, if your attendant care expenses exceed $17,196 it may be best to claim the costs of the care and forget about the disability tax credit. (*Warning:* In this statement we ignored the "3 percent of net income or $2,011" restriction in calculating medical expenses that qualify for a tax credit, which we discuss in Tip #59.)

Alternatively, it may be best to restrict your claim for care to $10,000 and claim the disability tax credit. Decisions, decisions.

Claim the Disability Tax Credit Supplement If Under 18

In addition to the disability tax credit amount, if you were under 18 at the end of the year and qualified for the disability tax credit, you can claim to an additional credit amount of $4,198 (2009 amount).

The maximum credit amount claim of $4,198 is reduced under the following circumstances:

- ✔ Another individual — say, a parent — claimed childcare expenses (Tip #54) or attendant care expenses (as a medical expense; Tip #59) on their tax return regarding you

- ✔ You included attendant care expenses as part of your "disability supports deduction" claim (discussed below) or as part of medical expenses you personally claimed (Tip #59)

If you're able to claim the disability tax credit amount of $7,196 and the full $4,198 disability supplement, it's the total of these amounts — $11,394 — that you enter on line 316 of schedule 1 of your tax return. The income tax savings on this amount is $1,709 (15 percent) of federal income tax plus the respective provincial or territorial income tax.

Claim the Disability Supports Tax Deduction

If you have a severe and prolonged mental or physical impairment, you're able to deduct the cost of an attendant and other expenses you incur for the purpose of going to school or work (employment or self-employment). Complete form T929, "Disability Supports Deduction," and claim your deduction on line 215 of your tax return. The form is available on the CRA Web site (www.cra.gc.ca/forms).

Eligible expenses

To qualify for attendant care expenses your attendant must be over the age of 18 and cannot be your spouse/common-law partner.

Amounts reimbursed by a non-taxable payment, such as insurance, are not eligible for the disability supports deduction. Also, you can't claim any expense you've claimed as a medical expense (Tip #59). No double-dipping!

In addition to attendant care, eligible expenses include Braille note-takers and printers, electronic speech synthesizers, optical scanners, page turning devices, reading services, real-time captioning services or sign-language interpretation services, talking textbooks and teletypewriters.

Restrictions on expenses

Of course, a limit is placed on the amount of expenses you can deduct. For going to work, it's the lesser of

- ✔ Your "earned income" for the year, and
- ✔ The qualified expenses you paid for during the year.

For purposes of the disability supports deduction, earned income includes your employment income, net self-employed income, taxable amount of scholarships, net research grants, and amounts received from the federal government to encourage employment.

If the disability support expenses are required for you to attend secondary school or a designated educational institution, the limit is the least of the following:

- Your income from other sources (up to a maximum of $15,000)

- $375 multiplied by the number of weeks in attendance

- The qualified expenses you paid for during the year

#62

Reduce Your Taxes by Claiming Tax Credits Regarding Another's Disability

● ●

*1*n this tip we look at the tax rules that let you transfer to your tax return a disability tax credit from your spouse/common-law partner, child, or other dependant.

Transfer Your Spouse/Common-Law Partner's Disability Credit Amount to You

If your spouse/common-law partner is disabled (and is certified as such by a qualified practitioner on CRA form T2201, "Disability Tax Credit Certificate" — see Tip #61), his or her disability amount can be transferred to you to the extent he or she does not need it to reduce her income tax bill to zero.

In addition to the disability amount, a spouse/common-law partner can also transfer the age and the pension credit amounts (Tip #64) and the tuition, education, and textbook credit amount (Tip #56).

To calculate the credit amounts that can be transferred from your spouse/common-law partner, complete schedule 2 of your tax return. In the identification area on page 1 of your tax return, be sure to report your marital status and your spouse's/common-law partner's name and social insurance number so your claim is not rejected.

Transfer Your Child's (Or Other Dependant's) Disability Credit Amount to You

You may be able to claim all or part of a child's (or other dependant's) disability amount that is not needed to reduce the dependant's taxes — because, say, the dependant's federal taxes are already zero. You can claim the unused portion if he or she lived in Canada and was dependant on you because of a mental or physical impairment. One of the following must apply:

✔ The dependant was your or your spouse/common-law partner's child, grandchild, parent, grandparent, brother, or sister and lived with you

✔ The dependant was your or your spouse/common-law partner's child, grandchild, parent, grandparent, brother, sister, aunt, uncle, niece, or nephew and

- You made a claim for the caregiver credit amount (see below) or the credit amount for an infirm dependant age 18 or older (see below) for that dependant or

- You could have made a claim for the caregiver credit amount or the credit amount for an infirm dependant age 18 or older, if the dependant had no income and was 18 years of age or older during the year.

Where the dependant is under 18 the disability supplement (Tip #61) can be transferred to a supporting individual in addition to the disability tax credit amount.

If you're required to make child-support payments for your child, you cannot claim a disability amount for that child.

In the first year you claim this amount, you must attach to your return a properly completed and certified form T2201, "Disability Tax Credit Certificate," for each dependant.

If you're splitting this claim for a disability amount transferred from a dependant with another supporting person, attach a note to your return including the name and social insurance number of the other person making this claim. The total claimed for one dependant cannot be more than $7,196, or $11,394 if the full disability supplement can be transferred as well.

If you have a child with a severe and prolonged impairment, you may qualify for the Child Disability Benefit (CDB). The CDB is a tax-free supplement to the Canada Child Tax Benefit and Children's Special Allowance. Ensure the CRA has form T2201 on file for your child and that you file your tax return so the government can assess your eligibility for this credit.

Claim Additional Tax Credits When You Support Dependants Age 18 or Older

In addition to your spouse/common-law partner, child, or other dependants being able to transfer their disability tax credit amount to you, two other tax credit amounts may be available to you.

Caregiver Credit Amount

If at any time during the year you maintained a dwelling, alone or with another person, where you and a dependant lived, you may be able to claim this $4,198 credit amount. The amount is claimed on line 315 of schedule 1 of your tax return. A full credit amount of $4,198 will provide you with $630 (15 percent) in federal income tax savings. The provinces and territories also offer tax savings when the caregiver credit amount can be claimed.

To claim this credit amount, your dependant must be one of the following:

- ✔ Your or your spouse/common-law partner's child or grandchild
- ✔ Your or your spouse/common-law partner's brother, sister, niece, nephew, aunt, uncle, parent, or grandparent

In addition, the dependant must be

- ✔ Age 18 or over at the time he or she lived with you
- ✔ Dependant on you due to mental or physical impairment, or, if he or she is your or your spouse/common-law partner's parent or grandparent, at least 65 years of age.

The details of the claim for a caregiver amount are to be noted on schedule 5 of your tax return. The maximum credit amount of

$4,198 is reduced dollar for dollar by the dependant's income in excess of $14,336. When your dependant's income reaches $18,534, the credit amount is reduced to nil.

The claim for the caregiver credit amount is different from the credit amount for infirm dependants age 18 or older, which we discuss in the next section. For you to be able to claim the caregiver credit amount, the dependant must have lived with you at some time during the year. This is not a requirement in claiming the credit amount for infirm dependants age 18 and older. Because the caregiver credit amount will always be greater than or equal to the credit amount for infirm dependants aged 18 or older — because of the dependant's income threshold tests — claim the caregiver amount if the dependant lived with you. You cannot claim both credit amounts.

If you and another person support the same dependant, you can split the claim. However, the total of your claim and the other person's claim cannot be more than the maximum amount allowed for that dependant.

Credit amount for infirm dependants age 18 or older

This credit is similar to the caregiver credit amount that we discuss in the previous section, except that no requirement exists that the dependant must have lived with you. As with the caregiver credit amount where you can claim the full credit amount of $4,198 the federal income tax savings will be $630 (15 percent) plus provincial/territorial tax savings. The credit amount available is to be noted on line 306 of schedule 1 of your tax return.

You cannot claim both the caregiver credit amount and the credit amount for an infirm dependant age 18 or older for the same dependant.

To claim a credit amount for an infirm dependant age 18 or older the dependant must have been dependant on you, or you and others, by reason of physical or mental impairment.

You cannot claim this credit amount if someone other than you is claiming the eligible dependant credit amount (line 305) for the same dependant. However, if you're claiming the eligible dependant credit amount, you may also claim the credit amount for infirm dependants age 18 or older on line 306. You cannot claim the credit amount for infirm dependants age 18 or over if you, or anyone else, have claimed the caregiver credit amount (line 315) for the same dependant.

The credit amount available to be claimed is reduced by the dependant's net income in excess of $5,956. The credit is completely eliminated when the dependant's net income reaches $10,154. Provide the details of the claim for an infirm dependant (name, age, net income, nature of infirmity) on schedule 5 of your tax return.

The dependant's income thresholds for the infirm dependant age 18 or older credit are lower than those for the caregiver credit amount. So, where the dependant lives with you the caregiver credit amount may result in a greater tax reduction.

If more than one person is supporting the dependant person, the available credit amount must be allocated between those supporting people. That is, the total credit amount claimed for one dependant cannot exceed $4,198.

A dependant relative may include your or your spouse/common-law partner's child, grandchild, parent, grandparent, brother, sister, uncle, aunt, niece, or nephew. To claim this amount the dependant must be:

- ✔ Age 18 or older at the end of the year

- ✔ A resident of Canada at some time during the year, if a credit amount is being claimed for a dependant other than a child or grandchild

- ✔ Dependant on you by reason of mental or physical impairment

- ✔ Dependant on you, or you and others, for support

Generally, an individual is dependant on you for support if he or she does not have income in excess of the basic personal credit amount — $10,320 in 2009 — and you have contributed to the maintenance of that person (food, shelter, and clothing).

You can claim the credit amount for infirm dependants age 18 or older in respect to children or grandchildren if they live outside Canada provided they depended on you for support. The CRA can ask you to provide proof of support paid. Dependants other than your children or grandchildren must have been residents in Canada at some time during the year.

Make Use of Registered Disability Savings Plans (RDSPs)

*T*hrough the *Income Tax Act* the government encourages us to save for retirement using *registered retirement savings plans* (RRSPs, Tip #42) and for education using *registered education savings plans* (RESPs, Tip #51). In that tradition, a plan now exists to assist a disabled individual — and parents and other supporters of a disabled individual — to save to assist in funding living expenses in the later years of a disabled individual's life. The plan is called a *registered disability savings plan,* or RDSP. In this tip we take a look at the plan, explain how you can determine whether you qualify, and suggest ways to make the most of it.

Know What an RDSP Is

A registered disability savings plan is a relatively new idea to assist in saving for the long-term security of an individual with a disability in a tax-efficient manner with additional funds added by the government. Sounds good! Let's investigate.

RDSPs

Essentially, the plan permits up to $200,000 to be contributed to a RDSP on behalf of a disabled individual, the RDSP beneficiary. No annual minimum or maximum contribution applies. The deadline for contributions each year is December 31.

An RDSP is set up by a plan holder in conjunction with a financial institution. The plan holder is usually the disabled individual or a parent or guardian if the individual is a minor or not legally competent.

Anyone can contribute to the RDSP of a specific individual with permission of the plan holder.

Contributions to an RDSP are not tax deductible. Investment income (interest, dividends, and capital gains) earned on investments held in the RDSP is not subject to tax while the funds remain in the plan. When withdrawn, the funds will be subject to tax in the RDSP beneficiary's (the disabled individual's) hands.

CDSGs and CDSBs

With RDSPs, the federal government has also created two programs:

- ✔ **Canada Disability Savings Grant (CDSG):** The government will match contributions to an RDSP on a 100 percent, 200 percent, or 300 percent basis. The matching percentage depends on the amount contributed and the family's income. The maximum annual government matching is $3,500.

- ✔ **Canada Disability Savings Bond (CDSB):** This bond is available to lower-income families that qualify for the CDSG regardless of the amount contributed to the RDSP.

To encourage long-term savings, the CDSGs and CDSBs are to remain in the RDSP for ten years. If not, they must be repaid to the federal government.

Assess Your Eligibility for an RDSP

An individual can be a beneficiary of an RDSP if he or she is

- ✔ Eligible for the disability tax credit (Tip #61)
- ✔ Under the age of 60
- ✔ A resident of Canada when the RDSP is set up
- ✔ The holder of a valid social insurance number (SIN)

Contributions to an RDSP can be made until the end of year in which the RDSP beneficiary turns 59.

Make the Most of the CDSG

The grant is paid annually. Therefore, rather than making a contribution of all available money upfront to defer the tax on the investment income, consider spreading out the contributions over a number of years to maximize the grants the federal government will add to the RDSP.

The grants are paid to the RDSP by the federal government annually until the beneficiary is 49 years of age. For the grants to continue the RDSP beneficiary must file annual tax returns or, where the beneficiary is under 19, the parents or guardian must file annual tax returns.

Understand the amount of the grant

The amount of the grant depends on the amount contributed to the RDSP and the beneficiary's family income.

For the purposes of the CDSG, family income depends on the age of the RDSP beneficiary:

- ✔ While the RDSP beneficiary is under 19, the grants are calculated based on the income of the beneficiary's parents or guardian, and
- ✔ When the RDSP beneficiary is 19 or older, the grant is based on the beneficiary's income.

If the beneficiary's family income is $77,664 or less during the year, the maximum grant is $3,500 calculated as follows:

- ✔ For the first $500 contributed the federal government will match the contribution on a $3 to $1 basis — 300 percent — up to $1,500 a year.
- ✔ On the next $1,000 contributed the matching contribution is on a $2 to $1 basis — 200 percent — up to $2,000 a year.

If the beneficiary's family income is $77,665 or greater, the maximum grant is $1,000; it's calculated as one dollar on each dollar contributed (100 percent) up to a maximum of $1,000.

The maximum lifetime grant is $70,000.

Maximize the annual grant

We did the math so you don't have to! The annual government grant to be paid to the RDSP is maximized when

- ✔ You contribute $1,500, if your annual family income is $77,664 or below
- ✔ You contribute $1,000, if family income is $77,665 or above

The Canadian Disability Savings Bond (CDSB)

Where the beneficiary's family income is $21,816 or less during the year (refer to the previous section for a definition of family income), each year the government will deposit $1,000 to the RDSP as CDSB, regardless whether any RDSP contributions are made in the year. Where the beneficiary's family income is between $21,816 and $38,832, the $1,000 payment is reduced as income increases to $38,832. If family income is $38,832 or greater no CDSB is paid.

The maximum lifetime CDSB payment is $20,000 per RDSP beneficiary. The eligibility requirements and the definition of family income for the CDSB are the same as those noted above for the CDSG.

RDSP Withdrawals

Two types of withdrawals or payments can be made from an RDSP:

- ✔ **Lifetime Disability Assistance Payments (LDAP):** These are annual payments from an RDSP that are designed to last a beneficiary's lifetime. After they begin they are to continue to be paid annually until the beneficiary dies or the plan is terminated. These payments can begin at any age, but must commence no later than the year in which the RDSP beneficiary turns 60.

  The LDAP has a yearly maximum that is calculated based on the value of the RDSP at the beginning of the year of the commencement of annual payments and the life expectancy of the RDSP beneficiary (as prescribed by the CRA).

- ✔ **Disability Assistance Payment (DAP):** These are lump-sum payments made to the RDSP beneficiary. DAPs may be requested when the beneficiary is at least 27. These payments are permitted only when the total contributions to the plan exceed the CDSGs and CDSBs received.

All CDSG and CDSB received from the federal government in the previous ten years must be repaid whenever funds are withdrawn from an RDSP.

Payments for an RDSP will not impact the taxpayer's income-tested benefits such as the following:

- ✔ The Goods and Service Tax/Harmonized Sales Tax (GST/HST) credit (Tip #23)
- ✔ The Canada Child Tax Benefit (Tip #52)
- ✔ Old Age Security (OAS) pension (Tip #64)
- ✔ Employment insurance (EI) benefits

All the provinces/territories have announced that in determining financial/disability assistance they will provide a full or partial exemption of RDSP assets and income.

#64

Make the Most of the Old Age Security (OAS) Program

*H*ey, this tip may not deal solely with income tax, but it's good news just the same because the Old Age Security (OAS), a monthly public pension payment, can be a source of money for you. Yes, OAS is subject to tax — and the scary part is that depending on your income level the tax may be 100 percent!

The OAS is available to most Canadians age 65 and over, even if they no longer live in Canada. The amount is adjusted quarterly for increases in the cost of living as measured by the Consumer Price Index; the maximum monthly OAS pension payment for October to December 2009 was $516.96. The OAS is administered by Human Resources and Skills Development Canada (HRSDC) with the assistance of Service Canada.

Look at Eligibility Criteria

Eligibility for an OAS pension is based on two criteria: age and years resided in Canada. OAS pension is not affected by your employment history, and you're entitled to receive it whether or not you have retired. Two categories of people are eligible for OAS:

- ✔ People living in Canada who are 65 or older, are Canadian citizens or legal residents and have lived in Canada for at least 10 years while adults and

- ✔ People living outside Canada who are 65 or older, were Canadian citizens or legal residents at the time they ceased to live in Canada and had lived in Canada for at least 20 years as an adult.

 Don't fall into either of these categories? You still may be eligible to receive OAS! Canada has a number of social security agreements with other countries. If you lived in one of these countries or contributed to its social security system, you may qualify for a pension from that country, Canada, or both. Need more information to determine whether you qualify? Contact HRSDC at 1-800-277-9914.

HRSDC's Web site at www.hrsdc.gc.ca will help too. You can also drop in to a Service Canada Centre; addresses can be found on Service Canada's Web site at www.servicecanada.gc.ca. (Note that these points of contact apply for all the questions you may have — or forms you may need — based on the information in this tip.)

Full or partial OAS pension

The main criterion in determining whether you're entitled to a full or partial OAS pension is the length of time you've been in Canada. A full OAS pension is available where you

✔ Lived in Canada for at least 40 years after your 18th birthday, or

✔ Were born on July 1, 1952, or earlier, and

- Lived in Canada on July 1, 1977,

- Lived in Canada for some period of time between your 18th birthday and July 1, 1977, or

- Lived in Canada for 10 years immediately prior to your OAS application being approved.

Don't qualify because you haven't lived in Canada for the past 10 years? Don't fret! You should still qualify for full OAS if you lived in Canada for the year immediately before your application was approved, or prior to those past 10 years, you lived in Canada as an adult for a period of at least three times the length of your absences during the past 10 years. (Go ahead — do the math!).

If you don't qualify for a full OAS pension, a partial pension may be available to you. The amount you would receive is based on the number of complete years you lived in Canada after turning 18.

Apply for OAS six months ahead!

To ensure your OAS payments start on time, apply six months before your 65th birthday. An application kit (ISP3000) is available from any Service Canada Centre, or call 1-800-277-9914. You can also print the kit from the HRSDC Web site at www.hrsdc.gc.ca. You can't apply online, but you can complete the form online, print it, sign and date it, and then mail it to a Service Canada Centre. If you apply after age 65, you can receive back payments up to 11 months.

Understand the OAS Is Taxable

Your OAS pension is taxable, and reporting the tax on your return is very simple. You'll receive a T4A(OAS) information slip summarizing the amount paid. Expect this slip to arrive in January following the year the OAS was received. If you're computer savvy, you can also see your slip online — follow the links on the Web site at www.hrsdc.gc.ca.

Include the amount noted in box 18 on line 113 of your tax return. Some tax may have been held back on the OAS pension payment to you; this amount will be noted in box 22 of the T4A(OAS). Be sure to include the withheld tax on line 437 of your return.

If you want to reduce the amount of tax that comes due on April 30 each year, you can request that tax be withheld from your OAS pension payments.

Be wary of the OAS "Clawback"

Much to the chagrin of seniors, our government believes that those with net income in excess of $66,335 (for 2009) do not need a full OAS pension. When a taxpayer has received OAS higher than his or her calculated maximum OAS entitlement, the excess amount must be repaid — or "clawed back". The amount that must be repaid is equal to 15 percent of net income in excess of $66,335 — stay tuned for an example. The clawback works by reducing monthly OAS payments to take into account an individual's expected repayment. High-income individuals do not receive any OAS at all. This withholding of OAS adds a measure of complexity to tax return preparation, as we explain below.

The CRA determines whether you have to make an OAS repayment based on information in your tax return. If you owe a repayment the CRA tells the HRSDC, which in turn adjusts your future monthly OAS payments. Assuming you file your 2009 tax return by April 30, 2010, the CRA should assess you by the end of June 2010. Based on your 2009 return, HRSDC will adjust your next 12 monthly OAS payments beginning with the one for July 2010 — your July 2010 payment may be significantly different from your June 2010 payment! In other words, HRSDC anticipates you will have to repay all or a portion of your 2010 OAS in an amount that is approximately what you had to repay for the 2009 OAS. Rather than paying you the OAS and then waiting for you to repay it as part of your 2010 tax return, HRSDC simply reduces the amount of your monthly OAS cheque.

What if your 2010 net income is lower than your 2009 net income? No worries . . . the government will pay any difference between what you received and what you were entitled to by decreasing your tax liability (or increasing your tax refund) on your 2010 tax return.

Say Jim turned 65 on January 1, 2009. He applied for OAS six months before his 65th birthday. (We have purposely made Jim's income exceed $66,335 to detail the calculation and impact of the OAS repayment on his tax return and tax liability.)

Let's work through an illustration of how Jim's OAS repayment (or "clawback") is calculated.

Old Age Security (OAS) pension (estimate)	$ 6,000
Other pension income	$70,000
Interest income	$ 2,000
Deduction for support payments made to former spouse	($5,000)
Net income before deduction for OAS repayment (line 234 on tax return)	$73,000
Net income before deduction for OAS repayment (as above)	$73,000
Less base amount	$66,335
Excess net income	$ 6,665
Net income before deduction for OAS repayment (as above)	$73,000
Less repayment — 15 percent on excess net income (line 235 on tax return)	$ 1,000
Net income after OAS repayment (line 236 on tax return)	$72,000

Jim will note the $1,000 of OAS he is required to pay back on line 422 of his 2009 tax return, and it will increase his 2009 tax liability or decrease his refund.

Protect your OAS! Based on an OAS maximum for 2009 of $6,060 when your net income is $107,692 or more, you'll repay all your OAS — a full OAS clawback! In other words, a 100-percent tax on your OAS. Use the tips in this book including pension splitting (Tip #68) to minimize your net income to minimize or eliminate your OAS clawback!

If you and your spouse elect to take advantage of the pension-splitting rules (Tip #68) you may find that the spouse in the lower tax bracket now has an OAS clawback or an increased clawback. The "lost" OAS due to the clawback (or increased clawback) needs to be weighed against the tax savings from electing to take advantage of the pension-splitting rules.

Apply for Other OAS Payments

In addition to a regular OAS pension, a taxpayer may be entitled to additional payments under the OAS program. None of the following payments are taxable but they must be reported on your tax return. The amount paid to you is noted in box 21 of the T4A(OAS) slip. The amount is to be reported as income on line 146 of your return and then deducted on line 250. To receive these special non-taxable OAS payments you must apply using form ISP3026:

- ✔ **Guaranteed income supplement:** The guaranteed income supplement (GIS) provides low-income seniors in Canada with supplementary pension payments in addition to the regular OAS pension. The GIS is based on your income and marital status.

- ✔ **The allowance:** The allowance is an additional amount paid to low-income seniors aged 60 to 64 with a spouse or common-law partner who receives the OAS and GIS. It's like an early OAS pension. To receive it, you must meet some residency requirements.

- ✔ **The allowance for the survivor:** Additional money is paid to low-income seniors aged 60 to 64 if their spouse or common-law partner has died and they meet residency requirements.

To continue receiving the GIS, the allowance, or the survivor's allowance, ensure you file a tax return by April 30 each year. Without a tax return on file, your payments will stop!

Know When to Take Your CPP/QPP Retirement Pension

● ●

*J*ust like Tip #64 on dealing with Old Age Security (OAS), we include this tip to ensure you make the most of your Canada Pension Plan (CPP) or Quebec Pension Plan (QPP) entitlement. (Be sure to also check out Tip #68, which details some tax saving available by "sharing" CPP with a spouse/common-law partner!)

After the OAS (Tip #64), the CPP (and its Quebec counterpart, the QPP) is a second level of public pension available to certain Canadians. However, unlike the OAS pension, which is available to all Canadians who meet certain residency requirements, you receive a CPP/QPP pension only when you've paid into the plan. If you earned employment or self-employment income during your working days, you most likely paid into one (or both) of these plans and can reap some benefits in your retirement years.

Available CPP/QPP Benefits

Table 5-1 lists the variety of benefits you can receive under the CPP/QPP and notes whether they're taxable.

Table 5-1   Summary of CPP/QPP Benefits and Taxation

Type of Receipt	Taxable?
CPP/QPP retirement pension	Yes
CPP/QPP disability pension	Yes
CPP/QPP child disability benefit	Yes — but taxed in child's tax return
CPP/QPP survivor benefit	Yes
CPP/QPP child survivor benefit	Yes — but taxed in child's tax return
CPP/QPP death benefit	Yes — but taxed in estate

Comparing CPP and QPP

The Quebec government administers the QPP on behalf of the residents of Quebec. Human Resources and Skills Development Canada (HRSDC), with the assistance of Service Canada, administers the CPP for the remaining nine provinces and three territories. With respect to most issues, the two plans operate in a similar fashion. For simplicity and conciseness, most of this tip deals with CPP issues.

For details on QPP contact Régie des rentes du Québec via its Web site (www.rrq.gouv.qc.ca) or toll-free phone (1-800-463-5185).

Report CPP/QPP Income on Your Tax Return

Each January, HRSDC sends CPP recipients a T4A(P) tax slip. (You can also see your slip online at www.hrsdc.gc.ca.) Enter the amount noted in box 20 on line 114 of your tax return. Amounts in the other boxes on the slip provide a breakdown of your sources of CPP. You don't need to report these amounts on your tax return, with the exception of box 16 — the disability benefit. Enter this amount on line 152 of your return, which is just to the left of line 114. Don't add box 152 when calculating your total income; the amount is already included in box 114.

The CPP Retirement Pension

The CPP is a monthly pension paid to individuals who have contributed to the CPP, or to both the CPP and QPP if they live outside Quebec.

Like OAS, you must apply to receive a CPP retirement pension. After you qualify to begin to receive CPP you're permitted to work as much as you like and your pension amount will not be affected. However, you can no longer contribute to the CPP. (This will change when the new CPP rules come into being in 2012. We discuss these proposed new rules later in this tip.)

To find out how much CPP you're entitled to at different start dates, contact HRSDC. Simply fill out form ISP1003, "Estimate Request for Canada Pension Plan Retirement Pension," with alternative start dates. The closer you are to the date you want your pension to begin, the more accurate the estimate will be. The form is available at any Service Canada Centre or online at www.hrsdc.gc.ca.

Apply for CPP six months ahead!

You can apply for your CPP retirement pension online at www.hrsdc.gc.ca. After you submit the application you'll be asked to print and sign a signature page and then send it to a Service Canada Centre. If you don't want to apply online, you can fill out the form by hand and mail it in. You need form ISP1000, and can find it in the forms area of the HRSDC Web site at www.hrsdc.gc.ca. You can also pick up an application at any Service Canada Centre, or call 1-800-277-9914 for a copy. HRSDC suggests you apply six months before you want your retirement pension to begin (much like the OAS, Tip #64).

As with the OAS, you may qualify for a CPP retirement pension that is based not only on contributions you have made to the plan, but also on contributions you have made to another country's social security system. This is good news if you were in Canada for only a short while before you retired but had previously worked in and paid social security taxes to another country. See the International Benefits section on the HRSDC Web site (www.hrsdc.gc.ca) for further information.

Get your money quicker! Have your CPP payment deposited directly to your bank account.

Take Your CPP Retirement Pension Early — or Late!

The CPP retirement pension is designed to be paid starting when an individual turns 65. However, you have the option of taking a discounted payment at any time between the ages of 60 and 64. The current rules are to be changed in 2012; for your convenience we've summarized the current rules and the proposed new rules.

Current rules

If you decide to start your CPP retirement pension before you're 65 years of age, the payments are reduced by 6 percent for each year (0.5 percent per month) that you're under 65. So if you decide to take your CPP at 60 you'll receive 70 percent of what your full entitlement would have been at 65.

To choose this option, you must have stopped working, or you must have been earning less than the monthly maximum CPP retirement pension for at least two months; this amount was $908.75 per month in 2009. When you begin receiving CPP you're no longer required to make CPP contributions. (If you're 65 or over no work cessation restrictions apply in collecting your CPP retirement pension.)

If you elect to start receiving your CPP retirement pension after age 65, you're entitled to an increased amount — again, 6 percent per year (or 0.5 percent per month). If you wait until your 70th birthday, your entitlement increases by 30 percent! The amount cannot be increased more than 30 percent — so, waiting until you're 71 or 72 will not get you a bigger CPP retirement pension.

How do you decide when to start taking your CPP retirement pension? HRSDC suggests you consider the following:

✔ Whether you're still working and contributing to the CPP

✔ How long you have contributed

✔ How much your earnings were

✔ What your other sources of retirement income are

✔ How your health is

✔ What your retirement plans are, including desired lifestyle

In general, if you're still working or don't need the extra cash flow the CPP will provide, you might want to wait to get a bigger pension later. On the other hand, if your health is poor or the extra cash flow will come in handy, you might opt to take your CPP early in order to maximize your situation.

Proposed new rules

In May 2009 new proposals were announced regarding receiving your CPP early or late; the proposals are to become effective in 2012. A major positive change is that you won't have to retire — or work for little income — to begin collecting your CPP early (between the ages of 60 and 64). However, you'll need to contribute to the CPP while you are working, and should you begin collecting CPP at 60 you'll receive only 64 percent of your entitlement rather than the current 70 percent. (As they say, "there's no free lunch!"). If you take your CPP late — say, at 70 — your CPP will be increased by 42 percent rather than the current 30 percent.

Know about Other CPP Benefits

In addition to the retirement pension, the CPP also provides CPP disability benefits and CPP survivor benefits.

CPP disability benefits

The CPP will provide you with a monthly pension if you've been a CPP contributor and are considered mentally or physically disabled. Your disability must be "severe and prolonged." HRSDC considers "severe" to mean that you cannot work regularly at any job, and "prolonged" to mean that your condition is long-term or may lead to death. The benefit comprises a flat amount plus a second amount based on the number of years you have contributed to the CPP. The maximum monthly disability benefit in 2009 was $1,105.99.

Payments can also be made to dependant children. If you become disabled, your child under 18 can qualify for a benefit. If your child is between ages 18 and 25, he or she will still qualify if attending school full-time. The maximum amount paid in 2009 was $213.99 per month per child.

You must apply for both the regular disability benefit and the children's benefit. Form ISP1151, "Application for Disability Benefits," is available online at www.hrsdc.gc.ca, or you can call 1-800-277-9914 or drop by a Service Canada Centre. Apply as soon as you consider yourself to have a long-term disability that prevents you from working at any job. The government will require a medical report from your doctor.

CPP survivor benefits

CPP survivor benefits are paid to your estate, surviving spouse/common-law partner, and dependant children. The three types of survivor benefits are the death benefit, the survivor's pension, and the children's benefit.

- ✔ **Death benefit.** The death benefit is a one-time payment to your estate. The maximum amount for this benefit is $2,500.

- ✔ **Survivor's pension.** Your surviving spouse/common-law partner can receive a monthly pension. The amount of the payment depends on how long you paid into the CPP, your spouse or common-law partner's age when you die, and whether he or she is receiving a CPP retirement or disability pension. The calculation is based on what your CPP retirement pension would have been had you been 65 at the time of death. This amount is then adjusted to take into account the age of your survivor. The maximum amount that can be received is 60 percent of what your retirement pension would have been — the 2009 monthly maximum is $545.25, or 60 percent of $908.75. To receive this amount, your survivor must be age 65 or over at the time of your death. If your survivor is younger, the payments are lower. (The maximum for a survivor under 65 in 2009 was $506.38.)

✔ **Children's benefit.** The children's benefit is a monthly payment to a deceased contributor's dependant children. At the time of the contributor's death, the child must be under 18, or between the ages of 18 and 25 and enrolled full time in a recognized educational institution. The maximum monthly amount in 2009 was $213.99. At least one of the child's parents must have been a contributor to the CPP. A child may get two benefits if both parents are deceased or disabled.

You must apply for CPP survivor benefits. Applications are available at Service Canada Centres, on the HRSDC Web site at www.hrsdc.gc.ca, or by calling 1-800-277-9914.

Splitting CPP Credits: CPP and Marriage Breakdown

CPP credits are used to determine the amount of your entitlement to a CPP retirement pension. Because spouses/common-law partners build up credits during a marriage or common-law relationship, when a marriage breaks down both can share in the CPP entitlements earned while they were together. CPP credits can be split even when only one spouse/common-law partner paid into the CPP. You or your ex or one of your lawyers can apply to HRSDC. For more on the tax implications of a marriage breakdown, see Tip #53.

Be Smart in Receiving Other Types of Pension Income

*Y*ou've worked hard, saved for retirement, and perhaps are a member of your former employer's pension plan. Now you're in the stage where you're receiving payments from the plan, or maybe taking out some of your retirement savings through withdrawals from an RRSP, RRIF, or similar retirement saving vehicle.

Understand the Pension Income You Receive

The dollar amounts of your various pension incomes are to be aggregated and reported on line 115 of your tax return. This is fairly straightforward — most pension income will be reported on T4A slips or other tax information slips.

Here are descriptions of the various types of pension income:

- ✔ **Payments from a former employer's or union's registered pension plan (box 16 of T4A slip).**

- ✔ **Payments from an RRIF — registered retirement income fund (T4RIF slip) — and payments from an annuity (T4A slip).** If you're under age 65, report these amounts on line 130 of your return — not on line 115. This is because these types of pension income do not qualify for the pension income credit (Tip #67) when you are under 65.

- ✔ **Certain annuity income.** If you've purchased an annuity with non-RRSP funds, the annuity payments you receive are part interest and part capital. The capital portion is not subject to tax because it represents a partial return of the purchase price that you funded with tax-paid dollars. The interest portion is usually taxed as interest (hey, this makes sense!). However, if you're age 65 or older and have receipts from a "mixed annuity" (an annuity payment in which the interest and capital portion are determined by tax rules), the interest portion is considered pension income and is reported on line 115.

Foreign Pension Income

Foreign pension income refers to any pension income received from a source outside Canada. A common type is U.S. social security paid to a resident of Canada. To receive this you would have worked in the U.S. at some time in your life. If you worked in the U.S. or any foreign country you may have been part of a foreign employer's pension plan. You also may have served in a foreign country's armed forces and be entitled to a pension. Most foreign pension income is subject to tax — but not all!

U.S. social security income

Include the full amount of U.S. social security income you receive on line 115. Of course, you'll need to translate the U.S.-dollar amount received into a Canadian-dollar amount!

On line 256 of your return, you can take a 15 percent deduction of the amount you received in U.S. social security. This results in only 85 percent of your U.S. social security being subject to tax!

Other foreign pension income

You include foreign pension income on line 115 of your tax return after applying the appropriate exchange rate. If the foreign country withheld tax from your pension payment, do not deduct the tax, but report the gross pension receipt. The foreign tax paid may qualify as a tax credit (referred to as a foreign tax credit) in calculating your tax liability.

Canada has a number of tax treaties with other countries. A treaty may adjust the amount of a foreign pension that is taxed in Canada. The CRA can assist you in determining whether any of your foreign pension is partially or completely exempt from Canadian tax; call 1-800-267-5177. To make this determination the CRA will ask for details about your pension, so keep any documents sent to you from the pension plan. If you determine that an amount is not taxable in Canada, it's best to include the income in your return on line 115 and deduct the amount on line 256.

Maximize the Age Amount and Pension Income Amount Tax Credits

• •

s we discuss in Tips #64, #65, and #66, you have to pay tax on your OAS, CPP, and other pensions. The silver lining is that you have a few ways to at least reduce the tax burden on your pension income. In this tip we look at how you can save tax by simply being 65 years of age or older and how you can claim a tax credit on the first $2,000 of certain types of your pension income. In Tip #68, we bring your spouse or common-law partner into your tax planning as we discuss CPP sharing and pension splitting.

Know How a Tax Credit and a Tax Deduction Differ

The age amount tax credit and the pension income amount tax credit are two of a number of non-refundable tax credits available to taxpayers. Non-refundable tax credits directly reduce the tax you owe — they don't reduce your taxable income. In this way they differ from tax deductions, which are subtracted in computing your taxable income. Examples of tax deductions include your RRSP contributions (Tip #42), eligible interest (Tip #47), and employment expenses (Tip #22).

These credits are referred to as "non-refundable" because if they exceed your tax liability you don't get a refund of the excess.

With a tax credit, all taxpayers are subject to the same tax savings. The tax savings from a tax deduction increases as your taxable income increases to be taxed in higher tax brackets.

Non-refundable tax credit *amounts* differ from non-refundable tax credits. The non-refundable tax credit is the actual federal tax reduction — or tax savings — available. The amount of the tax credit is based on the non-refundable tax credit amount available to you.

For all but one (the charitable donation tax credit, Tip #9) of the non-refundable tax credits, the federal tax savings is 15 percent of the non-refundable amount to which you're entitled. (A provincial/territorial tax savings also applies; the actual savings depends on what province/territory you live in.)

Maximize Your Age Amount Tax Credit

You qualify for the maximum age credit amount of $6,658 for 2009 if you were 65 years of age or older on December 31, 2009. The age amount is entered on line 301 of schedule 1 of your tax return. The maximum federal tax savings is $998.70.

Now for the bad news. Although the maximum credit amount is $6,658, it's reduced by 15 percent of your net income (from line 236 of your tax return) in excess of $32,312. The age amount you're able to claim is reduced as your income exceeds this level. If your income is $32,312 or less, you'll be able to claim the maximum age amount.

For example, suppose Alice turned 65 in 2009. Her net income for the year (as reported on line 236 of her tax return) is $35,000. Her age credit is reduced by $403: ($35,000 – $32,312 × 15%). This means she can claim $6,255 ($6,658 – $403) on line 301 on schedule 1 of her tax return as her age credit amount. Her federal tax savings will be $938 ($6,255 × 15%).

You're not entitled to any age amount if your net income exceeds $76,699. The age credit amount will work out to zero.

The lower your net income, the greater the tax savings of the age amount! To the extent possible, reduce your net income to maximize the age amount available to you — through income splitting (Tip #50), CPP sharing and pension splitting (Tip #68), and maximizing tax deductions through contributions to your own or a spousal RRSP (Tip #43).

Claim the Pension Income Credit Amount

You can claim up to a $2,000 pension income credit amount if you report pension and/or annuity income on line 115 or line 129 of your tax return. The maximum federal tax savings is $300.

Unfortunately, you can't be too quick in assuming you're entitled to the full $2,000 pension income amount! Only pension or annuity income you report on line 115 or 129 qualifies for the pension income credit amount.

Amounts such as Old Age Security (OAS) benefits, Canada/Quebec Pension Plan (CPP/QPP) benefits, Saskatchewan Pension Plan payments, death benefits, and retiring allowances do not qualify for the pension income amount. Non-annuity income you withdraw from your RRSP similarly does not qualify for the pension amount.

 If you're age 65 or over but do not have sufficient pension income to qualify for the full credit (that is, your eligible pension income is less than $2,000), you can create pension income by converting all or part of your RRSP to an RRIF or a life annuity. Or, you can purchase a life annuity with other available funds. The income from either of these investment vehicles is eligible for the pension income credit amount..

 Through pension income splitting (Tip #68) you may be able to create eligible pension income for your spouse/common-law partner so that he or she also can take advantage of this $2,000 pension income credit amount.

 If your spouse/common-law partner does not need all or a portion of the non-refundable tax credit that arises from the pension amount to reduce his or her federal tax to zero, it may be transferable to you (Tip #49).

 If you're under 65, the pension amount is available only when you've received payments from a pension plan and/or received annuity payments due to the death of your spouse — or if based on pension splitting you included these types of pension income on your tax return.

#68

Reduce Your Family's Tax Bill by Sharing CPP and Pension Splitting

• •

*I*ncome splitting — or income sharing, or shifting — is one of the best, and easiest, tax planning ideas we can offer.

The concept is straightforward. When possible — meaning when permitted by the *Income Tax Act* — split, share, or shift income earned by one family member with another family member who is taxed at a lower tax bracket than the family member who earned the income. The gross family income remains the same but the tax bite is reduced, leaving more money for the family to spend on groceries, vacations, home repairs, university tuition — you get the idea.

Sharing Your CPP Retirement Pension

Don't confuse sharing your CPP with the tax planning opportunity provided by pension splitting (also discussed in this tip).

In undertaking CPP sharing you and your spouse/common-law partner receive an equal share of the CPP retirement pension you both earned during the years you were together (not separated or divorced). If only one spouse/common-law partner is entitled to a CPP retirement pension, then the one CPP pension can be shared. Sharing your CPP does not increase or decrease the overall retirement pension to which you and your spouse/common-law partner are entitled. CPP sharing is simply undertaken to reduce the family's tax burden.

CPP sharing eligibility and how to apply

To share your CPP retirement pension entitlements, you and your spouse/common-law partner must both be at least 60 years of age, and you must request that your CPP retirement pension be shared.

The request is made on form ISP1002, "Application for Pension Sharing of Retirement Pension(s) Canada Pension Plan." You can download the form from the HDRSC Web site (www.hrsdc.gc.ca) or pick one up at any Service Canada office.

After the application is accepted, the CPP retirement pension cheques (or direct deposit) sent to you and your spouse/common-law partner will reflect the CPP sharing, as will the T4A(P) slip, "Statement of Canada Pension Plan Benefits," you receive at the end of each year to use in completing your tax return.

Stopping CPP sharing

The CPP sharing will stop when

- Either of you dies
- You become separated, divorced, or your common-law relationship ends
- You make a request to stop CPP sharing. Form ISP1014 "Cancellation of Pension Sharing for Canada Pension Plan Retirement Pension(s)" is be completed, signed by both spouses/common-law partners and mailed to nearest Service Canada office.

Sharing QPP retirement benefits

The Quebec Pension Plan (QPP) also contains provisions for sharing. However, different eligibility requirements apply than with the CPP. It's best to contact La Régie des rentes du Québec (www.rrq.gouv.qc.ca or toll-free at 1-800-463-5185).

Pension Splitting

In addition to sharing your CPP with your spouse/common-law partner as discussed above, you can also "share" or "split" other types of pension income.

Unlike in CPP sharing, with pension splitting you don't need to contact the payer of the pension income. The pension can continue to be paid to one spouse and the tax information slip (that is, the T4A, T4RIF) is issued solely to the actual recipient of the pension. No actual payment needs to be made to the other spouse. In other words, in using pension splitting you don't have to do anything except make a few new notations on tax returns and complete form T1032, "Joint Election to Split Pension Income."

Up to 50 percent of certain types of pension income can be split, shifted, or allocated from a higher-tax-bracket spouse/common-law partner to a lower-tax-bracket spouse/common-law partner. This results in the couple paying less tax! The tax paid by the lower-tax-bracket spouse/common-law partner will be less than the tax saved by the higher-tax-bracket spouse/common-law partner.

An example will make this a little clearer. Assume your taxable income is $180,000, including $50,000 of pension income from your former employer. At $180,000 of income you're in the top tax bracket (which begins at $126,265 for 2009). Let's say you live in a province/territory where the top tax rate is 45 percent and, to keep this really simple, that your spouse/common-law partner has no taxable income.

	You	*Spouse/ Partner*	*Total*
Retirement pension without pension splitting	$Nil	$50,000	$50,000
Tax rate	<u>45%</u>	N/A	
Tax	<u>$22,500</u>	$Nil	$22,500

Let's improve the situation. You and your spouse/common-law partner agree to pension split. You wish to shift the maximum $25,000 (the maximum is 50 percent of $50,000) to your spouse's tax return. As this will be your spouse's/common-law partner's only income it will be taxed in the lowest tax bracket which again varies by province/territory. In this example we assume 21%. (For 2009 the lowest tax bracket ends at taxable income of $40,726.)

	You	*Spouse/ Partner*	*Total*
Retirement pension with pension splitting	$25,000	$25,000	<u>$50,000</u>
Tax rate	<u>45%</u>	21%	
Tax	<u>$11,250</u>	<u>$5,250</u>	$16,500

The tax is reduced to $16,500 from $22,500 — a $6,000 saving!

The pension-splitting result is optimal when one spouse/common-law partner is in the highest tax bracket and the other spouse is in the lowest tax bracket.

The decrease in the higher-tax-bracket spouse's/common-law partner's income could cause his or her OAS clawback to be reduced or eliminated (see Tip #64 for more on the OAS clawback).

The increase in the lower-tax-bracket spouse's/common-law partner's income could cause him or her to have an OAS clawback or an increase in the current OAS clawback.

Because the lower-tax-bracket spouse/common-law partner will report a higher net income as a result of electing to pension split, the age credit (see Tip #67) available prior to pension splitting can be reduced or eliminated. (The age credit decreases as income begins to exceed $32,312.) As well, the higher-tax-bracket spouse's/common-law partner's claim for a spouse or common-law partner amount can be reduced or eliminated.

To decide whether an election to pension split makes sense, weigh these implications in light of the tax savings pension splitting can provide.

Determining whether you qualify for pension splitting

The pension splitting rules apply to Canadian residents who are married or in a common-law relationship at the end of the year. The maximum amount of eligible pension income that can be split is prorated in cases where a couple comes together during a year or one of the spouses dies.

You can split your pension income with your spouse even if he or she is under the age of 65.

Deciding whether your pension income qualifies for pension splitting

To make use of the pension-splitting rules the pension recipient must receive "eligible" pension income. To figure out what is eligible pension income it's easiest first to see what represents *ineligible* pension income for purposes of pension splitting:

✔ Old Age Security (OAS) payments

✔ Canada or Quebec Pension Plan (CPP/QPP). (Other rules apply for sharing this type of income; see our comments earlier in this tip.)

✔ Non-annuity registered retirement savings plan (RRSP) withdrawals

✔ Withdrawals from a retirement compensation agreement (RCA)

When the actual pension recipient is age 65 or over at the end of a year, the pension income eligible for splitting includes the following:

✔ Annuity payments from a registered pension plan (RPP)

✔ Annuity payments from a deferred profit sharing plan (DPSP)

✔ Registered retirement income fund (RRIF) and life income fund (LIF) withdrawals.

When the actual pension recipient is under 65 at the end of a year, the pension income eligible for splitting includes the following:

✔ Annuity payments from a registered pension plan (RPP)

✔ Amounts listed under "Eligible pension income for pension splitting" above if received by virtue of the death of a spouse/ common-law partner.

Knowing how to pension split

It's simple! The pension splitting rules are elective on an annual basis. Follow these steps:

1. The amount to be split is deducted on line 210 on the tax return of the spouse who actually received the pension — the high-tax-bracket spouse/common-law partner.

2. The amount is added to the income reported on the other spouse's/common-law partner's tax return — the low-tax-bracket spouse/common-law partner — on line 116.

3. The tax withheld on the actual pension payments to the high-tax-bracket spouse/common-law partner is allocated to the other spouse/common-law partner on the same basis as the pension income was split. (This removes the cash-flow burden of requiring the low-tax-bracket spouse/ common-law partner to come up with a significant amount of money on April 30!)

Both spouses/common-law partners must agree to partake in pension splitting and the amount to be split, and must complete and sign two copies of form T1032, "Joint Election to Split Pension Income." Each spouse/common-law partner must include the form with their tax return if paper filing. If electronically filing each spouse/common-law partner needs to keep a copy in case the CRA asks to see it.

Claiming an extra pension income credit

The rules for the pension income credit (Tip #67) were expanded when the pension-splitting rules came into being back in 2007. If both spouses/common-law partners are over age 65, then each will receive up to $2,000 in pension income credits. (If the eligible pension income is less than $2,000 the credit maxes out at the actual eligible pension income taxed to each spouse/common-law partner.) The result is that pension splitting may serve to permit another pension income credit amount of $2,000 in the family where the lower-tax-bracket spouse/common-law partner was not entitled to it previously.

The rules are a bit trickier if both spouses/common-law partners aren't over age 65. In that case, if the payments came from a registered pension plan (RPP) then each spouse/common-law partner is entitled to a pension credit regardless of age. However, in most circumstances payments from an RRSP or RRIF will not qualify for the pension credit in the hands of a spouse/common-law partner under age 65. In that situation, you may still benefit from paying less tax if each spouse/common-law partner is in a different tax bracket — you just won't benefit from the pension credit as well.

#69

Know That the U.S. Internal Revenue Service May Have an Interest in You

*W*e're guessing most of you are quite familiar with paying taxes to — and dealing with — the Canada Revenue Agency (CRA). However, a number of individuals who live in Canada also have the pleasure of filing an income tax return with the U.S. Internal Revenue Service — better known as the IRS.

Not to ruin the party, but if you die owning U.S. assets you can be subject to U.S. estate tax. Yikes! (We discuss U.S. estate tax in Tip #70.)

In this tip we will look at when you may need to file a U.S. income tax return.

Knowing When to File a U.S. Income Tax Return

You must file an income tax return with the IRS when you fit into one of the following categories:

✔ **You're a U.S. citizen:** U.S. citizens are required to file a U.S. income tax return (IRS form 1040), report their worldwide income on the return, and pay U.S. federal income tax no matter what country they live in.

✔ Canada's income tax treaty with the U.S. and the Canadian and U.S. foreign tax credit mechanisms are designed to avoid having taxpayers taxed twice on the same income. So, reporting the same income on your Canadian and U.S. income tax returns (adjusted for the different currencies, of course) does not mean you'll be subject to double tax. The CRA and IRS aren't *that* unfair.

✔ **You're a "green card" holder — or the holder of a U.S. Permanent Resident Card** These folks have the same U.S. tax filing rules as a U.S. citizen. (By the way, the card is no longer green.)

✔ **You're a Canadian resident considered by the U.S. to be a "resident alien" or "non-resident alien"** (We laughed too when we first heard the word "alien" used in discussing U.S. income taxes.)

Deciding if You're an Alien

In this section, we help you determine whether you're a resident or non-resident alien of the U.S. (It's not as straightforward as you might think!)

Resident alien

You're considered a resident alien of the U.S. if you meet the "substantial presence test" because of frequent stays in the U.S. and cannot claim the "closer connection exception" regarding your ties to Canada. You may find you're a resident alien if you've moved to the U.S. on a temporary basis for work. Resident aliens are taxed in the U.S. on their worldwide income and must file a U.S. income return (IRS form 1040) — just like a U.S. citizen.

Substantial presence test

This test is based on your physical presence in the U.S. over the last three years. You're considered substantially present in the U.S. when you were present during the current and past two years for at least 183 days. To determine the total days you were in the U.S., get out your calculator and add up the following (including partial days):

✔ Each day in 2009 counts as a full day

✔ Each day in 2008 counts as one-third day

✔ Each day in 2007 counts as one-sixth day

If you were in the U.S. for fewer than 31 days in 2009 you will not meet the substantial presence test.

Closer connection exception

If due to frequent vacationing in the U.S. you do meet the substantial presence test, then you'll be considered resident and required to file a U.S. tax return that reports your worldwide income.

However, you can avoid this tax filing if you're able to claim you were more closely connected with Canada in 2009 than with the U.S. because of your significant personal (home, family, assets, social, political, church, driver's licence) and business ties to Canada. A closer connection exception is available if you, as the alien

- ✔ Were present in the U.S. for fewer than 183 days in 2009,

- ✔ Maintained a permanent place of residence in Canada throughout 2009, and

- ✔ Complete and file IRS form 8840, "Closer Connection Exception Statement for Aliens," with the IRS by June 15, 2010.

Non-resident alien

You're considered a non-resident alien of the U.S. when you don't meet the "substantial presence" test or you do meet the substantial presence test but can claim an exception due to having a closer connection to Canada (refer to the previous section). This includes a large number of Canadians, often referred to as "snowbirds," who spend a great deal of time in the U.S. to avoid harsh Canadian winters.

A non-resident alien must file a non-resident U.S. income tax return (IRS form 1040NR) when, the individual

- ✔ Has U.S. employment income.

- ✔ Has a tax liability on U.S. source income including employment income, interest, dividends, and royalties.

- ✔ Is engaged in business that can produce income "connected" (the IRS's word) with the U.S. For example, renting out your condo in Boca Raton, Florida or your vacation home in Tempe, Arizona. You may earn income from renting the property or you may have a capital gain on sale.

Even though the Canada–U.S. tax treaty is designed to avoid you being taxed in both countries, the U.S. has the first right to tax rental income and capital gains regarding real estate located in the United States. A U.S. income tax return filing would be necessary and any U.S. tax paid would qualify for a foreign tax credit when completing your Canadian income tax return.

File U.S. Tax Returns on Time

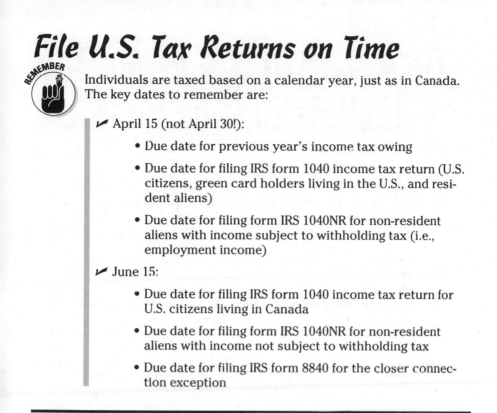

Individuals are taxed based on a calendar year, just as in Canada. The key dates to remember are:

✔ April 15 (not April 30!):

- Due date for previous year's income tax owing

- Due date for filing IRS form 1040 income tax return (U.S. citizens, green card holders living in the U.S., and resident aliens)

- Due date for filing form IRS 1040NR for non-resident aliens with income subject to withholding tax (i.e., employment income)

✔ June 15:

- Due date for filing IRS form 1040 income tax return for U.S. citizens living in Canada

- Due date for filing form IRS 1040NR for non-resident aliens with income not subject to withholding tax

- Due date for filing IRS form 8840 for the closer connection exception

Don't forget about state, county, and city taxes

Own property in the U.S.? If you're considered a resident alien, you may be required to file a state, county, or city tax return for the area in which you own property. For further information go to www.statelocal.net/index.cfm.

#70

Be Aware of U.S. Estate Tax Implications on Death

• •

*1*n this book we talk a lot about Canadian income tax, and we discuss potential U.S. income tax implications in Tip #69. Well, we have still another type of tax to comment on — U.S. estate tax.

U.S. estate tax is foreign (pun intended) to most of us because Canada doesn't have a comparable tax. (We understand from our grandparents that Canada used to have succession duties, which to us look a lot like an estate tax.) In this tip, we fill you in on what you need to know about U.S. estate tax.

Understanding U.S. Estate Tax

Here's how the Web site irs.gov defines *estate tax:* "Estate tax is a tax on your right to transfer property at your death." Hmmmm. We're not sure that's clear. How about simply calling it a tax payable on the value of your assets at the time of your death? (**Note:** The tax is based on the value of U.S. assets at the time of death and not only on accrued gain — so the cost of the assets has nothing to do with U.S. estate tax.)

The amount of tax, before deductions and credits, varies from 18 percent (on an estate of US$10,000) to 45 percent (on an estate of US$2 million or more). However, the good news is that estate tax credits are available and Canadian residents even get some special treatment.

Oddly, the estate tax rates are to be reset to zero for 2010 because the estate tax has been repealed for the year. Estate tax is to return in 2011 unless U.S. legislation comes on stream to alter this.

Know the assets that expose you to U.S. estate tax

Because our editor gave us just three pages for this tip we detail only the U.S. estate tax implications facing Canadians who are considered non-resident aliens of the U.S. (We comment on resident and non-resident aliens of the U.S. in Tip #69.)

A Canadian non-resident alien is subject to U.S. estate tax on the total value of his or her U.S. estate that includes the following:

- ✔ Shares of U.S. corporations (even if held in Canada)
- ✔ Real estate located in the U.S.
- ✔ Personal property such as cars and furniture in the U.S.

Claim credit against U.S. estate tax

Any U.S. non-resident (Canadian or otherwise) can claim an estate tax credit of US$13,000, which effectively means no U.S. estate tax applies on the first US$60,000 of a U.S. estate.

For Canadian residents the estate tax credit is increased to US$1,455,800 for 2009, but on a prorated basis. (The increased credit is due to the Canada – U.S. tax treaty; we first discuss the tax treaty in Tip #69.) The proration percentage is determined using the formula of

$$\frac{\text{U.S. estate}}{\text{World-wide estate}}$$

If your U.S. estate was 20 percent of your worldwide estate, you would be permitted a U.S. estate tax credit of US$291,160 (20 percent of US$1,455,800). This would make the first US$1,104,536 of your U.S. estate tax free.

Enjoy the small estate exemption

A provision in the Canada – U.S. tax treaty provides relief to Canadian residents with worldwide estates worth less than US$1,200,000. When this is the case the U.S. estate tax will generally apply only to real estate located in the U.S.

Filing Tax Returns

The U.S. estate tax can affect two tax returns. The first — and most obvious — is the U.S. estate return (which is completely separate from the U.S. income tax return). The second return that may be affected is the final personal Canadian tax return of the deceased.

Prepare a U.S. estate tax return

A U.S. estate return for non-residents of the U.S. is IRS form 706-NA, due nine months after the date of death. The return must be filed if the deceased's U.S. estate was worth more than US$60,000 at the time of death. A return needs to be filed even if the U.S. estate tax liability is zero.

To take advantage of the provisions of the Canada – U.S. tax treaty you must provide the details of the deceased's worldwide assets to the IRS in this return.

Claim a foreign tax credit on the deceased's Canadian income tax return

Where a deceased taxpayer has paid U.S. estate tax, the tax paid qualifies for a foreign tax credit on the deceased's final Canadian income tax return. However, the credit is available only up to the extent of the Canadian taxes payable on the deceased U.S. source income in the year of death.

Undertake Estate Planning

*E*state planning sounds ominous. We know that "estate" and "death" are terms that often go together — much like death and taxes. However, in this tip our goal is to point out that estate planning involves more than just income taxes.

Estate planning is a component of financial planning. It focuses on minimizing the work and difficulties faced by executors while maximizing the wealth passed to heirs. Estate planning is far more than simply having an up-to-date will. In fact, drafting your will should be the last thing you do in documenting your estate plan — all the other steps should be taken care of first.

In Tip #72 we dwell on the income tax implications of dying, and in Tip #74 we point out the probate fee exposure your estate may have.

Decide What Your Estate Is to Do

The first step of an estate plan requires you to decide your estate's purpose:

- ✔ Who are the beneficiaries/heirs to your estate? Family members? non-family individuals? charities? Who is to get what?

- ✔ Should your estate be dispersed on death or should it carry on? Who will see that your wishes are met?

- ✔ Are funds to be kept aside for a specific purpose? A disabled child's care? a grandchild's education?

- ✔ Are there assets you wish to be shared after death, such as the family cottage?

After you determine your estate's objectives, design and enact a plan to ensure the objectives are reached. It's vital here to assess the income tax and probate consequences; luckily for you, we highlight them in Tips #72 and #74.

Build Your Estate Planning Team

Your estate plan will involve a number of professionals working together on your and your family's behalf:

- ✔ **A lawyer** to draft a will, powers of attorney, and trust agreements, and to ensure the estate plan is compliant with relevant succession, estate, trust, and other laws including family law,

- ✔ **An accountant** to point out and calculate income tax and probate exposure on death and to ensure tax elections and personal, estate, and trust tax returns are prepared and filed by the due dates, and

- ✔ **An insurance specialist** to advise on alternatives in having life insurance as part of your estate plan. In Tip #72 we explore how life insurance can be an effective way to fund a tax liability on death to avoid or minimize the liquidation of an estate's assets to pay an income tax bill.

Reduce Income Tax at Death

● ●

*A*void planning for your estate and you can leave a significant income tax liability upon your death. As death and death taxes occur at the same time, you may find that in this situation a significant portion of your income is taxed in a top tax bracket and therefore loses about 45 percent to the CRA.

In this tip we challenge you to look at your income tax exposure at death and then to undertake some tried, tested, and true (and legal!) estate planning ideas to minimize the tax to maximize the value of your estate being passed to your heirs. (We expect the CRA is not one of your desired heirs!)

In Tip #74 we look at minimizing your exposure to provincial/territorial probate fees (or "estate administration taxes").

Understand the Relationship of Death and Taxes

Without trying to be brazen, when you die you leave the Canadian tax system. On death you're subject to tax for the very last time. The tax rules are generally drafted so that any accrued gains or income you have at the time of your death are subject to tax. A general exception to these rules occurs when your assets are passed on to a spouse/common-law partner. Here the tax can usually be deferred until the death of the surviving spouse/common-law partner.

Capital gains and recapture

For income tax purposes you're considered to have sold all your assets at the time of death. (Again, an exception is available when property is passed to a spouse/common-law partner.)

The "sale" proceeds are deemed to be the value of the assets at your death. The excess of proceeds over the cost is a capital gain of which 50 percent is taxed. If your assets include rental properties there may also be "recapture" of prior-year depreciation claims (or capital cost allowance — CCA in tax lingo; see Tip #32). Recapture is fully taxed.

The tax liability arising on the deemed capital gains and/or recapture must be funded from other sources. As a "sale" occurred strictly for income tax purposes you did not receive any cash to pay the tax. In the worst case the estate is forced to sell an asset to pay a tax bill. This works against you if one of the objectives of your estate (Tip #71) is to keep the cottage in the family after you pass on.

RRSPs and RRIFs

On death your registered retirement savings plans (RRSPs) and/or registered retirement income funds (RRIFs) are considered deregistered and, unless the beneficiary of your plan is your spouse/common-law partner, the full value of each plan is included in the income reported on your final personal tax return.

At least most RRSPs and RRIFs provide immediate access to cash, to fund the tax liability by having the plan liquidate the holdings. However, the remaining value to be passed on to your heirs can be dramatically reduced.

Live Rich, Die Poor

Live it up while you're alive and leave the coffers empty when you shuffle off this mortal coil — this is the estate planning motto! A proper estate plan will permit you to live the life you deserve, but on death you may find you don't legally own a lot of assets — or you're poor on paper — meaning a low income tax exposure. Perfect!

A way to avoid taxes on death would be to rid yourself of all assets (including RRSPs and RRIFs) before you die. However, you still have to live! Your estate plan must allow you to live comfortably until your death and have access to assets you enjoy — like the family cottage. You want to ensure you have enough funds to live on, and you *don't* want to get involved with your children's squabbles over your assets. You also do not want to face a large tax liability now. What to do?

Estate Planning Tools

Although it's never pleasant to think of our own demise, the thought of paying less tax usually brightens our day. In this section, we look at a number of ways you can reduce the income tax exposure you may have at death.

Early inheritances to your children and grandchildren

If an objective of your estate is to pass assets to your children, why not do it now? The kids may prefer some money sooner rather than later — especially if they have an outstanding mortgage.

In passing funds on to your adult children you can do an outright gift (a true early inheritance) or you can lend funds and forgive the loan on or before death.

Gifts

When you give cash to an adult child no income tax implications exist for you, regardless of how the money is used. If you liquidate securities to make the cash gift you may incur capital gains, which would be subject to tax in the year of liquidation. This tax may be lower than on your death, plus you have the cash to pay the tax, and moreover your current tax rate may be substantially lower than your tax rate in the year of death. (Another thought is that in a poor economic market selling may be more attractive in terms of reducing your tax on the gain and letting the market "uptick" be taxed at a later time in your child's hands should she re-invest the funds you give to her.)

Consider establishing a trust in which you add cash to fund investments on behalf of your grandchildren. (Don't be afraid of trusts! See Tip #73.) When the grandchildren are under 18 the interest or dividends earned on the investments will continue to be taxed in your hands. However, any capital gains can be taxed in the grandchildren's hands. Because only 50 percent of capital gains are taxed, an individual can have $20,640 of the capital gains and pay no income tax thanks to the $10,320 basic personal tax credit amount we're all entitled to. So, here you can reduce the size of your estate and reduce the *extended* family tax bite.

Loans

Rather than giving funds to your adult children, you can make a loan. The loan can be set up so it's forgiven no later than at the time of your death. During your lifetime this offers you some control as you can "call" the loan. The loan can be interest-free if your adult child uses the funds to pay down a mortgage, pay for your grandkid's tuition, fund a vacation, buy a new car, and so on.

Should your adult children invest the funds, the income attribution rules would have you, not your adult child, pay tax on the investment income if the funds were lent on an interest-free or a below-market-rate basis.

Undertake an "estate freeze"

As your assets grow in value so does the tax liability you will face on death. As part of your estate plan you can implement steps to allow this growth to continue (stock and real estate markets willing, of course) but to not have the growth accrue to your hands. This is accomplished by exchanging a "growth asset" for a non-growth asset.

In doing the exchange this will "freeze" the growth in your hands and the tax liability that has accrued as at the time of the exchange. The growth of your asset from the time you acquired it to the time of the exchange or freeze will be subject to tax, but not until your passing.

The growth after the time of the exchange or freeze accrues to someone else — your heirs. When the growth accrued to you is frozen, so is your tax liability. At the time of the exchange or freeze the future tax liability can be estimated and steps can be taken to plan for its payment on your death. Often, you can purchase life insurance (which we discuss later in this tip); on your death the insurance proceeds are used to pay the tax liability, and the estate stays intact.

Portfolio of investments

A portfolio of growth investments (stocks, mutual funds, real estate, and so on.) can be transferred to a private family owned corporation on a tax-free basis. (Well, it's actually a tax deferral because the accrued gain at the time of the transfer will be taxed on your death — but not until then!) In return for your portfolio of investments you receive preferred shares of the corporation. The preferred shares would have a value equal to the value of the portfolio transferred to the corporation and this value will not grow. The value of the preferred shares would be frozen. The preferred shares would be voting and dividend paying to allow you to control the corporation (that is, the decisions concerning the portfolio of investments) and to take funds out for living expenses.

Your heirs, perhaps your children, would subscribe for the common shares (or "growth shares") of the corporation for a nominal amount, say $100. The future growth of the investment portfolio will accrue to the common shareholders and will be taxed in your heirs' hands when they sell or are deemed to sell the common shares of the corporation on their death.

For more on the tax benefits of corporations, see Tip #30.

Family business succession

An estate freeze is a common technique used by family businesses. It's often coupled with passing the business to a second generation. The common shares, a growth asset, owned by parents, are exchanged on a tax-free basis (well, again, tax-deferred as noted above) for preferred shares. New common shares are then purchased by the sons and daughters of the second generation. The parent's tax liability is frozen and steps are undertaken to provide the funds to pay this liability at death. The preferred shares are inherited by the children who become the sole owners of the business. The procedure repeats itself when time comes to pass the business on to the third generation.

Make charitable donations and bequests

In Tip #75, we provide details on the advantages charitable donations and bequests offer in minimizing income taxes on death when they are part of your estate plan. There is tax savings available when charitable donations are made in your year of death or after your death by virtue of a bequest in your will.

To arrange your affairs to make a bequest, contact the "planned giving" department of your favourite charity.

If you begin funding a charitable donation to be given on your death (say, a life insurance policy), you can receive an official receipt for yearly charitable contributions (say, annual life insurance premiums) while you're alive.

Reduce exposure to U.S. estate tax

In Tip #70 we discuss the implications of dying while owning U.S. assets (such as shares of U.S. corporations and real estate located in the U.S.) and the potential exposure to U.S. estate tax.

If you own U.S. assets you can undertake strategies to minimize or eliminate the potential U.S. estate tax you may be subject to. It's best to contact a U.S. estate tax specialist for further advice in this area.

If you're considering purchasing a U.S. property, see a U.S. estate tax specialist *before* you make the purchase.

Purchase life insurance

Life insurance can be a handy estate planning tool. Life insurance itself does not reduce your exposure to income tax on death — it's simply used as a means to fund a tax liability on death so the estate does not have to be crippled to pay the tax.

Life insurance is most effective when an estate is quite illiquid — say, because the majority of the estate is made up of a cottage or other real estate holdings.

A life insurance death benefit payment is not taxable.

Because life insurance is, in effect, a benefit to your heirs, let them pay the annual premiums.

Have a power of attorney

A power of attorney — sometimes called a living will — lets your "attorney" make health and financial decisions for you when you can't. We discuss the importance of having an up-to-date power of attorney in Tip #76.

Make sure your will is up to date

We consider this the last step in your estate plan because you need to visit all the other estate planning steps first. In other words, your will is done after you've decided on the objectives of your estate and implemented strategies to meet these objectives while at the same time minimizing your tax and probate exposure. (We discuss probate exposure in Tip #74).

Use Trusts in Your Tax and Estate Planning

*T*rust us — a trust is not solely for the old or rich, overly complex, a "tax scam," or exorbitantly expensive to set up or maintain. A trust can be a very effective tax and estate planning tool, as we cover in this tip.

Understanding What a Trust Is

A *trust* is an arrangement that separates control and legal ownership of an asset from its actual beneficial ownership. In plain English, this means the asset is owned and controlled by someone other than the person(s) that benefits from the asset (say, in the form of income and/or capital gains derived from the asset).

Here's an example of a trust. The parents of a very young child die but leave funds (perhaps via life insurance) to care for the child. Because the child is so young it's not prudent to give the funds directly to the child. Therefore, an arrangement is set up (a trust) where the funds are made available to the child (the beneficiary) but control of these funds rests with others (the trustees) to ensure the funds are prudently saved and spent. The trustees have a legal duty to ensure the funds are used properly and solely for the benefit of the child.

For income tax purposes a trust is a separate taxpayer. A trust must file its own special tax return (a "T3 income tax return" versus a "T1 income tax return" an individual files) if it has income, and it may or may not be required to pay income taxes. Where the trust has a lower tax rate than the trust beneficiary(ies) it makes sense to have the trust pay the tax. Where the beneficiary(ies) of the trust is subject to tax at a rate lower than the trust then best to have the trust allocate its income and capital gains to the beneficiary(ies) so they would be subject to tax and not the trust.

A trust can be used for many other reasons other than tax planning, including the following:

✔ Avoiding family disputes

✔ Assisting in managing another's affairs

✔ Controlling children's money

✔ Providing for a child's education and/or special needs

✔ Providing for the succession of a family business

A trust arrangement is documented in a *trust agreement,* which is drafted by a lawyer. Unlike when a company is incorporated, a trust agreement does not require government approval to be set up. A trust agreement remains a private document.

The trust agreement will note the trust's name (say, the Jones Family Trust) as well as the names and powers of the trustees. The trustees can be given strict guidelines on how the trust is to be run and which beneficiaries get what and when, or — as is the case with most modern trusts — the trustees are given discretion in terms of managing the trust assets and distributing income to the beneficiaries.

Getting to Know Who's Involved in a Trust

A trust requires the involvement of three people. We introduce you to these fine folks in this section.

Settlor

The person who sells or gifts assets (i.e., investments, money) to a trust is the trust *settlor.* Usually, the settlor's "job" is complete after the trust is settled. A settlor of a trust can be a parent who wishes to pass on assets to children.

The settlor cannot be able to have the trust property returned to him- or herself. If so, the trust will be considered "reversionary" and the tax benefits expected from the trust will not be available.

The sale or gift of assets to a trust is considered a disposition for tax purposes. If the asset has an accrued capital gain, it could trigger a tax liability. However, this tax may be less than the tax liability that occurs later in life, or at death. (A capital gain will not arise where assets are transferred to a trust that is a spousal, alter-ego, or joint spousal/partner trust. We discuss these trusts near the end of this tip.)

Beneficiaries

The individual or individuals who will reap the rewards from the trust assets are the "beneficial owners." Often children are beneficiaries of a trust, especially if they are under 18. The future appreciation in the trust assets will be taxed in the trust or the beneficiaries' hands and *not* the settlor's hands. This is of great advantage where the settlor is at a higher tax rate than the beneficiaries.

Trustees

Trustees manage or control the trust assets on behalf of the beneficiaries. This permits a parent to minimize a potential tax liability without giving assets directly to a child who, at least in the eyes of the parents, may not act responsibly.

Investigating Common Trusts

Trusts fall into two categories: testamentary and inter-vivos (or living) *trusts*. A testamentary trust is created on the death of a settlor, and a living trust is created while the settlor is still alive (hence the name). Each category of trust is taxed differently. In this section, we take a look at the most common types of *testamentary and inter-vivos trusts*, and explain when they're best used for reducing taxes and/or other purposes.

Inter-vivos income-splitting trust

The term *income splitting* — or, as it's sometimes called, *income sharing* or *income shifting* — is used to describe the plans or steps taken to shift income from a higher-tax-rate family member to a lower-tax-rate family member. The family income remains the same but the family income tax burden is decreased, leaving more after-tax income for family living expenses. (We discuss the tax savings available with income splitting in Tip #50, and look at CPP sharing and pension splitting in Tip #68.)

The idea here is that parents transfer investments to a trust in which the children are beneficiaries. The income earned on the investments is then taxed in the children's hands. Because the children are expected to be in a lower tax bracket than the parents, the family is better off on an after-tax basis.

Working against this objective are the income tax provisions called the "attribution rules." These rules essentially state that no matter who receives the income, it's taxed in the hands of the person who made or funded the investment. In other words, the income earned on the investment asset is "attributed" to the individual who funded the investment. However, there are exceptions to the attribution rules:

- ✔ Attribution of interest or dividends occurs only if the child beneficiary is under 18. Therefore, no attribution occurs when the beneficiaries are adult children.

- ✔ No attribution of "income on income" applies. Interest and dividends earned on the reinvestment of interest and dividends does not attribute.

- ✔ No attribution of capital gains applies. Because only 50 percent of capital gains are taxed, a trust beneficiary could be subject to tax on $20,640 of capital gains in 2009 but pay no tax because of the $10,320 basic personal tax credit amount available to all individuals.

- ✔ No attribution of interest and dividends applies, even when the beneficiaries are children under 18, where funds are loaned, rather than gifted, to the trust. The loan must be made at a market rate of interest and the interest on the loan must be paid within 30 days of the end of each calendar year. The individual lending the funds — say, a parent — would include the interest received in his or her personal taxable income and the trust would deduct the interest costs in determining its taxable income because the interest is being incurred to earn income. (We discuss the deductibility of interest in Tip #47.)

- ✔ For this strategy to work effectively in shifting income from a parent to a child, the trust assets need to have an investment return greater then the interest rate on the loan.

Testamentary spousal trust

As this trust is "testamentary" it is created by a will. On death, the assets of the deceased are transferred to a spousal trust on a tax-free basis. The trust must permit only the surviving spouse/common-law partner to receive the income of the trust assets until his or her death. A spousal trust has three main advantages:

- ✔ Just as with assets bequeathed directly to a spouse/common-law partner, the deceased spouse/partner on death does not face capital gains and the associated income tax in respect of assets transferred to a spousal trust on death. The income tax on the accrued capital gains on the assets of the deceased is deferred until the death of the surviving spouse/common-law partner.

✔ Like any trust, it has trustees to manage it. Where the spouse/ common-law partner of the deceased has little financial experience this permits an element of control.

✔ A testamentary spousal trust is taxed at the same tax rates as an individual. Therefore, the same graduated rates apply. This permits tax savings when the spouse/common-law partner of the deceased is taxed at a higher tax bracket than the trust. Therefore, less tax, more funds for the surviving spouse/ common-law partner.

Multiple testamentary non-spousal trusts

Like a spousal trust, these trusts are taxed at graduated tax rates. The beneficiaries are often children. Separate trusts are created (usually one per child) as opposed to one trust. This allows to the tax savings of the graduated levels of tax to be multiplied. We discuss this in Tip #76 in the context of choosing your heirs.

Alter-ego and joint spousal/partner inter-vivos trusts

You need to be at least 65 to establish these trusts. Assets can be transferred to these trusts without triggering income tax on the accrued capital gain at the time of transfer. In the case of an alter-ego trust the tax on the accrued gain is deferred until your death. Where a joint spousal/partner trust is used the tax can be deferred until the death of the second spouse/common law partner.

Use of these trusts don't decrease your income taxes at death (or on the death of your spouse/common-law partner) but these trusts work extremely well to minimize your probate exposure on death (see Tip #74).

These trusts also have other advantages:

✔ **They can serve as a will substitute:** Because the assets are in a trust they are not part of your estate and do not pass to your heirs as the result of a will. The assets will pass according to the trust agreement. Compulsory succession rules can be avoided. These assets are not subject to a will that could be contested.

✔ **They can enhance privacy:** A probated will is a public document. Using these trusts prevents the public from knowing the value of your estate and who your beneficiaries are.

✔ **They can serve as a power of attorney substitute:** Co-trustees or successor trustees can act on your behalf if you become unable to manage the assets of the trust. A power of attorney (see Tip #76) is not needed for assets owned by a trust.

Reduce Probate Fees at Death

• •

*P**robate* is a court certificate ("letters probate" or similar) that validates a will and confirms the executor named is authorized to deal with your assets after your death. Most financial institutions will not release assets of the deceased to the beneficiaries of the will until they are provided with letters probate.

Probate fees (or, "probate tax") — or "estate administration tax" (the modern name) — are the cost of obtaining letters probate. Ontario, British Columbia, and Nova Scotia have the highest probate fees in the country.

Probate fees are based on the value of the assets in the estate. Obviously, the lower the value of the estate subject to probate the lower the probate fee. In this tip, we look at some ways you can organize your affairs now to reduce your probate exposure later.

Understanding the Relationship between Probate Fees and Income Taxes

Generally, planning for income tax minimization has priority over the planning for probate minimization — especially because probate fees in many of the provinces and territories are not a significant cost. (Table 74-1 breaks down the probate fees for Canada.) In other words, do not let the "probate planning tail" wag the "income tax planning dog".

Sometimes conflict can occur between a recommended income tax strategy and a probate plan. Again, it's often best to go with the tax idea and accept that the probate fee be paid.

An example of where probate planning is less important than income tax planning is the home you live in, which may be exposed to probate on your death. However, you want to ensure that if you undertake steps to avoid this you do not lose the potential principal residence exemption (see Tip #46) to shelter the income tax on the capital gain that can arise on death. (We discuss the potential income taxes you can have on death in Tip #72.)

Determining Whether Probate Will Be Required

Not every will needs to be probated. Whether your will needs to be subject to the probate process will depend on what assets are involved, the legal ownership of the assets, and the custodian of the assets at the time of your death.

Assets that don't usually require probate include personal and household effects, vehicles, and life insurance proceeds. Additionally, as we discuss in the next section, the following assets can also be excluded from the probate fee calculation:

- ✔ RRSPs, RRIFs, and TFSAs with a designated beneficiary
- ✔ Shares of a private corporation, and
- ✔ Assets owned jointly

Without planning, if some of your assets are subject to probate then *all* of your assets can be subject to probate. So it's important to separate your assets between those subject to probate and those not. (We cover just how to do that in the remainder of this tip.)

 Talk to a lawyer and the custodian of your assets (perhaps the financial institution holding your investments) to find out who will request to see letters probate and on what assets.

Reducing your Estate Subject to Probate

In this section we comment on a number of strategies you can use (perhaps in combination) to reduce the value of your estate that will be subject to probate.

Designate a beneficiary of your RRSPs, RRIFs, and TFSAs

When a beneficiary is noted in the documentation of these plans, upon your death the funds will flow directly to the designated beneficiary. The funds do not first go into the estate and then out to the beneficiary. Because these funds do not become part of the estate, no applicable probate fee applies.

Own assets jointly

When you own assets jointly, say with a spouse/common-law partner or an adult child, the asset will pass directly to the joint owner(s) on your death. Again, because the assets do not first go into the estate, the asset is not included in the value of the assets on which the probate fee is calculated.

Transfer assets to an alter-ego or joint spousal/partner trust

When you're 65, you can transfer your assets to an alter-ego trust. Or, if you have a spouse/common-law partner, you can make use of a joint spousal/partner trust. (Refer to Tip #73 for an explanation of these types of trusts.) The assets remain under your control, and all the income and capital gains they generate is taxed in the same way as without using the trust — both while you're alive and on death. Should you transfer a home to one of these trusts, the principal residence exemption continues to be available. The transfer of the assets to these types of trusts does not trigger a tax liability because the assets are considered "sold" to the trust at a value equal to the tax cost of the assets.

Because upon death the "legal" owner of the assets is a trust — and not you — the assets will not be part of your estate and, again, not subject to probate. The assets pass to your intended beneficiaries by virtue of the trust document and not by your will. Of course, the trust and the will beneficiaries can be the same if you wish. We discuss trusts and how they may fit into your income tax and estate planning ideas in Tip #73.

Transfer assets to a family owned private corporation (a holding company)

To transfer your shares of a private corporation to your heirs on your death it is expected that the directors of the private corporation would not request to see letters probate to approve the transfer.

A financial institution, such as an investment management company responsible for holding the corporation's portfolio of marketable securities, would not request letters probate in this instance as no impact occurs on the investments held by the corporation. The investments continue to be held by the same owner — the private corporation. A corporation does not "die." (For more on corporations, check out Tip #30.)

You can transfer investments and other assets to a corporation without triggering a tax liability provided the proper income tax election is documented and filed with the CRA. (We touch on this briefly in Tip #72 regarding undertaking an "estate freeze.")

Have two wills

Draft up two wills: one that covers the assets subject to probate and another for the assets that are not subject to probate.

A common probate plan for an individual with the majority of his or her wealth in investments is to transfer the investments to a private corporation or "holding company". (Again, we touched on this in Tip #72 in connection with carryout an "estate freeze.")

In consideration for the investments the individual receives back shares of the holding company. A will is prepared that solely addresses the shares of the holding company held by the individual. A second will is prepared to cover all the other assets owned by the individual.

On death, the second will may need to be probated. However, the value of the estate represented by this will is minimal because the bulk of the individual's wealth is represented by the first will, which does not need to be subject to the probate process. The probate fee will be based solely on the second will, which may represent a very small portion of the individual's full estate.

Make Charitable Donations Part of Your Estate Plan

*I*n Tip #71 we discuss the whys and whats of estate planning, and we extend our discussion to the hows of estate planning in Tips #72 to #74. In this tip, we carry on the "how" theme to show you how charitable donations can assist in your estate planning.

A lot of estate planning deals with the preservation of the wealth you've generated during your lifetime. Depending on your financial position, you — or perhaps your spouse/common-law partner, should they outlive you — could face a significant income tax bill on death. One of the ways to reduce this tax bill, and maybe to meet other objectives of your estate plan too, is to make charitable donations in the year of your death, at the time of your death and after your death.

Charitable Donations Made in the Year of Death

In Tip #9 we note that the maximum amount of charitable donations you can claim in a year is restricted to 75 percent of the net income figure reported on line 236 of your tax return. However, in the year a person dies this limit is 100 percent of the person's net income. Moreover, if the donations exceed the 100 percent limit in the year of death the excess donations can be carried back to the previous year to be claimed. The donation restriction for that year is retroactively increased to 100 percent. To use this provision, an adjustment request (CRA form T1ADJ "T1 Adjustment Request) to that year's return is sent to the CRA.

Include Charitable Donations in Your Will

If you want donations to be made to charities on and/or after your death you can set this up in your will. Simply include a clause in your will stating that specific charities are to receive certain dollar amounts. Alternatively, a charity can be a full or partial beneficiary of your estate. In this case, the amount the charity will receive is not known until the estate has made its final distribution.

Where funds are donated to a registered charity or charitable foundation by virtue of a will, the tax credit can be claimed on the final personal tax return of the deceased— no matter the timing of the donation This is very advantageous as the final personal tax return of the deceased can have a significant income tax liability. (The potential for income tax at death is discussed in Tip #72.)

Donate RRSPs, RRIFs, TFSAs, and Life Insurance to Charities

You can name a registered charity or charitable foundation as the beneficiary of an RRSP, RRIF, TFSA, or insurance policy and obtain a tax credit for the donation in the year of death. Where the beneficiary is stated in the documentation of the plans — rather than in a will — you can reduce the probate exposure of your estate. We discuss probate, also called estate administration tax, in Tip #74.

When a gift of a life insurance policy is made, it may also be possible to claim the insurance premiums as charitable donations as they are paid in the years while you are alive.

Prepare a Power of Attorney and a Will

*C*ertainty.

The main reason for having an up to date power of attorney and will is simply to ensure that you and your assets are efficiently handled in the exact way you wish and that those left with the task are trustworthy and have your best interests at heart.

In this tip we focus on the completion of your estate planning. Here, we detail the merits of allowing another to act for you when the need may arise and to ensure your estate wishes are clearly communicated to your heirs.

When your plans and intentions are written down it means not only that you can relax, but also that your family can too. Everyone is aware that things are in place when needed, both while you're alive and on your death.

Your Power of Attorney

The benefit of having a will (which we discuss below) is well rec-ognized in that it ensures your wishes are met on and after death. However, for a will to come into play, well, you have to, ahem, die. If you become incapable of making decisions while you are alive, a power of attorney will allow someone you trust to make decisions on your behalf and in your best interests.

Simply put, in designating someone to be your power of attorney you are authorizing them to act for you as your "agent" to deal with decisions that you need to make but may be unable to do so.

 The "attorney" in "power of attorney" does not need to be a lawyer. However, you're best off having a lawyer draft your power of attorney for you.

Ensure your power of attorney is up to date, and redo it any time your selected attorney should become unable to act as such.

You can have two separate powers of attorney:

- ✔ **A power of attorney for property:** Actually, what you want is to have a "continuing" or "enduring" power of attorney for property. Having the power of attorney be continuing or enduring allows the power of attorney to continue should you become mentally incapable. This power of attorney allows someone to act for you while you're mentally competent, and also when you're not.

- ✔ If there are income tax decisions, elections, returns to be completed, signed and filed to take advantage of the tips in this book the person having your the power of attorney can see to it that all these tasks are completed to benefit you and your heirs.

- ✔ **A power of attorney for personal care:** Here, the power of attorney only has "power" when you're incapable of making personal care decisions such as medical treatment, the decision to move to a nursing home, nutrition, hygiene, and the like.

Your Will

The writing (or updating) of your will should be one of the last, if not the last, steps in implementing your estate plan. It's time to look at your will after you've completed the earlier estate planning steps (as detailed in Tips #71 to #75) of deciding on the objectives of your estate and have implemented the ways the objectives are to be met — early inheritance gifts, planned giving to charities, transferring assets to a corporation, purchasing life insurance, designating beneficiaries of your RRSPs, RRIFs, and TFSAs, owning assets jointly, use of trusts, and so on. In drafting your will you must consider each asset that is to become part of your estate.

Although you may be tempted to use a will kit as an inexpensive way to prepare a will, we don't recommend it. Working with a lawyer will ensure that your will is tailored to your needs *and that all of your assets are considered.*

Have an accountant look at a draft version of your will before you "go final." (No, we are not looking for work here!) Your lawyer may be great on estate law and the necessary wording of a will but he or she may not be up on the tax and estate planning strategies available to you, your spouse/common-law partner, and your family.

If you die without a will — called dying *intestate* — it will be stressful for those you leave behind. Transferring your assets can be costly, and there will be delays. You have no control on who looks after your affairs, nor can you ensure your assets will end up as you wished — or even whether all assets you own have been considered. Don't die without a will!

Making a trust the beneficiary of your will

Many wills provide for the individual's wish to bequeath all his or her assets to a spouse/common-law partner, and that should the individual outlive the spouse/common-law partner, the assets are to be passed on to adult children. The will of the other spouse/common-law partner would read the same. The estate objective is that the assets "stay in the family" — the assets first move to the surviving spouse/common-law partner and then to the adult children.

You can ensure your assets stay within your family and reduce the post-death income tax burden through the use of a trust. As we note in Tip #73, testamentary spousal trusts and multiple non-spousal testamentary trusts can be created in will. The advantage is that the trusts are taxed as a separate taxpayer and the income is subject to tax at the same graduated rates as individuals are. And where the tax rate of the trust is lower than the tax rate of the estate beneficiary, an opportunity exists for tax savings!

Instead of making your spouse/common-law partner the beneficiary of your estate, consider using a testamentary spousal trust. Continuing, should you outlive your spouse/common-law partner, then have your assets go to a number of testamentary trusts — say, a separate trust where the beneficiary is a different adult child. Again, your objective for your assets to first pass to your spouse/common-law partner and then to your adult children has been met (plus there is the potential to minimize the tax on future investment income)... Remember, the beneficiaries of each trust are entitled to the trust assets.

Reviewing and updating your will

Review your will periodically — every five years at least, and also at times when a major change occurs in your life circumstances, including the following:

- ✔ Divorce

- ✔ Death of a spouse/common-law partner

- ✔ Second marriage

- ✔ Illness

- ✔ Child/grandchild becoming disabled

- ✔ Children getting married

- ✔ Children with marital concerns

All of these twists in life will likely cause you to revisit your estate objectives, perhaps change your current estate planning techniques, and alter your will.

Part VI
The Part of Tens

"Death and taxes are for certain, Mr. Dooley, however, they're not mutually exclusive."

In this part . . .

Every Dummies book offers a few lists of top tens to wrap things up, and this book is no exception. First, we offer some valuable suggestions on ways that you can reduce your taxes year-round — not just in a frenzied panic come tax-time. Finally, we provide you with some helpful hints on how you can reduce the chances that the tax auditor will come calling. That's one visit you can do without!

Top Ten Year-Round Tax-Saving Strategies

*I*n this tip we run through our "greatest hits" — our top ten most effective tax-saving strategies. If you're employing all these strategies you get an A+ from us tax nerds for having your taxes managed all year long!

Open a TFSA

The (now not so) new tax-free savings account (TFSA), launched January 1, 2009, is the ideal place to put up to $5,000 of savings and earn tax-free income and/or gains for life. Withdrawals aren't taxed, don't negatively affect your eligibility for government-tested benefits, and can be re-contributed the following calendar year. (See Tip #41 for more.)

Maximize Your RRSP Contributions

Take advantage of one of the last great tax shelters. An RRSP is an arrangement that allows you to save for your retirement on a tax-friendly basis. Funds you contribute are not taxed until you withdraw them. The maximum contribution you can make for 2010 is $22,000; for 2011 onward the amount is indexed. (Check out Tip #42 for more info.)

Set Up a Spousal RRSP

The primary benefit of a spousal RRSP is that funds withdrawn can generally be taxed in the hands of a lower-income spouse. (Again, Tip #42 has the scoop on contributing to RRSPs.)

Think about Opening an RDSP for a Disabled Person

If you or someone you care about has a disability, consider opening up a registered disability savings plan (RDSP). Contributions to RDSPs, limited to $200,000 over the disabled beneficiary's lifetime, may be augmented by up to $90,000 in Canada Disability Savings grants and bonds. (Tip #63 has more on RDSPs.)

Earn Tax-Efficient Investment Income

If you've maxed out your TFSA and RRSP contributions, consider tax-efficient investment income outside these tax-sheltered plans by investing in Canadian dividends, which are eligible for the dividend tax credit (Tip #34), and capital gains, which are only half taxable (Tip #38).

Open Up RESPs for Your Kids

Don't forget to make at least $2,500 of contributions to each child's registered education savings plan (RESP) this year to take advantage of the $500 Canada Education Savings Grant. You may also be able to catch up on missed CESGs from prior years. (Get schooled about RESPs in Tip #51.)

Explore Pension Splitting

If you've received pension income in the year, be sure to investigate whether splitting up to half that income with your spouse or partner makes sense when you file your tax return. (Tip #68 will help you make that decision.)

Consider Income Splitting

A spousal income-splitting strategy (which we cover in Tip #50) — where the higher-income spouse or partner loans funds to the lower-income spouse or partner to invest — may be ideal given the record low prescribed interest rate, which is currently set at 1 percent.

Donate "In Kind" to Charity

When planning your charitable giving for the year, consider donating appreciated securities directly to your charity of choice.
You get a tax receipt for the full value of the securities that you donated and pay no tax on any accrued capital gains. (Tip #10 has what you're after.)

Plan Now to Avoid a Tax Refund

If you regularly get a large tax refund each spring — say, because you're eligible for the child tax credit; see Tip #49 — consider applying for a reduction of tax at source using CRA form T1213. (You'll need to complete the form each year.)

#78

Top Ten Ways to Reduce the Risk of a CRA Audit

*W*hat are the two most dreaded words in the English language? Okay — aside from "root canal." For many it's "tax audit." Chances are if you're reading this chapter you're looking for ways to reduce your risk of getting anything other than a thank you note — called a Notice of Assessment in tax speak — from the CRA.

If you do happen to receive something more than a Notice of Assessment in the mail — perhaps a request for more information — the first line of defence is to avoid breaking out in a sweat. You see, you should understand that there's a difference between an audit and a request for more information — also called a "verification procedure." The CRA may ask to see confirmation of receipts that don't have to be sent with your return, such as childcare expenses and tuition, but that's not an audit. In fact, most individuals are never audited; they simply receive requests for additional information. Here are ten pointers to help you avoid becoming CRA's next audit target.

Audit Your Own Return

Make sure you double check your return before you send it in. Check first for mathematical accuracy. Make your life easy and use tax software or an online service to ensure your numbers add up properly. Also check you've included all relevant information (like your SIN and address). Avoiding simple mistakes is the first step in keeping the CRA from reviewing your return more closely.

Report All Your Income

Make sure you've reported all your income, including interest and dividends from all your accounts. If you forgot something, you can be sure the taxman will eventually find it. You see, the CRA gets a copy of all the information slips you receive and they cross check them by computer to make sure everything is reported. One handy tip is to compare this year's return to last year's to ensure you haven't missed anything.

Have a Reasonable Expectation of Profit

Be careful if you run your own business and are reporting a loss on this year's return. To claim these losses, you must be running your business with a reasonable expectation of profit. If not, these losses can be denied. The tax collector only flags your return the first year you report business losses, but if you continue to report losses for the next two or three years you should expect to hear from the CRA. Avoiding recurring losses can be as easy as reducing your largest expense over time, which, if you own your own business, is usually interest expense. Pay down your loans as diligently as possible and prepare a forecast to be able to show the taxman how you expect to earn a profit.

File Your Tax Return

Some people argue that the only way to ensure your tax return doesn't get audited is simply not to file a tax return at all. After all, the CRA can't audit what isn't there. To these people we say — try again. In fact, every year CRA sends out countless letters to individuals asking that they file a return — proof the taxman knows who these people are. Non-filers risk not only getting caught and getting hit with interest and penalties, but also going to jail. In addition, if the CRA has to ask you to file a return we can guarantee they'll have a closer look at it when you finally do. So make sure you file every year — ON TIME! And if you've been a non-filer in the past remember it's never too late to make things right.

Be Consistent with Your Expenses

Claims for expense deductions must be reasonable, and the expenses must be incurred to earn income. This means that claiming your personal expenses not only is a bad idea — it's not allowed under our tax law. If you own your own business, make sure your expenses are consistent from year to year. Of course you must still be able to support expenses claimed, but a significant jump in meals and entertainment or travel costs may just catch the taxman's eye.

Don't Cheat

Sounds simple enough, right? Well, those of you who are tempted to cheat should be aware that the taxman has ways of tracking you down. The CRA has identified industries that have, in the past, had a higher incidence of cheaters, including construction, subcontractors, unregistered vehicle sales, auto repair, direct sales, childcare, cleaning, and restaurants. If you're in one of these industries don't be offended by our comments. You're probably above board with your tax filings! But not everyone is — and we wanted you to know you're more likely to hear from the CRA.

Some of you like to voice your opinions on blogs and various other online forums — and that's fine. But be aware that the CRA may be paying attention to your online musings. If the taxman takes notice of your comments he may just check your tax filings to close the loop.

Think Twice about Taking Cash Under the Table

Many people think that taking cash payments for services will get them out of paying tax. What the taxman doesn't know won't hurt him — right? Don't be so sure. There is no shortage of Canadians who are willing to quietly report you for offering your services on a cash basis. In one instance we're aware of, a business owner offered a customer services at a discount if he paid cash. Unfortunately the customer worked for CRA. Ouch! The business owner's tax affairs we're examined and he was eventually reassessed for years of underreported income plus interest and penalties.

Learn from Your Mistakes

If you're caught cheating, it's almost guaranteed the CRA will look at that particular item again the next year. Suppose, for example, that you receive a request to substantiate your childcare expenses, and find that — by accident or design — you've overstated your expenses. You can be sure the CRA will ask you to submit your receipts the next time around — perhaps even for the next couple of years. The moral of the story? You have absolutely no excuse for getting caught making the same mistake twice.

Don't Give the Taxman Something to Audit

Some tax returns have very little worth auditing. An employee with one T4 slip has less chance of being audited than a self-employed person with significant expenses. The CRA likes to flag the more risky items to get more bang, so to speak, for its time spent assessing. Items such as losses from tax shelters, significant interest deductions, rental or business losses, and clergy residence deductions (believe it or not) have an increased likelihood of being flagged for an audit. These deductions may be legitimate, but if you choose to complicate your tax affairs by reporting deductions that can be higher risk be sure you have the information necessary to back up your claim — just in case the taxman comes knocking.

Keep Your Fingers Crossed

Even if you do everything right on your returns you may be selected for an audit or receive a request for information because of just plain old bad luck. Each year the CRA selects taxpayers at random, and uses the results of these audits or requests to determine where people make the most mistakes and in which areas people most often cheat. So even if you've crossed all your t's and dotted your i's, you may still receive an unwelcome letter in the mail on CRA stationery. Don't assume you've done anything wrong — just be sure you can prove you did it right.

Index

• D •

BUSINESS & PERSONAL FINANCE

978-0-470-83878-5   978-0-40-83818-1

Also available:
- Buying and Selling a Home For Canadians For Dummies 978-0-470-83740-5
- Investing For Canadians For Dummies 978-0-470-16029-9
- Managing For Dummies 978-0-7645-1771-6
- Money Management All-in-One Desk Reference For Canadians For Dummies 978-0-470-15428-1

- Negotiating For Dummies 978-0-470-04522-0
- Personal Finance For Canadians For Dummies 978-0-470-83768-9
- Small Business Marketing For Dummies 978-0-7645-7839-7
- Starting an eBay Business For Canadians For Dummies 978-0-470-83946-1

EDUCATION, HISTORY & REFERENCE

78-0-470-83656-9   978-0-7645-2498-1

Also available:
- Algebra For Dummies 978-0-7645-5325-7
- Art History For Dummies 978-0-470-09910-0
- Chemistry For Dummies 978-0-7645-5430-8
- French For Dummies 978-0-7645-5193-2

- Math Word Problems For Dummies 978-0-470-14660-6
- Spanish For Dummies 978-0-7645-5194-9
- Statistics For Dummies 978-0-7645-5423-0
- World War II For Dummies 978-0-7645-532-3

FOOD, HOME, GARDEN, & MUSIC

8-0-7645-9904-0   978-0-470-15491-5

Also available:
- 30-Minute Meals For Dummies 978-0-7645-2589-6
- Bartending For Dummies 978-0-470-05056-9
- Brain Games For Dummies 978-0-470-37378-1
- Gluten-Free Cooking For Dummies 978-0-470-17810-2

- Home Improvement All-in-One Desk Reference For Dummies 978-0-7645-5680-7
- Violin For Dummies 978-0-470-83838-9
- Wine For Dummies 978-0-470-04579-4

GRAPHICS & DESIGN

978-0-470-45318-6   978-0-470-52967-6

Also available:
- Dreamweaver CS4 For Dummies 978-0-470-34502-3
- Flash CS4 For Dummies 978-0-470-38119-9
- Google SketchUp 7 For Dummies 978-0-470-27739-3

- Manga Studio For Dummies 978-0-470-12986-9
- Photoshop CS4 For Dummies 978-0-470-32725-8
- Photoshop Lightroom 2 For Dummies 978-0-470-34539-9

GREEN/SUSTAINABLE

978-0-470-84098-6   978-0-470-17569-9

Also available:
- Alternative Energy For Dummies 978-0-470-43062-0
- Energy Efficient Homes For Dummies 978-0-470-37602-7
- Green Building & Remodeling For Dummies 978-0-470-17559-0

- Green Business Practices For Dummies 978-0-470-39339-0
- Green Cleaning For Dummies 978-0-470-39106-8
- Green Your Home All-in-One For Dummies 978-0-470-40778-3
- Sustainable Landscaping For Dummies 978-0-470-41149-0

HEALTH & SELF-HELP

978-0-471-77383-2   978-0-470-15732-9

Also available:
- Breast Cancer For Dummies 978-0-7645-2482-0
- Depression For Dummies 978-0-7645-3900-8
- Healthy Aging For Dummies 978-0-470-14975-1

- Improving Your Memory For Dummies 978-0-7645-5435-3
- Neuro-linguistic Programming For Dummies 978-0-7645-7028-3
- Pregnancy For Canadians For Dummies 978-0-470-83945-4
- Understanding Autism For Dummies 978-0-7645-2547-6

HOBBIES & CRAFTS

978-0-470-28747-7   978-0-470-29112-2

Also available:
- Crochet Patterns For Dummies 97-0-470-04555-8
- Digital Scrapbooking For Dummies 978-0-7645-8419-0
- Home Decorating For Dummies 978-0-7645-4156-8
- Knitting Patterns For Dummies 978-0-470-04556-5

- Oil Painting For Dummies 978-0-470-18230-7
- Origami Kit For Dummies 978-0-470-75857-1
- Quilting For Dummies 978-0-7645-9799-2
- Sewing For Dummies 978-0-7645-6847-3

HOME & BUSINESS COMPUTER BASICS

978-0-470-49743-2   978-0-470-11806-1

Also available:
- Blogging For Dummies
  978-0-470-23017-6
- Excel 2007 For Dummies
  978-0-470-03737-9
- Office 2007 All-in-One Desk
  Reference For Dummies
  978-0-471-78279-7

- PCs For Dummies
  978-0-470-46542-4
- Web Analytics For Dummies
  9780-470-09824-0

INTERNET & DIGITAL MEDIA

78-0-470-25074-7   978-0-470-52567-8

Also available:
- eBay For Canadians For Dummies
  978-0-470-15348-2
- Facebook For Dummies
  978-0-470-52761-0
- Search Engine Marketing For
  Dummies 978-0-471-97998-2

- The Internet For Dummies
  978-0-470-12174-0
- Twitter For Dummies
  978-0-470-47991-9
- YouTube For Dummies
  978-0-470-14925-6
- WordPress For Dummies
  978-0-470-40296-2

MACINTOSH

78 0-470-27817-8   978-0-470-43541-0

Also available:
- iMac For Dummies
  978-0-470-13386-6
- iMovie '09 & iDVD '09 For
  Dummies 978-0-470-50212-9
- iPhone For Dummies
  978-0-470-53698-8
- MacBook For Dummies
  978-0-470-27816-1

- Mac OS X Leopard For Dummies
  978-0-470-05433-8
- Macs For Seniors For Dummies
  978-0-470-437797-7
- Office 2008 For Mac For
  Dummies 978-0-470-27032-5
- Switching to a Mac For Dummies
  978-0-470-46661-2

PARENTING

8-0-471-77386-3   978-0-471-79146-1

Also available:
- AD/HD For Dummies
  978-0-7645-3712-7
- Baby & Toddler Sleep Solutions
  For Dummies 978-0-470-11794-1
- Overcoming Dyslexia For
  Dummies 978-0-471-75285-1

- Parenting For Dummies
  978-0-7645-5418-6
- Pregnancy For Canadians For
  Dummies 978-0-470-83945-4
- Teaching Kids to Read For
  Dummies 978-0-7645-4043-1
- Type 1 Diabetes For Dummies
  978-0-470-17811-9

PETS

9780764584183

9780470068052

Also available:
- ✓Birds For Dummies
  9780764551390
- ✓Boxers For Dummies
  9780764552854
- ✓Cockatiels For Dummies
  9780764553110

- ✓Ferrets For Dummies
  9780470127230
- ✓Golden Retrievers For Dummies
  9780764552670
- ✓Horses For Dummies
  9780764597978
- ✓Puppies For Dummies
  9780470037171

PROGRAMMING & SECURITY

978-0-470-31726-6

978-0-470-55093-9

Also available:
- ✓Excel 2007 VBA Programming For
  Dummies 978-0-470-04674-6
- ✓Firewalls For Dummies
  978-0-7645-4048-6
- ✓iPhone Application Development
  For Dummies 978-0-470-48737-2

- ✓JavaScript & Ajax For Dummies
  978-0-470-41799-7
- ✓PHP & MySQL For Dummies
  978-0-470-52758-0
- ✓Twitter Application Developmen
  For Dummies 978-0-470-56862-0

RELIGION & INSPIRATION FOR DUMMIES

978-0-7645-5391-2

978-0-470-19142-2

Also available:
- ✓The Bible For Dummies
  978-0-7645-5296-0
- ✓Comparative Religion For
  Dummies 978-0-470-23065-7
- ✓Islam For Dummies
  978-0-7645-5503-9

- ✓Judaism For Dummies
  978-0-7645-5299-1
- ✓Saints For Dummies
  978-0-470-53358-1
- ✓The Torah For Dummies
  978-0-470-17345-9

SPORTS & FITNESS

978-0-471-76871-5

978-0-470-83828-0

Also available:
- ✓Exercise Balls For Dummies
  978-0-7645-5623-4
- ✓Coaching Hockey For Dummies
  978-0-470-83685-9
- ✓Fitness For Dummies
  978-0-7645-7851-9

- ✓Rugby For Dummies
  978-0-470-15327-7
- ✓Ten Minute Tone-Ups For
  Dummies 978-0-7645-7207-4
- ✓Yoga with Weights For Dummie
  978-0-471-74937-0

G